Haim Fireberg, Olaf Glöckner (Eds.)
Being Jewish in 21st-Century Germany

Europäisch-jüdische Studien
Beiträge
European-Jewish Studies
Contributions

Edited by the Moses Mendelssohn Center
for European-Jewish Studies, Potsdam,
in cooperation with the Center for Jewish Studies
Berlin-Brandenburg

Editorial Manager: Werner Treß

Volume 16

Being Jewish in 21st-Century Germany

Edited by
Haim Fireberg and Olaf Glöckner

DE GRUYTER
OLDENBOURG

This publication has been generously supported by the Friedrich Naumann Foundation for Liberty (Jerusalem) and the Moses Mendelssohn Foundation (Erlangen).

ISBN 978-3-11-060766-6
e-ISBN (PDF) 978-3-11-035015-9
e-ISBN (EPUB) 978-3-11-039574-7
ISSN 2192-9602

Library of Congress Cataloging-in-Publication Data
A CIP catalog record for this book has been applied for at the Library of Congress.

Bibliographic information published by the Deutsche Nationalbibliothek
The Deutsche Nationalbibliothek lists this publication in the Deutsche Nationalbibliografie; detailed bibliographic data are available in the Internet at http://dnb.dnb.de.

© 2018 Walter de Gruyter GmbH, Berlin/Boston
This volume is text- and page-identical with the hardback published in 2015.
Typesetting: Michael Peschke, Berlin
Printing: CPI books GmbH, Leck

♾ Printed on acid free paper
Printed in Germany

www.degruyter.com

Table of Contents

Preface
A Word from the Editors of this Volume —— 1

Legacy, Trauma, New Beginning after '45
German Jewry Revisited

Michael Wolffsohn
Jews in Divided Germany (1945–1990) and Beyond
Scrutinized in Retrospect —— 13

Michael Elm
The Making of Holocaust Trauma in German Memory
Some Reflection about Robert Thalheim's Film *And Along Come Tourists* —— 31

Julius H. Schoeps
Saving the German-Jewish Legacy?
On Jewish and Non-Jewish Attempts of Reconstructing a Lost World —— 46

Migration as the Driving Factor of Jewish Revival
in Re-Unified Germany

Eliezer Ben-Rafael
Germany's Russian-speaking Jews
Between Original, Present and Affective Homelands —— 63

Julia Bernstein
Russian Food Stores and their Meaning for Jewish Migrants in Germany and Israel
Honor and 'Nostalgia' —— 81

Elke-Vera Kotowski
Moving from the Present via the Past to Look toward the Future
Jewish Life in Germany Today —— 103

Fania Oz-Salzberger
Israelis and Germany
A Personal Perspective —— 117

Culture and Arts – Reflecting a New Jewish Presence

Hanni Mittelmann
Reconceptualization of Jewish Identity as Reflected in Contemporary German-Jewish Humorist Literature —— 131

Karsten Troyke
Hava Nagila
A Personal Reflection on the Reception of Jewish Music in Germany —— 142

Zachary Johnston
Aliyah Le Berlin
A Documentary about the Next Chapter of Jewish Life in Berlin —— 152

Ghosts of the Past, Challenges of the Present: Germany Facing Old-New Anti-Semitism

Monika Schwarz-Friesel
Educated Anti-Semitism in the Middle of German Society
Empirical Findings —— 165

Günther Jikeli
Anti-Semitism within the Extreme Right and Islamists' Circles —— 188

H. Julia Eksner
Thrice Tied Tales
Germany, Israel, and German Muslim Youth —— 208

Towards New Shores: Jewish Education and the Religious Revival

Olaf Glöckner
New Structures of Jewish Education in Germany —— 231

Walter Homolka
A Vision Come True
Abraham Geiger and the Training of Rabbis and Cantors for Europe —— 244

Authors and Editors —— 251

Index —— 254

Names Index —— 257

Preface

A Word from the Editors of this Volume

In the last four decades, and especially since 1990, international migration has profoundly changed the profile of receiving (destination) nations all over the globe, while also deeply influencing conditions in migration exit (origin) countries. The change has been particularly felt in European countries, which in the past were quite homogeneous from a national, ethnic, linguistic, and often religious point of view. The influx of large numbers of immigrants from different countries and continents irreversibly challenged the concept of the classic nation-state with the emergence of a variety of new, culturally- and nationally-diverse frameworks within European societies.

Trans-border movements and its relation to issues of identity and culture are by no means new to Jewish historiography. On the contrary, it could be said that modern Jewish identity and culture as such were created by transnational migrations, at least in Europe and other Western countries. Thus, a particular Jewish identity developed in Europe over a period of almost 200 years, as a cross-national entity based on solid religious traditions, in ongoing conflict with the emerging nation-states and their exclusive aspirations. This phenomenon was used by nationalists and anti-Semites, who exploited it politically, blaming the Jews of 'cosmopolitanism', which, they claimed, undermined their local and national loyalty. It was seldom perceived as a political contribution in the construction of new transnational identities for the general population. Among Jews, the tension between a parochial heritage and universal perspective was fruitfully rendered into a combination of communal identity and societal adaptation, one that defines Jews in every modern European country in the broadest range of possible degrees.

Cultural diversity is never conflict-free. However, Jews in the modern era have demonstrated that the results shouldn't be dissolution of societal solidarity on the one hand, or withdrawal into isolation on the other, but rather a transformation of identities and values into a kaleidoscope within a given society. This outcome is known as the 'Jewish global identity' or in other words – 'Jewish Peoplehood.'

Since the middle of the nineteenth century, Jews have experienced massive influxes of migration for different reasons, such as escaping pogroms, wars and hunger in Eastern Europe, but also a search for a new cultural and professional future in the New World and in *Eretz Israel* (the Land of Israel). The largest and most vibrant Jewish demographic center of that time was still situated in Eastern Europe. In the course of the twentieth century, however, Eastern European Jewry was shaken and stricken in a devastating way – in particular by the Nazi-German organized Holocaust, but also by 70 years of State Communism in the USSR and by 40 years of similar political repression in the countries of the so-called socialist "East Bloc." Jewish community life lost most of its structure and vitality and to this day we have witnessed a constant outflow of Jews from the East, while the State of Israel and the communities in North America and Western Europe have become the new, vibrant Jewish centers of the late twentieth century.

At the turn to the New Millennium, something surprising happened in the heart of Europe, something that sparked disapproval and amazement across borders. Germany, the country of the Nazi thugs and Holocaust murderers, masters of barbarity and crime in the Second World War became not only a leading country of the European Union, but also an attractive destination for émigrés from the crumbling Soviet Union. No later than the mid 1990s it had become clear that tens of thousands of former Soviet Jews (*Halachic* Jews, non-*Halachic* Jews, and non-Jewish spouses) who left their homeland have not headed to Israel or to America, rather they have gone precisely to that country that was responsible for the Holocaust. One must admit that by the end of the twentieth century, a general respect has grown towards the visible German transformation from a cruel militaristic, trigger-happy and intolerant state, into a stable democracy, seemingly cosmopolitan and open-minded towards other ethnicities, cultures, and religions. This was a new Germany, no doubt, yet who had ever seriously believed in a Jewish wave of migration back to this country of Goethe and Bach, as well as of Hitler, Eichmann, and Goebbels?

Surprisingly, no small number of former Soviet Jews decided to take this route. In 1990, on the eve of a vast migration from the FSU, the Jewish communities in Germany numbered around 29,000 registered people. In 2013 the Jewish communities numbered approximately 101,400 registered members. The official data reveals that in the heydays of migration, up until 2004, some 220,000 Jews (*Halachic* Jews and non-*Halachic* Jews) and non-Jewish members of their families had immigrated to Germany. As a result, the Central Council of Jews in Germany (*Zentralrat*) now consists of 108 Jewish communities that are organized in 23 regional associations. In addition, 24 communities are organized under the roof of the Union of Progressive Jews in Germany (UPJ).

It would be correct to assess that the ex-Soviet Jewish influx into Germany, especially during the 1990s, prevented the disappearance of all the few small, weak, and outdated Jewish communities in Germany.

All Jewish congregations, from (ultra-) orthodox and conservative to (ultra-) liberal, are present in contemporary Germany. Quite a few new synagogues have been built, Jewish schools and kindergartens opened. Jewish cultural centers attract Jews and non-Jews in nearly the same intensity, Jewish museums are in construction, and even three rabbinic schools have opened their gates in recent years.

Politicians, intellectuals, social scientists, and other scholars try to get to the bottom of this phenomenon: How will the unexpected influx from the former Soviet Union affect Jewish life in Germany in the long run? What does it mean for the single individual – to be a Jew in twentieth century Germany, in the so-called Berlin Republic? What happens 'on the ground' in local Jewish communities, what are the current demographic trends among Jews? What happens in Jewish arts, music, literature, and social networks? Is it possible nowadays to live not only side-by-side, but also jointly with the non-Jewish German population? What makes a typical Jewish identity here, and not to be forgotten: How safe is it to live as a discernable Jew in Europe's currently most vibrant country?

All these questions were intensively discussed at an international conference, titled: *From Rejection to Acceptance – To be Jewish in 21st Century Germany*, hosted on February 10–12, 2013 by the Kantor Center for the Study of Contemporary European Jewry at Tel Aviv University, in cooperation with the Moses Mendelssohn Center for European-Jewish Studies at Potsdam University, the Friedrich Naumann Foundation for Liberty – Jerusalem, and Beit Hatfutsot, the Museum of the Jewish People, at Tel Aviv University.

The organizers wanted to shed light on Jewish life in present-day Germany from a host of different perspectives – for example, achievements and challenges of the Jewish communities, Jewish cultures and sub-cultures, ties with the German Christian majority and with other local minorities; the consequences of Jewish demographic changes (including the Israeli migration); interrelations between different Jewish congregations and organizations; and also their relations with the Federal Government and other political bodies. One important goal was also to examine levels of anti-Semitism and xenophobia in contemporary German society, and finally on the dynamic of German-Israeli relations in the last decades.

Our hypothesis was that in large part, Jewish immigrants had integrated successfully into the general society, and in many cases had become leading actors in society, culture and economics, while at the same time struggling to maintain their unique Jewish cultural and communal identity. The participants were asked to highlight the social, cultural, demographic, economic, and political processes, which brought about the integration of Jewish immigrant groups into contemporary Germany, both into the Jewish communities as well as into the general social fabric. We hope we laid a foundation for more comprehensive studies on immigration and society in Germany in general, and on new forms of Israel-Diaspora relations.

The conference volume at hand reflects important aspects of ongoing discussion on how Jews in Germany could succeed in developing new thriving life after the Holocaust. It also shows how the ex-Soviet-Jewish influx into reunified Germany has not only stabilized local Jewish community life but also radically changed its self-understanding and 'internal compass.' We learn about the new self-confidence of the Jewish community but at the same time also about growing threats of renewed anti-Semitism, racism, and xenophobia that raise questions about the future. The volume tells us about revivals and new beginnings in Jewish culture, arts, philosophy, and – yes – also of a return of multifaceted Jewish religion. Finally we encounter ideas about how new structures and opportunities of Jewish education help the Jewish veterans and immigrants – 'old' and 'new' to come together and to undertake this daring and courageous attempt to reconstruct Jewish Life in twenty-first century Germany.

Michael Wolffsohn's article on *Jews in Divided Germany (1945–1990) and Beyond: Scrutinized in Retrospect* examines the development of Jewish life in divided Germany after the Second World War, and the effect on the Jewish community in the wake of the fall of the Eastern Bloc and the unification of Germany. Wolffsohns conclusions are in a way very provocative. "Germany's new Jewry has become and will increasingly be a community of Jews without Judaism", he predicts: "with a vocal and growing Orthodox minority, and a much smaller but also very active liberal mini-minority." Wolffsohn also assumes that another phenomenon, a parallel Jewish world will develop in Germany, trying to be an alternative to practicing forms of Judaism: "Israelism." "But", he continues, "such 'Israelisms' culminate in a farce, not an Israeli reality. It is an absurdity, and an absurdity cannot be the ingredients for strengthening identity." Although it is not a 'farewell eulogy' to the future of Jewish life in Germany, it will be interesting to follow the connections that may be created by the 'Israelists' and the expanded Israeli community in Germany in the coming years.

Michael Elm deals in his article *The Making of Holocaust Trauma in German Memory. Some Reflection about Robert Thalheim's Film "And Along Come Tourists"* with the question of the Holocaust as a present traumatic event in German contemporary life. Elm investigates the notion of trauma which has been established through the course of West and East German history and asks, using the example of Robert Thalheim's movie *And Along Come Tourists (Am Ende kommen Touristen)*: "Which historical narrative could be helpful in building trust between non-Jewish Germans and Jews today?" The answers are complicated and not clear-cut. In the movie "a young non-Jewish German and a Pole discuss the heritage of Auschwitz without including explicitly a Jewish perspective. The question arises – whether the position of the 'Jewish other' has to be addressed in such a narration or not." According to Elm, "the emphasis on the German-Polish perspective is – from a narrative point of view – by no means excluding the Jewish experience." That means: "Still the barriers between the collective memories remain difficult to overcome."

Julius H. Schoeps in his article *Saving the German-Jewish Legacy? On Jewish and non-Jewish attempts of reconstructing a lost world* addresses the social and cultural alienation of contemporary Jewish population in Germany from the great contribution of the Jews in this country in every life's aspect. "Some of the new immigrants from the CIS who today make up 90 percent of the membership in Germany's local Jewish communities, are indeed interested in the German-Jewish legacy, yet this does not necessarily have anything to do with their own sense of identity." Schoeps thinks that "*cultural* Jewish continuity in Germany cannot be artificially reconstructed even 70 years after the Holocaust." One decisive question remains, however: Schoeps believes "that the integration of the outstanding Jewish contribution of the past into the new German society fabric is a mission that lies at the foot of the Germans, not the Jews. As long as this question remains significant in the dialogue between non-Jews and Jews in Germany, normalcy will remain a distant prospect."

In contrast to this, **Eliezer Ben-Rafael** describes in his article *Germany's Russian-speaking Jews: Between Original, Present and Affective Homelands* quite different perceptions. Ben-Rafael writes, "There was, in essence, no Jewish community [...] in Germany when Russian Jews began arriving in Germany, and today they constitute the overwhelming majority (90 percent) of the Jewish population of Germany." In contrary to scholars that predict the vanishing of Jewish identity among the Russian-speaking community, Ben-Rafael claims: "Russian-speaking Jews in Germany also participate in transnational-diaspora structures, which bind them to their counterparts in Jerusalem, Moscow, and New York. [...] Russian-speaking Jews, whatever their hesitancies regarding what 'Jewishness' means, rely on Jewish education to transmit to the young what should make Jewish life and interest in Israel meaningful." These findings might be even more significant for the children of the immigrants, the so-called 1.5- and the second generation.

Julia Bernstein in her article *Russian Food Stores and their Meaning for Jewish Migrants in Germany and Israel: Honor and 'Nostalgia'* deals with the process of integration into a new society through preservation of food habits from the former 'home-land.' The text is based on a comparative study that was conducted in Germany and Israel. Sticking to food habit, concludes Bernstein "in the migration process obviously contribute to 'living memories,' yet they do much more: They also 'make a place' for a virtual home that preserves social status and stabilizes the self-esteem of customers [...] Food consumption in the migration process seems to promote contouring collective 'we'-identities."

Elke-Vera Kotowski compares in her article *Moving from the Present via the Past to Look toward the Future: Jewish Life in Germany Today* between the Jewish populations in Germany in the 1930s and today, and asks whether with all the obvious differences between the two periods "there are any links connecting those Jews who lost their homes during the Nazi period in Germany, and those Jews who are searching for a new beginning in Germany today?" Kotowski shows that "exiled German Jews of the 1930s who were religious or strongly connected to Jewish tradition, often were eager to join or even to establish *Liberal* (i.e. Reform) Jewish communities." They influenced the receiving societies and helped to shape their destiny, but many felt alienated to the majority society. But Kotowski also concludes that "not only the German-Jewish émigrés from the 1930s but also Russian-Jewish newcomers from the 1990s have unpacked their suitcases." However, it "seems that the second generation of immigrants will be able to participate in Germany's society with great success."

Fania Oz-Salzberger deals in her article *Israelis and Germany: A Personal Perspective* with a phenomenon that for many Israelis (and maybe even to many "bio-Germans") – not to speak of the Jewish communities in Germany – is difficult to digest. It means, the almost mystical attraction of Germany (and Berlin in particular) to *Sabras* (young native Israelis), that pushes so many to visit, to live for different periods of times among Germans and even to emigrate to Germany. Oz-Salzberger studied the various social networks of Israelis in Berlin (either in real life or virtual networks) in order to find the common characteristics that bond all Israelis in Germany in general and Berlin in particular. Although she found that "many of the current Hebrew-speaking residents of Berlin whom I have met in recent years, Jews as well as Arabs, are enchanted, fascinated, and sometimes even obsessed with the dark past." Yet, according to Oz-Salzberger, "Berlin remains problematic for them, and they live their problematic life in it as a matter of choice; because life is not meant to be simple, and because this urban, highly cultured, intense global-polis is not offering its newcomers either harmony or simplicity. It is not part of the deal."

Hanni Mittelmann deals in her article *Reconceptualization of Jewish Identity as Reflected in Contemporary German-Jewish Humorist Literature* with the question of humor and humoristic Jewish-German literature that tries to reflect Jewish life in contemporary Germany on one hand, and on the other tries to reshape Jewish identity and culture by the young generation of Jews in Germany. In contrast to the post-War generations, Mittelmann explains, the new generation of writers is "no longer afraid of Germany," and deals with wide range of topics, from politics to sex. The contemporary literature, Mittelmann concludes, "releases the Jews from their role as victims, and attempts to free Germans from fear of their own shadow."

Singer and poet **Karsten Troyke** in his article *Hava Nagila* (the name of a popular Hebrew song that means 'Let us rejoice') shares with us "*A Personal Reflection on the Reception of Jewish Music in Germany.*" Troyke suggests "there was not the slightest interest in Jewish music in Germany after 1945." Yet, for different reasons, Troyke claims, the 1980s witnessed a big change and "many young people in East and West Germany suddenly started singing Yiddish songs." In the United States, young Jews had already started to do so. This later became known as the 'Klezmer revival'." It burst out of its Jewish roots and became a well-established multifaceted genre, although the boom seems to have passed the zenith already. Troyke himself has sung Yiddish songs around the world but "only in three countries I did find large non-Jewish audiences. These countries were Sweden, Poland and – Germany."

The American movie director and producer **Zachary Johnston** shares with us in his article *Aliyah Le Berlin (Making Aliyah to Berlin): A Documentary about the Next Chapter of Jewish Life in Berlin* his insights on the emergence of a diaspora of Israeli youth in Berlin. In many ways – second only to Fania Oz-Salzberger (see her article in this volume) – he is one of the pioneers in identifying the phenomenon that he follows in his documentary, and he had done it well before it became a hot issue in the Israeli media in 2014. Johnston challenges the common Israeli set of values about migration. "One cannot use the term '*aliyah*' out-of-context without eliciting a knee-jerk response due to its value-loaded nature of the word, which is tied to the 'ascent' of Jews to Israel," writes Johnston, and he adds: "Perhaps, this new age of Israeli and Jewish exploration in Germany has a higher purpose that has yet to be ascertained, that down the road the concept of *aliyah* will receive a something deeper, stronger, and broader meaning for the nation of Israel and its citizens."

Monika Schwarz-Friesel in her article *Educated Anti-Semitism in the Middle of German Society: Empirical Findings* claims that "the experience of the Holocaust and dealing with the lethal ideology that led to Auschwitz did not bring the strategies of verbally dehumanizing and demonizing the Jews to an end. Such strategies prevail and are frequently used in modern discourse even by highly educated people from mainstream society." Obviously this goes hand-in-hand with the rise of anti-Semitic manifestations in Europe during the last decade. "The articulation of traditional anti-Semitic stereotypes", adds Schwarz-Friesel, "by projecting them on Israel has increased significantly." One of the dominant strategies of dealing with actual anti-Semitism in German public discourse, Schwarz-Friesel writes, is to deny its very existence. She also concludes, based on her studies that "the age-old basic Jew hatred is alive in the middle of German society and that is by no means a sole phenomenon among Right- or Left-wing extremists."

Günther Jikeli in his article *Anti-Semitism within the Extreme Right and Islamists' Circles* stresses that "antisemitism has long been a part of the extreme Right and Islamist movements. However, [...] often takes indirect forms. In the case of the extreme Right, it is frequently embedded in revisionist positions on the Second World War. Islamists, on the other hand, voice anti-Semitic positions with references to Israel, anti-Jewish excerpts from Islamic scripture, and hostile attitudes towards Western societies in the context of an alleged 'war against Islam.'" Jikeli underlines his observation that "the extreme Right and Islamists are not isolated from mainstream society; similar attitudes are widespread, and exist beyond the membership of organizations associated with extreme Right and political Islam."

Julia Eksner analyses in her article *Thrice Tied Tales: Germany, Israel, and German Muslim Youth* the complicated attitudes of Muslim youth in Germany with Jews and with Israel and vis-à-vis their German 'homeland'. –"The argument made here", writes Eksner, "is that German Muslim youth's positioning against Israel is by no means a 'natural' or 'cultural' given; rather, Muslim youth's responses are structured by preexisting discursive relations in Germany." Her conclusions back that of other authors in this book that anti-Semitism is well rooted in the German culture and in contemporary German society, especially in its anti-Israeli form. "In effect", Eksner concludes, "German social and discursive context legitimizes and encourages both the critique of Israel and Muslim youths' anti-Israeli attitudes as 'normal and acceptable', thus channels expression of anger at their disenfranchisement from the object much closer to home (both literally and figuratively) to a 'legitimized' transnational object – the State of Israel, and, by implication, its (Jewish) citizens."

Olaf Glöckner in his article *New Structures of Jewish Education in Germany* deals with the burden of preserving traditional religious Jewish education in Germany in an era of secularism and large non-religious Jewish population that migrated to

Germany after the fall of the Iron Curtain on one hand, and the dominance of the German state's educational systems on the other. Many Jews in Germany express their wish to learn more about Judaism, religion, arts, philosophy and the legacy of history – but often lack the opportunity for this on-site. Glöckner argues that "in summary, it can be said that the Jewish educational system in Germany has undergone impressive advances during the last 15 to 20 years [...] ranging from Jewish religion, tradition, and history, to the State of Israel, Jewish culture, and Hebrew mastery – being offered to different age groups." Nevertheless, Glöckner stresses that it is of vital importance to settle the imbalance in comprehensive Jewish education between relatively strong Jewish centers and the relatively weak sub-centers of the Jewish periphery. He also refers to the huge importance of finding a way to improve the accessibility of teenagers to Jewish education.

Walter Homolka sums in his article *A Vision Come True: Abraham Geiger and the Training of Rabbis and Cantors for Europe* how a new generation of young men and women – very often from Eastern Europe – have discovered the world of Jewish Theology anew and are preparing to bring this world (back) in order to revitalize communities across Germany and beyond. With the School of Jewish Theology, opened in 2013 at the University of Potsdam, the training of Liberal and Conservative rabbis has finally received an academic theological framework within the German university system. "In 1836", Homolka writes, "Abraham Geiger demanded the establishment of a Jewish theological faculty as the litmus test of Jewish emancipation in Germany." More than 170 years later, this test has finally begun to be proven successful.

We hope that these articles can be a modest contribution towards a better understanding of contemporary Jewish life in Germany, which is undergoing surprising and dynamic changes at present, yet still faces decisive challenges in the near future.

In conclusion, we wish to thank all the organizations and individuals that contributed their knowledge, time, and means to the success of the conference and made it possible to publish this volume about contemporary Jewish life in Germany. It has been a pleasure to cooperate with all of you in this important endeavor: The Kantor Center for the Study of Contemporary European Jewry at Tel Aviv University; the Moses Mendelssohn Center for European-Jewish Studies at Potsdam University; the Friedrich Naumann Foundation for Liberty – Jerusalem, for its generous financial support; Beit Hatfutsot, the Museum of the Jewish People; The Goren-Goldstein Diaspora Research Center, Tel Aviv University; The Tel Aviv University Research Authority. Special thanks are given to the dedicated staff of the Kantor Center: Ronith Greefeld, Talia Naamat and Adrian Gruszniewski for their contribution. Last and not least we thank Liora Shani of Beit Hatfutsot and her staff for their valuable support. Special thanks is given to Daniella Ashkenazy for her excellent editorial work.

Haim Fireberg and Olaf Glöckner

Legacy, Trauma, New Beginning after '45
German Jewry Revisited

Michael Wolffsohn
Jews in Divided Germany (1945–1990) and Beyond

Scrutinized in Retrospect

Reconstruction of history is more than just adding more or less impressive stories. This is true of the history of Jews in post-War Germany, as well. Therefore, I prefer empirical facts instead of wishful thinking one way or the other. All subchapters presented here are based on my decade-long research on the issue.[1]

Jewish history after 1945 in the 'Two Germanies' is thrilling and touching. Nevertheless, one should keep in mind that at least until 1990 Jews in Germany consisted of tiny, little communities. The German Democratic Republic (GDR) in East Germany had become almost *"judenrein"* – mainly for all-German (Nazi) historical reasons, but also due to self-inflicted anti-Jewish and even more so for anti-Israeli policies of the GDR. From 1945 to 1990, West German Jewry was the prime player, although this as well carries its own reservations: From a global Jewish and, of course, a global non-Jewish perspective, German Jewry after 1945 has been almost a non-entity in general, including West Germany. So is this "much ado about nothing" – or something? If the measure is not quantity but rather historical importance – Germany is still relevant. We are involved. Our story is being told. *Nostra res agitur* ('It's our case, it matters to us').

Political Geography

After the Second World War, West Germany had been the easternmost place in Western Europe. Thus, for geographical reasons, West Germany became the 'number one haven' for any refugee from Eastern Europe, including Jews. Most Jewish Holocaust survivors did not wish to stay in Eastern Europe, for two reasons: They wanted to flee its traditional, vehement, and often again deadly bourgeois-agrarian as well as newly Communist-led anti-Semitism. Thus Jews moved to West Germany, first and foremost to the American Zone and this for

---

[1] See: Wolffsohn, Eternal Guilt?, 1993; Wolffsohn / Puschner, Geschichte der Juden in Deutschland, 1992; Wolffsohn, Die Deutschland-Akte, 1995; Wolffsohn, Meine Juden – Eure Juden, 1997; Wolffsohn / Brechenmacher, Deutschland, jüdisch Heimatland, 2008; Brenner (ed.), Geschichte der Juden, 2012.

good reason. The British Zone was not the most suitable place to go to; fearing that Zionist activists would immediately recruit these Jewish newcomers and turn them into either anti-British or anti-Arab fighters in Palestine, the influx of Jews was not welcomed in the British Zone. The French were even poorer than the British Zone; the small French Zone situated in the far west of West Germany was fundamentally unattractive to those who sought refuge, rescue, and revitalization.

West Germany's easternmost place was West Berlin which formally did not belong to West Germany, but 'the West' was present there, and even devastated Berlin was there – partly gruesome, sinister, partly metropolitan flair. Moreover, Berlin was the geographical center of a lucrative East-West black market economy attracting displaced persons without means.

Munich, the Bavarian capital in the relatively-flourishing American Zone was also a popular refuge for Jewish Holocaust survivors fleeing Eastern Europe. From a historical and moral perspective, both Berlin and Munich were odd choices. After all, it was Berlin, Germany's capital, where the Holocaust and the Second World War had been planned, and Munich had been the 'capital' of the Nazi movement, the so-called *"Hauptstadt der Bewegung."* The essentials for survival do not always conform with memories, or in this case – historical associations.

Another geographical point should be kept in mind. In keeping with a dominant Diaspora Jewish tradition, the Jewish influx to West Germany targeted cities – large urban centers, not only Berlin and Munich but also Frankfurt, Cologne, or Stuttgart. There was a distinct pattern in the way East European Jewish refugees went from Holocaust hell camps to "displaced persons" (DP's) camps in West Germany, then migrated finally towards urban centers.

Despite the fundamental rupture of German Jewish history caused by the Holocaust – the new, originally non-German Jews who populated post-Holocaust Germany, exhibited – consciously or unknowingly – yet another German-Jewish geographical-demographical pattern: They moved to the 'right side of the tracks.' In other words, they preferred middle- and upper-class areas and boroughs such as Olivaer Platz, Wilmersdorf, or Charlottenburg in Berlin and – later, as their economic situation improved – Grunewald, Zehlendorf, and Dahlem. By settling in these better-off areas, Jewish newcomers declared their upward mobility – whether consciously or unknowingly following the same geographical-demographical path taken by German Jews up until 1933. This was in sharp contrast to many non-Jewish immigrants – mostly Turks – who came to Germany since the 1960s. In post-war East Germany (the GDR), despite the differences in the regime and the state of the economic, here as well the Jewish pattern was identical: East Germany's Jews settled/resettled in urban centers, first and foremost Berlin, and also in the more desirable urban residential areas.

Dissolution, "Final Solution", and Resurrection

To properly understand what transpired among German Jewry between 1945 and 1990 it is important to step back and put things in a wider frame of reference of German-Jewish history, beginning with the age of Jewish Emancipation. To position our short time-span in the perspective of the nineteenth and twentieth century, I suggest dividing German-Jewish history into three periods that can be defined by keywords: *Auflösung* ('dissolution'), *"Endlösung"* ('Final Solution') and *Auferstehung* ('Resurrection'). The period of dissolution of traditional Jewish structures and gradual emancipation spanned the years 1800 to 1933. This was followed by the era leading up to and including the "Final Solution" during the years 1933 to 1945. Lastly, we witness a period of German-Jewish resurrection that began in 1945. The end of the war heralded a totally new chapter in German-Jewish history, which rightly should be divided into two stages: The first, the Displaced Persons period. The second stage (since 1948) was ushered in by the establishment of the State of Israel, and the advent of a German-Jewish-Israeli triangle, in lieu of the traditional bilateral German-Jewish relationship stretching from the nineteenth century up to 1948.

West Germany (FRG)

As noted above, the years 1945 to 1948 were dominated by the displaced persons experience, and most DP camps were located in the American Zone, especially in Bavaria. Like many non-Jews, many desperate Jewish Holocaust survivors eked out a living in post-war Germany by engaging in illegal black-market activities – however in the case of the Jews this fueled old prejudices of 'sly Jews.' At the same time, one witnesses the first signs of re-establishment of local German-Jewish communities – a resurrection of Jewish life, although most members of the community had no intrinsic links – cultural or ancestral – to Germany's past German-Jewish legacy.

In 1950, the Jewish Agency confronted German Jews with an ultimatum: They should leave Germany – the country of their people's murderers – within six months, otherwise they could expect to be ostracized by Israel and Diaspora Jewry. Heinz Galinski, the President of West Berlin's Jewish community boldly rejected the Jewish Agency initiative. Not only was the community not ostracized; the reconstruction of Jewish institutional life was accelerated. Nevertheless, forging coherent and vibrant communities 'from within' was a great challenge. Post-war German Jewry was typified more by material growth than spiritual growth – to use a Jewish idiom: more *kemach* ('flour') than *torah* (Jewish education or other spiritual and intellectual pursuits). This trend, of course, is not limited to German Jewry alone.

The early 1950s were dominated by German restitutions to Jewish victims inside and outside Germany – including *shilumim* ('reparations') to the State of Israel for those who had been murdered. This made it easier for Jews in Germany to accept German bids for atonement through monetary compensation and made it easier to ease any guilt for being in Germany at all. Gradually, daily routine began to push aside the past, at least outwardly, among both Jews and non-Jews. Yet, events 'intruded' in this process: The capture, trial, and execution of Adolf Eichmann, one of the inner circle of Holocaust perpetrators, strongly affected historical minds in Germany during the early 1960s, returning shadows of the past. Public and Jewish awareness of the Holocaust continued to be re-awakened time and again by other events. First there was the 1963 Auschwitz trial in Frankfurt, followed by the 1964 debate on the statute of limitation with regard to crimes against humanity. While 1964/65 deliberations over diplomatic relations between West Germany and Israel enveloped German-Jewish inhabitants, this remained mainly a bilateral affair between Bonn and Jerusalem, less so an inner German-Jewish issue. On the eve of the June 1967 Six-Days War, the military build-up towards war was perceived as an existential threat to Israel's very existence, greatly alarming Germany's Jewry who viewed the Jewish state as a safe haven should they ever need one. Anxiety was even more marked during the Yom Kippur War. Jewishly, things went from bad to worse in October 1973, and not only on an emotional level; German-Jewish confidence in its traditional ideological beacon – the Social Democratic Party of Germany (SPD) was shattered by Willy Brandt's (Social Democrat) and Walter Scheel's (liberal Free Democrat) coalition seeking to prevent American arms being re-supplies to Israel from German soil.

In essence, the Six Day War was a watershed that signaled the beginnings of tensions and estrangement for the German-Jewish community: Many younger members of the SPD began actively to support the increasingly anti-Zionist and anti-Israeli New Left. By the early 1970s, the boundary between the democratic Left and the terrorist Left had been blurred, marked by the Leftist plot to blow up West Berlin's main Jewish community center on 9 November 1969 (which at the time was holding an event commemorating the thirtyfirst anniversary of Kristallnacht, with all the 'moves and shakers' of the Jewish community in attendance) – a terrorist attack foiled by a defective detonator.

However, even in the German political mainstream attitudes were changing. Since 1969 Willy Brandt's new *Geschichtspolitik* ('history as politics') orientation introduced two new dimensions to German-Jewish-Israeli relations. The first was a more relaxed SPD-German approach to the Third Reich in general and the

Jewish world in particular. (Given the fact that the SPD as a party and Brandt personally had fought Hitler, such 'shaking off of culpability' was viewed by many as logical and gained popularity in Germany's political marketplace of ideas, since it liberated the SPD's German supports of guilt.) This change of attitude was coupled by Brandt's repositioning of West Germany in the Cold War to take a more independent, East-leading politic (*Ostpolitik*) which jeopardized Bonn's traditionally pro-Israel Near East (*Nahost*) political orientation. (The catalyst for 'distancing from Israel' was Bonn's need to cozy-up to Moscow, which supported the Arabs.) German-Jewish representatives were soured by another 'encounter' with the Brandt-Scheel administration; when Brandt came to Warsaw in December 1970, he impressed the enlightened world by kneeling down at the Warsaw Ghetto Memorial, however, the German-Jewish community felt slighted that Brandt refused to include any prominent Jew in his delegation.[2]

The German-Jewish relationship (with Israeli as an ever-present third arm) did not improve under Chancellor Helmut Schmidt (SPD), Brandt's successor (1974–1982). The tough-lipped Schmidt provoked more than one incident with Israel, often using this or that prominent Diaspora Jew as a 'sidekick' (to legitimize his positions) – his absolute favorite being embracing and quoting Nahum Goldmann (the head of the World Jewish Congress between 1948 and 1977 and president of the World Zionist Organization between 1956 to 1968, David Ben-Gurion's personal nemesis).

There were a series of incidents signaling the change of orientation and distancing from Germany's Holocaust legacy towards a 'let bygones be bygones' attitude, perhaps the most unforgettable the 1985 "Bitburg controversy" sparked by Chancellor Kohl's visit to the German military cemetery in Bitburg together with American President Ronald Reagan – a cemetery where Waffen SS soldiers, among others, were buried. The visit sparked an acrimonious confrontation between the Reagan Administration and the American Jewish community, and protests to the Kohl government by the Jewish community in Germany – both to no avail. The visit was a landmark event on the slippery slope down to moral equivalency that lumped together Holocaust victims and SS soldiers (and more and more, Germans as a whole) as victims of Nazism ("the human wreckage of totalitarianism," to quote Reagan).

One year later, the "singularity" of the Holocaust became a bone of contention in what became known as the *Historikerstreit* ('historians dispute') provoked by German historian Ernst Nolte, who framed the Holocaust as merely a part of totalitarianism and mass murder in the twentieth century, arguing the Holocaust

---

[2] For details and documentary evidence see Wolffsohn / Brechenmacher, Denkmalsturz? Brandts Kniefall, 2005.

was not German-specific and that Hitler and Stalin were part of a continuum of this phenomenon. This dispute was far more than an internal academic controversy. It also radiated on the relations of the German and Israeli government and the German Jewry in general.

When in the night of the 9 November 1989 the Berlin Wall fell, followed by German reunification, this became another turning point. Old fears were sparked anew: Would a reunified Germany become *judenrein*? Would reunification mark the beginning of a Fourth Reich...or an "open society" in Karl Popper's sense? History has already given the answer. The Jews gave their own answer, as well: More than 200,000 Jews from the Former Soviet Union optimistic to make a new beginning elsewhere 'invaded' Germany since the early 1990s – and have happily stayed, throwing their lot with Germany's future.

East Germany (GDR)

The majority of Germany's pre-1933 Jewry had traditionally been liberal, a significant minority with strong socialist or even communist leanings. Thus, it is no wonder that the "first socialist state on German soil" attracted prominent, intellectual 'old fellows' among Holocaust survivors, such as the poets Anna Seghers, Stefan Heym, and Stephan Hermlin.[3] The GDR-Jewish (and Israeli) honeymoon ended like the Soviet-Israeli one, in late 1948 only to be followed by an unbridled anti-Zionist campaign that lasted until Stalin's death in March 1953. Compared to other East Bloc countries where anti-Zionism had undeniable anti-Semitic undertones (and overtones), the GDR's was tamer – but anti-Semitism's presence was strong enough to lead to an exodus of the vast majority of GDR-Jews to West Berlin or West Germany. After all, *Judenlisten* (lists of Jews) of dissidents targeted as 'enemies of the regime' due to suspected Jewish or Zionist leanings or for merely being Jewish, had been prepared by the authorities in 1953 and 1967. We know this from other East Bloc countries, as well. These lists were by no means a "Schindler's List"; on the contrary. As a result, the GDR became almost *"judenrein"*, except for tiny local enclaves. Their leadership (if Jewish at all) and its rank-and-file were systematically undercut by the East German secret service (the *Stasi*) right up until the dismantling of the GDR. Simultaneously, East Germany played a vanguard role in supporting Palestinian and other anti-Zionist and anti-Semitic terrorist organizations – from the Palestinian PLO and PFLP to the arch-terrorist Carlos and the West German "Red Army Fraction" (RAF).

---

[3] For details, documents and references see: Wolffsohn, 1995.

By the mid-1980s, when GDR state leadership realized that their country was or would soon go bankrupt, they became prone to an old anti-Semitic myth – Jews were not only perceived as tremendous wealthy, but also wielded tremendous 'political clout' and Jews, in essence, "ran Washington." Thus, East Berlin's leaders claimed East Germany was 'the only truly antifascist German state' and sent their Jewish comrades to convince American Jews – and through them Capitol Hill and the White House, to extend Most Favored Nation status to the GDR. In the end they failed, however, some leading American Jews were sucked into the narrative of the possible resurgence of fascism in Germany. Edgar Bronfman, then President of the World Jewish Congress, aligned himself against unification despite the fall of the Berlin Wall in 1989, and threw his support behind preservation of 'Two Germanies.' Jewish anxieties, not just German-Jewish ones about German unification were understandable for a host of reasons, but support behind preservation of an anti-Semitic and anti-Zionist state like the GDR was politically absurd and blind. Finally it failed, because it was a minority position.[4]

Demographic trends and shifts

The exact figure of Holocaust survivors in Germany is not known. We depend on more or less informed estimates that hold that in 1945 there may have been about 3,000 survivors in all four Allied Zones. This small number swelled within a short time due to the huge post-1945 East-West migration: Those "displaced persons" (DPs), roughly 500,000 to 600,000, who had escaped murderous post-Holocaust anti-Semitism in countries of Eastern Europe such as Poland. After the establishment of the State of Israel, the number of DPs dwindled. Only a small portion, some 30,000, remained on German soil. For them, future relations with the non-Jewish population appeared difficult. Obviously, the Germans did not want or were afraid of having Jews in their country,[5] and the remaining Jews remained reluctantly. In addition to their "survivor guilt," of having lived while others perished, they felt guilty for staying in Germany. They remained for two reasons. One, they felt guilty towards the rest of the Jewish world which, in turn, frowned upon their decision to live in the "country of the perpetrators," and for decades, Germany's post-1945 Jewry was stigmatized by Israel and the rest of the Jewish world. Besides a antagonistic Jewish world, Germany's 'new Jews' also felt guilty towards themselves – for remaining Jews lived a kind of schizophrenic life torn

---

4 Again see Wolffsohn, 1995.
5 Wolffsohn, 1997.

between growing economic wealth and the dissonance between governmental pampering and increasing social gentile openness, parallel to persistent and resistant clusters of anti-Semites. The burden of this hardly happy mental state was passed from Holocaust survivors to the second and third generation. Yes, there were post-1945 Jews born in Germany, but not that many. By 1989, the 'New German-Jewish' community had grayed and seemed doomed to gradually die out – physically or biologically on its own, not by liquidation. About 28,000 Jews lived in Federal Germany on the eve of the downfall of the Iron Curtain.

But then a sort of 'miracle' followed. The Israeli-American Jewish campaign "Let my people go!" gradually pried open the gates of the Soviet Union for Jews from the mid-1970s to 1989. Most went to the United States, some went to Israel but a minority chose West Berlin and West Germany. Reacting to Israeli pressure, the United States introduced quotas for these immigrants in 1989, after peaceful revolutions in Eastern Europe succeeded in bringing down the Communist regimes. Thus, US officials did not consider Eastern Europeans as political refugees anymore. Like it or not, many of those former Soviet Jews who could no longer gain entry into the Land of Golden Opportunities and did not want to go to the Promised Land – Israel – as a default headed for reunified Germany.

Leaving ethical debates aside,[6] the fact is approximately 220,000 former Soviet Jews came to United Germany between 1991 and 2013. Only half of them joined Jewish institutions (i.e. congregations, communities). These figures are indicative of the numeric revolution that has taken place since Germany's reunification, but the statistics are also indicative of the emergence of a second, new and now dominant Jewish stratum in Germany: Upon the remnants of German-German Jewry (almost totally extinguished by 1945, by death or by taking flight) and the thin stratum of the influx of post-Holocaust Polish-Jewish into West Germany and West Berlin, there is now a second, dominant stratum comprised of immigrants raised in an atheist Soviet milieu, largely ignorant of any Jewish tradition. These 'New-New' German Jews were – in many cases Halachically-Jewish but Jewishly they were culturally and spiritually illiterate and distanced from any expression of their Jewishness.

The implications were obvious, if there was to be any Jewish continuity: Such 'formally Jewish' newcomers had to be molded into 'spiritual Jews' by virtue of their association with Jewish communities, which half of them did not even join.

---

6 Historically, this may be as absurd (or even abominable considering they were given exit visas based on requests to 'repatriate to their Jewish homeland') but who has the right to put them in the docket and what entitles others to judge them? Do collective priorities (Rousseau's 'general will' or Kant's philosophy) take precedence over individual's rights to pursuit of happiness ('individual will' and freedom of choice)?

This nominally-Jewish half did not care about its Jewishness at all, at least not institutionally. The other half did join, but most had no affinity for the religious facets of Jewish communal life. They viewed the community instrumentally – for its welfare benefits and social opportunities.

This state of affairs presented new challenges: On the one hand, this new German Jewish demographic significantly bolstered German Jewry numerically, but in terms of Jewish identity it poses a new problem rather than the solution to the unanswered question of how to save post-Holocaust German Jewry. Contrary to the new Polish-German Jews, these New-New German Jews from the former Soviet Union have come to Germany voluntarily but they need to absorb *Jüdischkeit* ('Jewishness') as well as Germanness. *Jüdischkeit* it may be possible to 'teach,' but their *Deutschheit* ('Germaness') they have to develop themselves. Their Jewish predecessors, however, have for the most part been unable and unwilling to serve as mentors. Thus, the new demographic seemed to be left to determine its own German-Jewish identity – which has yet to develop. What shape will it take? Will they be Germans? Jews? Russians? A combination or all three? Nothing? Or nothing new? Jewish historians are not prophets, and only time will tell.

For a long time, a 'Jewish future' in East Germany seemed to be a complete illusion. Between 1946 and 1949 about a thousand long-time Communists, most intellectuals, had returned to what they perceived and believed to be 'the better Germany.' By 1953, however, most of the other East German Jews had already left. The "better Germany" went from bad to worse and, together with other Soviet Stalin-dominated states, persecuted Jews as Jews between late 1948 and Stalin's death in March 1953. The 17 June 1953 uprising crushed brutally by the GDR authorities and the Red Army did not encourage anyone to remain in what was heralded to be "Germany's first workers and farmers state." By the fall of the Berlin Wall, only approximately 400 Jews remained in the GDR, roughly 300 in East Berlin. The local Jewish communities outside of East Berlin consisted of a few dozens members, many elderly. The Russian Jewish influx up from the early 1990s prevented structural collapse.

Today, compared to the overall population in Germany, Jews remain a very small minority, although they are visible, vocal, and enjoy an audience among some Germans. They are not listened to because they have much to say or to contribute. They are listened to because of the six million of their brethren who are silent or have been silenced by German hands. Thus today's German officialdom wants to 'make amends by listening,' even if German-Jewish officialdom's messages have little to contribute. Yet, this is waning – particularly as the 'voice' of Germany's and Western Europe's Muslim population amplifies, driven by both demographic growth and growth in confidence to be heard.

Leaders and Biographies

In the context of this discussion, it is insightful to note some of the most prominent and influential personalities who have left an imprint on the Jewish community. Such leadership qualities are present particularly in the biographies of Jewish leaders in the post-War period, no matter how difficult it was (and maybe still is) to find a 'center of gravity' Jewishly-speaking – stability, balance, and orientation in a country so overshadowed by the Holocaust. The following is an unflinching attempt to put their legacies in retrospect – their leadership styles and their outlooks, their strong points and their weak points, their successes and their failures.

Heinz Galinski

Judged historically and strategically, Heinz Galinski was the pivotal German Jewish leader after 1945. From 1949 to his death in 1992 he served as President of (West) Berlin's local Jewish community. From 1954 to 1963 he headed the Jewish-German community's roof organization – the Central Council of Jews in Germany (Zentralrat der Juden in Deutschland) retaking the helm again between 1988 and 1992.

He was an autocratic personality – authoritarian, a difficult individual, a bitter man. Critics who chafed under his arrogant and high-handed leadership called him "Galle Galinski" due to his vexing personality. Others branded him "liverish Galinski" for his temperament. And there were a host of other tags Galinski earned in the course of a career. Like so many politicians (Jewish and gentile alike) he was egocentric and a man of action who had to be at the center of things at all times – be it strategic planning and action on behalf of the community, or punching tickets for an event or serving as master of ceremonies at a Hanukah ball. He 'ruled' the community with a strong hand but was a democratically-elected leader. A running joke during his lengthy tenure at the helm asked rhetorically: "Whose rule lasted longer: Emperor Hirohito of Japan or Heinz Galinski?" He was not a well-liked individual – neither within the *Zentralrat*, nor among his gentile interlocutors and the German public-at-large. Openly, German officials flattered Galinski; behind his back they complained and moaned and disliked him.

Criticism and jokes at his expense aside, it should be underscored (very important and unfortunately not recognized as a matter of course): Heinz Galinski was 'lily-clean' as a public servant. No graft. No corruption, whatsoever. Not the slightest manifestation of underhanded conduct. One might say, with hindsight, that he was the switchman of postwar German Jewry.

Nevertheless, his moral fiber had been contested. A rumor spread shortly after German Unification that Galinski may have worked for the *Stasi* – the GDR state security apparatus. Even his purported codename circulated: "IM Reb" ("Reb" – short for rabbi). No journalist, political scientist, politician, or historian wanted to investigate the rumor, and risk being labeled 'anti-Semitic' if evidence was found. Thus, the rumor has hung in abeyance ever since. I hesitated to delve into the matter myself – not because of charges of self-hatred that would no doubt be fired at me by Jews and gentiles as a descendant of Holocaust survivors and IDF veteran for 'laundering dirty laundry in public' should the charges turn out to be true. I hesitated because of the love-hate-relationship which typified my longstanding personal relationship with Galinski. Finally and reluctantly I did the documentary archival research. The outcome (much to my relief): "Much ado about nothing."[7] Yes, "IM Reb" did exist but IM Reb was not Heinz Galinski. IM Reb was one of East Berlin's former rabbis who had come from Hungary and like most other GDR rabbis worked for the *Stasi*. Galinski's record was unmarred.

Heinz Galinski can be credited with two fundamentally-important, effective, strategic achievements as a community leader: One may like them or not, but the importance of their outcome cannot be overestimated. When in 1950, the Jewish Agency demanded and the Israeli government aligned itself with the ultimatum that all Jews in Germany leave the country within six months, most local Jews were intimidated and silent. The demand only exacerbated their already bad conscience: Yes, indeed – How could they remain in Germany 'of all places' and 'after all that' or 'despite all that'? Heinz Galinski retorted loud and clear with an Obama-like message of "Yes, we can." This was the gist of the German-Jewish leader's response: Galinski said that like other Jews in Germany, he had not survived Auschwitz only to be told by fellow-Jews or others where to live or where not to live. It was none of the Jewish Agency's business or that of other institutions' or persons' to interfere with individual self-determination. No ostracizing of Jews in Germany followed. Year-by-year, the German-Jewish community became more a matter of fact. Unpopular, disputed... but undeniable, immovably a matter of fact that was ultimately accepted, uncontested, as an integral, and by now pivotal player in the mosaic of Diaspora Jewry.

Heinz Galinski's second strategic achievement was that he masterminded and oversaw Soviet-Jewish immigration to Germany since 1991. Again, he was at odds with other Diaspora Jewish communities and Israeli institutions over this – but 'on the ground' he won the day and without him postwar German Jewry would have been lost.

---

7 Wolffsohn, 1995.

Werner Nachmann

Werner Nachmann, Galinski's predecessor, led the Central Council between 1969 and 1988. His term was unspectacular and not worth mentioning in historical perspective; however, revelation after his death of what transpired 'below the radar' of the Jewish community, changed this picture and created a huge problem for the community.

Against the backdrop of German-Jewish history up until 1945, there was a fixation in considering any German-Jewish representative as a moral beacon – above scrutiny, certainly by Germans, ignoring the frailties real collectives of real human beings, Jewish or gentile, can harbor. Thus, doubts about human virtue were unthinkable when it came to the remnants of German Jewry. In May 1988, four months after Werner Nachmann's death the truth became known: Nachmann, who had been put on a pedestal, came crashing to the ground, tarnishing the collective image of the Jewish community with him. Held up as a paragon of virtue, no one – neither the Jews nor the Germans – 'thought the unthinkable,' that Jewish politicians are as human and fallible as gentile ones. Lamentably, Werner Nachmann had gotten confused with the boundaries between private and public money. For whatever reason, he kept German restitution transfers to Holocaust survivors for himself. Maybe he thought that any German-Jewish money belonged to the most-senior German-Jewish representative. Whatever his reasons, Nachmann had kept about 33 million Deutschmarks in restitution for himself. Unfortunately and quite ironically, expectations of 'paragon of virtue status' status-behavior remains an unhealthy premise underlying German-Jewish existence – a Werner Nachmann legacy.

Ignatz Bubis

Ignatz Bubis, the long-time President of the Frankfurt Community, succeeded Galinski in 1992 and stood at the helm of the *Zentralrat* until his death in 1999. He was the best Jewish communicator in postwar Germany. In fact, he was something like a German-Jewish Ronald Reagan in this sense. Contrary to the vexing "Galle Galinski" Bubis was perceived as grand 'charmer.' This was a welcome change that relaxed German-Jewish nerves. Bubis repeatedly pointed out that he was a 'German citizen of Jewish religion' (deutscher Staatsbürger jüdischen Glaubens). The gentile German world reacted enthusiastically – as if they had found the Holy Grail or at least that this was a German-Jewish 'first' after 1945. It was not, of course. What Bubis said, others had declared many times before. So had Karl Marx, the long-time editor of the Jewish weekly Allgemeine, and so had Hendrik van Dam who had worked as General Secretary of the *Zentralrat* from 1950 to this death in 1973. So had Werner Nachmann and many others, prominent and less prominent German Jews, not to mention the pre-1933 Jews who defined themselves as 'Germans of the Mosaic Persuasion.' The overwhelming applause Bubis received for his declarations was important not because it was a real first; but because it was perceived as one – indicative of the German-Jewish relationship as well as of the human comedy in general: What matters is perception not plausible facts. So, yes, the Bubis era was an era perceived as the era of German-Jewish détente – with some clouds that did not disturb this sunny picture.

The first cloud appeared before Bubis' *Zentralrat* presidency. His role as a businessman and real estate speculator was, to put it mildly, somewhat disputed, but Bubis' reputation took an unexpected turn in 1985 when Rainer Werner Fassbinder, the famous film-producer, wrote a play whose protagonist did not remind just a lunatic fringe of Ignatz Bubis and his commercial practices. The problem was that Fassbinder's text in *Der Müll, die Stadt, und der Tod* ('Garbage, the City, and Death') was so shallow, superficial, and openly and aggressively anti-Semitic that rehabilitated Bubis by turning him into a kind of martyr.

Another cloud was linked to 'other times and other places' – the GDR in 1951. At the time, Bubis had been convicted for black-marketeering during the early post-War years.[8] Such a verdict in an openly anti-Semitic trial on exaggerated or trumped-up charges, with an almost openly anti-Semitic jury, with clearly anti-Semitic witnesses – such a conviction was worthy of something close to knighthood. Consequently, Bubis, like many other GDR convicts, asked to be rehabilitated following German unification. Most applications were no more than a formality, and the same was expected with regard to Bubis. Bubis, however, was not rehabilitated.[9] Legal as well as political officials were upset and wanted to keep this fact secret or at least keep it low-profile. They could not keep it completely secret but they were largely successful in burying the embarrassing incident since it remained unknown to the public-at-large, both Jewish and gentile. The refusal to clear him also remained beyond the interests of historians, journalists, and politicians who may have been happy 'not to know' so as not to be troubled with some darker spots on the beaming light of the moral beacon – a paragon of virtue that Orthodox Jews would label *mita'am* – best translated as clean 'by virtue of his office, not by merit.'

If this was not enough, there was another dark spot in Bubis' record, pointed out by one of Germany's top investigative journalists, Hans Leyendecker from *Süd-*

---

[8] Zatlin, The Bubis Trial in Dresden, Boston University 1951, unpublished paper, presented at a Conference on German Jews since 1945, Munich University, Historisches Kolleg, December 2009, Courtesy of the author.
[9] Personal information to the author by then-acting Saxonian Minister of Justice, Steffen Heitmann, and the leader of the CDU parliamentary group in the Hesse legislature, Dr. Christian Wagner.

deutsche Zeitung formerly with *Der Spiegel*: allegations that Bubis had (perhaps linked to his general black-market activities) illegally sold gold for the Degussa gold handling firm, alluding that the gold had been taken from Holocaust victims.[10] To make his investigation iron-clad, Leyendecker asked to see the relevant Degussa files in the firm's archives. Access was denied. It was also denied to me: First, I was told that such files do not exist, later I was informed that these files did, in fact, exist but that the Bubis family denied access.[11]

Problems with Leadership

Whatever the merits and demerits of Galinski and Bubis, their paler predecessors or successors and Nachmann's moral as well as material flaws, all these individuals chosen to lead not only suffered from drawbacks that flawed their political leadership; they also lacked an intellectual dimension or Jewish spiritual side to guide the community, let alone vision. Heinz Galinski was the only German-Jewish leader who indeed had a vision, although a political one: the renewal of a Jewish community in Germany – "despite all Nazi megacrimes." All the other Jewish leaders, except for the unfortunately low-key Salomon Korn (Frankfurt am Main) did not have or offer any vision – neither political nor spiritual. Therefore, it should come as no surprise that consequently and contrary to German-Jewish tradition up until 1933 and general Jewish values reflected in the *Am HaSefer* ('People of the Book') tradition, the general milieu within Germany's Jewish communities has remained, at best, a-intellectual if not anti-intellectual. No vision. No visionaries. From where can German-Jewish draw guidance? So far, it has not come from Jewish persons in leadership positions or communal institutions. Up to now, lamentably, most German-Jewish leaders have been ridiculed behind their backs by most German and Jewish intellectuals. Why? Because, in the long run, you cannot play the intellectual if you are not intellectual. Time will tell if relatively new Jewish academic and religious institutions such as the liberal Abraham Geiger Kolleg and the conservative Zacharias Frankel College (both at Potsdam University) or the neo-Orthodox Rabbinical College of Berlin, the latter supported by the Ronald S. Lauder Foundation, can reverse this long-lasting negative trend.

---

10 Hans Leyendecker, in: Süddeutsche Zeitung, November 13, 2003.
11 This correspondence is accessible to the academic public, the media, or any other interested person at the archives of the Institut für Zeitgeschichte (Institute for Contemporary History), Munich, Michael Wolffsohn Papers.

This raises an interesting question: Can there be German Jewish existence with no 'Jewish' substance? It is highly questionable whether independent Jewish intellectuals in Germany who have not joined any Jewish community in the past, will begin to do so. Such free spirits, Jewish or not, are by definition independent personalities and do not join institutions which by nature demand discipline and obedience. You cannot square the circle. Germany does not lack Jewish intellectuals. But, Jewish intellectuals such as Marcel Reich-Ranicki, Richard Löwenthal, Ernst Fraenkel, Wolfgang Hildesheimer, Edgar Hilsenrath and others of their caliber do not join congregations. At best they may visit, but they do not join them.

No serious autobiography nor any scholarly biography has been published to date on any of the previous leaders of post-War German Jewry. This comes to no surprise. Career-wise, especially for newcomers, it would be suicidal to publish a serious work that would include the darker side of this or that German-Jewish leader. Paying attention to historical rather than day-to-day issues, their respective so-called 'autobiographies' (and other publications) carry little intrinsic value – positive reviews in certain prestigious dailies notwithstanding. Suffice it to say, dailies have their own standards and agendas; spiritual and intellectual leaders of the People of the Book have to live up to more ambitious intellectual – even 'theological' standards.

In general, serious research on post-1945 German Jewry started much later than general historiography of the FRG. On the other hand research on pre-1945 Germany as well as non-German Jewry has boomed. The reason is self-evident: Until 1945 the boundaries between black and white are clear. Moreover, most potential researchers have been at a loss how to evaluate the contempt for Germany's new Jewry of the Jewish world and Israel. While this contempt has been overcome gradually, its documentation and interpretation constitutes a mine field for researchers who want to get a job or keep it. True, avoiding unsavory or unpopular topics is not singular to the study of German-Jewish topics, but to date, perceptions and studies on Jewish issues have often succumbed to overstatement, often swinging between either adoration or distortion. Distortion dominated until 1945, adoration thereafter. Complex realities have not been sought. German-Jewish issues and studies are still à la recherche du temps perdu ('In Search of lost Time'). Beyond career considerations, archival access is a major barrier to serious examination of the historiography. Degussa is a case in point that reflects the scope of the problem for any serious historian.

Searching for New Identity

Inside the Jewish community of a reunified Germany, the pursuit of a new collective identity circles around questions such as: Can Jewish religion function as a common denominator for Germany's Jews? Are there competing ideas and 'alternatives'?

According to surveys, roughly fifty percent of FRG-Jewry has not been outspokenly Jewish-oriented, to put it mildly. This is one side of the coin. The other is that most of the communities are run or maintained according to Orthodox rites and rituals. True, Progressive (Reform) and Conservative Judaism have been able to make some inroads, but in quantitative as well qualitative terms, the inroads of streams such as 'Chabad Orthodoxy' have been far more spectacular.

This institutional dominance by Jewish orthodoxy in a mostly secular, religiously indifferent, and even ignorant Jewish community will inevitably lead to internal polarization with an insurmountable institutional advantage for the Orthodox line. Why? Uncommitted Jews will no longer remain in or join Orthodox communities. We will, therefore, see increasingly Orthodox German-Jewish congregations or institutions with small liberal pockets and an un- or rather de-institutionalized and, in the long-run, 'de-judaized' Jewish collective. A Jewish collective characterized solely by its Jewish roots or origins will arise. It will not be defined by Jewish substance, nor by Jewish religion, nor history or the sense of togetherness – unless the anti-Semitism of the outside world pushes them back into their religious or secular Jewishness. Such an anti-Semitic rise, however, is highly unlikely. Islamist anti-Jewish terror may be another force for renewed 'Jewishness' – a more likely scenario, whose emergence can already been felt. But this too is no positive Jewish self-determination or autonomy. It is negative heteronomy.[12]

To conclude: Germany's new Jewry has become and will increasingly be a community of Jews without Judaism, with a vocal and growing Orthodox minority, and a much smaller but also very active liberal mini-minority. There just may be another Jewish 'lifebelt' left: Israelism instead of Jewish religion. But 'Israelism' in and of a Diaspora community is somewhat odd, if not absurd. It is nice to wave the Israeli flag, say *Shalom* or even *Hag Sameh* and sing *Hevenu shalom alehem* plus *Hava nagila*. But such 'Israelisms' culminate in a farce, not an Israeli reality. It is an absurdity, and an absurdity cannot be the ingredients for strengthening identity.

---

[12] Heteromomy: in philosophy, an action that is influenced by a force outside the individual that lacks moral free choice or self-determination.

Research and Outlook

The state of empirical research on the Jews in today's Germany and recent decades is clearly inadequate. The most recent handbook on post-1945 German Jewry is a summary of 'statements' on the social and economic situation of FRG-Jewry – not the results of empirical research! Moreover, its content is suboptimal, having ignored the 1970s as well as the 1980s, or the earlier decades for that matter.[13] An unconvincing explanation is given: After the Holocaust, gentiles and Jews had been reluctant to collect separate statistical data on Jews. This is a methodological absurdity: Almost every Jewish community has had its social divisions and every division has had its own organizational framework and officialdom who kept records. Moreover, this 'excuse' seems blind to the fact that a central social agency of, by and for FRG-Jewry does exist, namely the Central Welfare Institute for Jews in Germany.

We realize that while passing over this fact, some post-1945 academic publications on Germany Jewry pretend to be real research rather than impressionism presented by academics. Much is said and published about FRG-Jewry, less is researched. I add the sad fact that this also holds true for statements and publications on Israel. Academic tools are available, but they are not applied by all academics.

Nevertheless even without detailed data and studies, it is safe to state (based on the appraisals of longtime informed participant-observations, one of anthropology's best tools) that various generational and geographical groups since 1945 have witnessed clear upward mobility. This generalization is also valid with regard to the influx of Jewish émigrés from the former Soviet Union who have arrived since the 1970s and, much more so, since 1991. To put it unequivocally: The longer they have lived in Federal Germany the better off they are. The chronological summary is linked to the generational one: Upward mobility on the macro-level is evident from first generation of immigrants to second-generation offspring and so forth. True, at the beginning, the majority of former Soviet Jews faced huge economic and social problems, not just the challenge of acculturation. Welfare authorities and social workers within their respective communities have had a hard time responding to these challenges, yet, on the whole, they have succeeded. This success, however, turned out to be a mixed blessing: Individually, for needy persons, it was a definite success. These perspectives – material wealth and comfort – are not a very encouraging harbinger for any future growth and blossoming of German-Jewish life. There is yet another challenge: Intermarriage.

---

[13] Goschler / Kauders, Dritter Teil: 1968–1989 Positionierungen. In: Brenner (ed.). Geschichte der Juden in Deutschland, 2012, p. 295.

Since the late 1940s FRG-Jewry has held the Jewish "world record" with mostly 70 to 80 percent intermarriage.[14] Intermarriage has usually been considered as the beginning-of-the "end of the road," a kind of self-inflicted liquidation process. Is this so in German Jewry today, or not? Only time will tell. But in fact, the existential question remains: How will FRG-Jewry – and modern contemporary Jewry elsewhere in the Diaspora, cope with new open societies? Will they prevail?

References

Brenner, Michael (ed.). *Geschichte der Juden in Deutschland. Von 1945 bis zur Gegenwart.* Munich: C. H. Beck, 2012.

Goschler, Constantin, Anthony Kauders. Dritter Teil: 1968–1989 Positionierungen. In *Geschichte der Juden in Deutschland. Von 1945 bis zur Gegenwart*, Michael Brenner (ed.), pp. 295–378. Munich: C. H. Beck, 2012.

Leyendecker, Hans. "Das Echo der Vergangenheit," *Süddeutsche Zeitung*, November 13, 2003. http://www.sueddeutsche.de/wirtschaft/degussa-das-echo-der-vergangenheit-1.903032 (accessed August 21, 2014).

Wolffsohn, Michael, Uwe Puschner. *Geschichte der Juden in Deutschland, Quellen und Kontroversen*. Munich: Bayrischer Schulverlag, 1992.

Wolffsohn, Michael. *Eternal Guilt? Forty Years of German-Jewish-Israeli Relations*. New York: Columbia University Press, 1993 (German Edition with Uwe Puschner: *Ewige Schuld? 40 Jahre deutsch-jüdisch-israelische Beziehungen*. Munich: Piper, 1988).

Wolffsohn, Michael. *Die Deutschland-Akte. Juden und Deutsche in Ost und West. Tatsachen und Legenden*. Munich: Edition Ferenczy bei Bruckman, 1995.

Wolffsohn, Michael. *Meine Juden – Eure Juden*. Munich: Pieper, 1997.

Wolffsohn, Michael, Thomas Brechenmacher. *Denkmalsturz? Brandts Kniefall*. Munich: Olzog, 2005.

Wolffsohn, Michael, Thomas Brechenmacher. *Deutschland, jüdisch Heimatland. Die Geschichte der deutschen Juden vom Kaiserreich bis heute*. Munich: Pieper, 2008.

Zatlin, Jonathan R. The Bubis Trial in Dresden. Boston University: 1951, unpublished paper; presented at a Conference on German Jews since 1945, Munich University, Historisches Kolleg, December 2009.

---

[14] Wolffsohn / Puschner, 1992, p. 210 with data from 1951 to 1988. For more recent data see Statistisches Jahrbuch Deutschland (Statistical Abstract Germany).

Michael Elm
The Making of Holocaust Trauma in German Memory

Some Reflection about Robert Thalheim's Film *And Along Come Tourists*

If one were to inquire in present-day Germany whether the Holocaust constitutes a traumatic event in German history, a majority of the population would most probably answer in the affirmative. What seems self-evident today is, of course, the result of a long and winding road which connects the German past with the present and – it goes without saying – is still under construction. The chapter at hand investigates the notion of trauma which has been established through the course of West and East German history and asks the question – with the help of Robert Thalheim's movie *And Along Comes Tourists* (*Am Ende kommen Touristen*)[1]: Which historical narrative could be helpful in building trust between non-Jewish Germans and Jews today?

The Holocaust as a Cultural Trauma in German Memory

The memory of the Holocaust in Germany is not a perpetrator trauma as one could assume. A perpetrator trauma requires that the perpetrators themselves recognize their wrongdoing or, for instance, that soldiers may suffer from Post Traumatic Stress Disorder (PTSD) after their military service, as in the case of the Vietnam War, which triggered the development of the medical category PTSD. In the case of Germany after the Second World War, the majority of soldiers, policemen, or prison guards who were involved in murdering European Jews did not seem to have suffered from such symptoms, nor did they ponder or agonize over the morality of their actions.[2] This begs the question: How did the notion of a 'Holocaust trauma in

---
1 And Along Come Tourists (Am Ende kommen Touristen), directed by Robert Thalheim, [2007] 2008.
2 The so called "First Auschwitz Trial" in Frankfurt from 1963 to 1965, where 22 members of the extermination camp administration, mainly in low ranking positions, were charge for murder, can serve as an example of this attitude. None of the accused uttered a word of excuse or regret. Confer: http://www.auschwitz-prozess.de/ (accessed January 10, 2013).

Germany' come into being and what does it imply? I would suggest that the current state of German collective memory is better described as 'a cultural trauma within the society of the perpetrators.'

The concept of cultural trauma is embedded in a social theory, which provides more sophisticated means to understand the recent changes in German collective memory because the concept accentuates the artificial side of the trauma construction in German society.[3] I will not only focus on this well-known process of building a new collective memory – with Auschwitz as its negative core – but also on the challenges of such an identity construction that arise for a third or fourth generation in Germany after the war. Not many films deal with the latter problem in a substantial way. I have chosen Robert Thalheim's film *And Along Come Tourists* because I see it as an attempt to investigate the consequences of acknowledging historical responsibility for these age groups. The film sheds some light on what might come after denial, questioning, rebellion, acknowledgement, memorialization, and routinization in German and European memory politics and culture.

To remember the Holocaust as a traumatic event in Germany is an invented tradition – an invention that is useful and necessary, because it has helped to create and stabilize a much needed mindset in postwar Germany. The very existence of this mindset is an expression of what I will describe later as a new twist in Germany's relation to modernity. In the paragraphs that follow I outline some stages in the development of this cultural trauma with respect to German films. Cinema is not a mirror; rather it provides societies with powerful audio-visual narratives of history, which interfere in and communicate with existing cultural narratives in art and society. Thereby influencing the narrative framework from which people draw their historical and social identities.

Cinematic Significations of How to Remember What

For a long time the collective memory in Germany was divided between an official, public memory and a private memory that runs through families. This cleavage can be found in both German states (both East and West Germany) despite remarkable differences in other aspects of memory politics. While the acknowledgment of responsibility was part of the official memory in almost every part of West Germany society, the private memory claimed victimhood and suffering for the Germans themselves. In fact, one might understand the development of

---

[3] Alexander, Trauma, 2012.

German memorial cultural much better, if one starts with the splitting of remembrance into a private and a public memory. These two memories overlap in what I would label a 'seduction narrative.' According to this narrative, the Germans were seduced and betrayed by Hitler and his elite. Cinematically this divide found expression in the depiction of the myth of the innocent *Wehrmacht*, which is portrayed in many successful West German productions such as *The Devil's General (Des Teufels General)*[4], *Stalingrad: Dogs, Do You Want to Live Forever (Hunde, wollt ihr ewig leben?)*[5], as well as the comparably critical TV-Production *Am grünen Strand der Spree* ('On the Green Riverside of the Spree')[6] until more recent films such as *The Downfall (Der Untergang)*[7]. This constellation allowed being critical of the Nazi regime without blaming a wider German population. As we know, the image of the *Saubere Wehrmacht* ('Clean Wahrmacht') was publicly defended until the mid-1990s when the exhibition *Crimes of the Wehrmacht* stirred a heated debate all over Germany. Sonja M. Schulz claims in her recently published study about National Socialism and film that up until today no feature film has chosen the crimes of German Police units or the *Wehrmacht* as a central subject.[8]

A decisive medial step towards acceptance of the Holocaust as a traumatic event in German history was made through the broadcasting of the American television mini-series *Holocaust* in early 1979. The encounter between the German-Jewish Weiss family and the German-Christian Dorf family broke through the filter of public and private memory and allowed for identification with the victims. Millions of Germans watched the melodramatic account which was criticized for its reduction of the Holocaust to the fate of a single Jewish family but also praised for its wide appeal. The mini-series marked the transition from rejection of the historical crime, to a melodramatic understanding of it.[9] Thus,

---

4 The Devil's General (Des Teufels General), directed by Helmut Käutner, [1955] 2009.
5 Stalingrad: Dogs, Do You Want to Live Forever (Hunde, wollt ihr ewig leben?), directed by Frank Wisbar, [1959] 2001.
6 Am grünen Strand der Spree – Große Geschichten, directed by Fritz Umgelter, [1960] 2014.
7 The Downfall (Der Untergang), directed by Oliver Hirschbiegel, [2004] 2004.
8 Schulz, Der Nationalsozialismus im Film, 2012, p. 504. According to Schulz there were plans by Romuald Karmakar to make a movie about Police Battalion 101. They have not been realized yet only the documentary *Land der Vernichtung* was produced in 2004, originally meant to be a pilot study, Schulz, 2012, p. 316.
9 Reichel, Erfundene Erinnerung, 2004, pp. 250–263. Interestingly enough the Bundeszentrale für politische Bildung ('Federal Agency for Civic Education' BpB), a major, state-sponsored educational organization, suggested a different ending of the mini-series. The US-American version closes with the emigration to Israel of the Zionistic son of the Weiss family who joined the partisans during the war. The BpB argued that the Zionistic narrative could be understood in a redemptive manner by a German audience, so the German version was televised *without* this ending, emphasizing the catastrophe and not the way out of it.

the series promoted an understanding of the Holocaust as a traumatic event in German history. Identification with the victims became possible. Obviously other changes were needed to accomplish this shift in German memorial culture. German society underwent quite a few developments, from the payment of reparations in the 1950s by the Adenauer government, to the widespread reception of the Eichmann trial in Jerusalem as well as the Auschwitz trials in Frankfurt from 1963 to 1965. It experienced the generational rebellion of the students of 1968 and the genuflection of Chancellor Willy Brandt in front of the Warshaw Ghetto Uprising monument in December 1970 and many more sociopolitical and sociocultural developments before German society was able to transform its view to the past.[10]

With regard to this transformation process, there is also a reasonable difference between *The Downfall* and the others cinematic productions that were mentioned. *The Downfall* did not have to acknowledge the past, because other movies and the German society-at-large had done that. It could focus on the inner condition of German society at this historical last stage of Nazism and of the history of reception. The film's director Oliver Hirschbiegel stated in an interview that the film was meant as an exploration of the Hitler myth. He wanted to show the human side of Hitler in order to deconstruct his demonic media image. Especially those aspects of his personality which were both attractive for a large part of the former German population and which were not challenged in recent media representations needed to be confronted. Therefore it could be understood as an intervention in what I have termed the 'seduction narrative.' Unfortunately it failed in many respects. One of them was the firm's failure to deconstruct the Nazi propaganda image of Hitler himself as a fatherly figure.[11] Other movies – for example, Dani Levy's *My Führer – The Really Truest Truth about Adolf Hitler (Mein Führer – Die wirklich wahrste Wahrheit über Hitler)*[12] – tried to mock the attitude of historical authenticity which prevailed in *The Downfall* and tried to establish a more ironic narrative and aesthetic style in depicting Hitler as a cinematic character and the artistic decision of the director in *The Downfall* to attempt to 'replicate' the historical milieu down to the physical characteristics and personal mannerisms and speech patterns of Hitler himself in the name of 'historical authenticity'? It is, indeed, rather obvious that the majority of cinematic productions about the Nazi period tend to hide behind a

---

10 For a comprehensive approach of these changes in German memory politics confer: Olick, What Does It Mean to Normalize the Past. In: Olick (ed.), States of Memory, 2003; Giesen, The Trauma of Perpetrators. In: Alexander (ed.), Cultural Trauma and Collective Identity, 2004.
11 For a more in-depth analysis of Hitler's image in cinema confer: Elm, Man, Demon, Icon. In: Machtans / Ruehl (eds.), Hitler – Films from Germany, 2012.
12 My Führer – The Really Truest Truth about Adolf Hitler (Mein Führer – Die wirklich wahrste Wahrheit über Hitler), directed by Oliver Hirschbiegl, [2007] 2007.

wall of historical facts and an illusionist attitude of unmediated access to historical reality. The strategy to mock such pathetic images of 'the Führer' and narrations about the Nazi past is even more visible in Walter Moers Bunker animation or, for instance, in the various spoofs with bogus subtitles on Bruno Ganz's Hitler performance in *The Downfall* that can be found on the Internet. One of the most popular is about Hitler trying to find a parking space in Tel Aviv.[13] I regard these attempts to ironize historical realism, as an expression of generational discontent with a memorial culture that has become quite static – and not only in Germany. For instance, Quentin Tarantino's *Inglourious Basterds*[14] can be regarded as a more recent approach in counterfactual history on the matter.[15]

Now, even though we can identify major deficits in the dealing with the past, the main problem of German memorial culture is not to acknowledge historical guilt, because this is what *has* been achieved. The problem is rather to understand the consequences of it. Auschwitz has indeed become an integral part of German identity. Even if a minority of citizens do not want to recognize the importance or even want to reject this part of German history, they have to take it into account. Memorialization and routinization are essential parts of the German collective memory for good reasons. In my understanding, the difficulties to integrate such a monstrous past in one's own personal identity as a German citizen are still underestimated. Furthermore Auschwitz requires a reflection far beyond personal guilt. Karl Jaspers, Hannah Arendt, Theodor W. Adorno, and many others have started this ongoing critical project. As a result of it, German identity has been challenged and haunted, driven (theoretically) to the need to take on a post-conventional[16] shape. The post-conventional aspect in German identity formation implies an obligation to reflect one's own social and cultural origin, to question normality as a convention. In this sense, the understanding of the Holocaust as a cultural trauma triggers a shift in German modernity. Politically this shift found its expression through a different notion of nationality from an ethnic understanding to a more democratic and pluralistic one. The general rift in German identity formation is both a result of and an impetus for memorial culture and not an undisputed reality on the ground in present-day Germany. The

---

13 N.N., Holocaust Survivors Protest Hitler Tel-Aviv Parking Parody, http://www.liveleak.com/view?i=bed_1234973320 (accessed 25 March, 2015).
14 Inglourious Basterds, directed by Quentin Tarantino, [2009] 2009.
15 Hückmann, Vengeful Fiction. In: Elm / Kabalek / Köhne (eds.), The Horrors of Trauma in Cinema, 2014.
16 The expression is taken from Lawrence Kohlbergs well-known concept of moral development, where it also signifies the last stage in moral development of an individual. The latter aspect of the concept with its normative implications and hierarchical structure does not apply to the discussion at hand, see: Kohlberg, Die Psychologie der Moralentwicklung, 1996.

challenge to integrate a difficult cultural heritage into one's own identity needs to be accompanied by an ongoing public debate, educational programs, and a discourse in political philosophy which are able to maintain the coherence of long-term developments. For instance I would argue that Jürgen Habermas' theory of communication action and discourse ethic is very much the political philosophy of this historical constellation. It represents a social theory (*Gesellschaftstheorie*) which questions the standards of rationality in favor of public debate and moral reasoning. Interestingly enough, the 'everyday life' approach of Robert Thalheim's movie – when it comes to historical responsibility – displays some similarities to Habermas' life world concept as a basic (uncircumventable) realm for normative orientation.[17] Memorial culture should not downplay the artificiality of its origin as an invented tradition nor disregard it as something only negative. The universalistic impetus echoes a tendency in the society of the perpetrators that has to be accompanied by a particularistic one to chronicle the destruction of Jews and Jewish life in Germany and all over Europe.

And Along Come Tourists

There are a few cinematic productions which reflect the complexity of this memorial culture. One of the more advanced endeavors is Robert Thalheims *And Along Come Tourists*. This third-generation narrative expresses the difficulties of integrating the German past in one's own identity and everyday life, against the background of a highly routinized memorial culture. The plot tells the story of Sven (Alexander Fehling), who does his civil service at a youth hostel and education center (*Jugendbegegnungsstätte*) near the Auschwitz memorial site. His main assignment is to help a Polish survivor, Stanislaw Krzemiński (Ryszard Ronczewski). The elderly survivor works at a restoration facility and testifies from time to time for visitors of the memorial site. Krzemiński's restoration task is to maintain the suitcases that are part of the exhibition in Auschwitz. Skillfully, Thalheim addresses the generational divide between 'living memory' (Maurice Halbwachs)[18] and the aspiration of institutionalized remembering. At the end of the movie, we will get to know that Krzemiński promised the deported people when they arrived at the ramp of Auschwitz, to take care of their suitcases and return them in good condition. According to the staged mindset of the survivor, they are not just parts of an exhibition but items that should be usable for living persons.

---

17 See: Jürgen Habermas, Von den Weltbildern zur Lebenswelt, 2012.
18 Maurice Halbwachs, The Collective Memory, 1980.

This attitude clashes with a memorial culture that is depicted throughout the film with a tendency to reify its objects, among them also the survivor himself, for the representation of a painful but somehow mastered past.

The character of Sven is dramaturgically designed to show the tension between these two different approaches to the past. His character serves in the cinematic narration as a mediator between the living memory of the survivor and the institutional efforts of society. In a more general way, he moderates between memory and cultural trauma. We will see that the character undergoes a maturation process from a passive towards an active historical attitude.

The dramaturgical design of Svens character is introduced in the opening sequences when Sven first meets Krzemiński and is welcomed by the director of the youth hostel and education center Klaus Herold (Rainer Sellien). In the first sequence, Sven enters Krzemiński's apartment where he is supposed to live and – because he is exhausted from the journey to Oświęcim – finishes the old man's milk in the refrigerator. Krzemiński is not amused by this behavior and mocks in Polish, whether his apartment has become a youth hostel now. In the second sequence Herold briefly explains to Sven, what his job obligations are in the education center. Herold emphasizes that the facility is not only a hostel but offers 'educational experiences'[19]. We will see that the clash between everyday necessities and the monumental shadow of the past is a reoccurring pattern throughout the movie.

Fig. 1: Krzemiński (Ryszard Ronczewski) at his restoration work.
(Foto: X Verleih AG, Berlin, 23/5 Filmpoduktion GmbH)

---

[19] And Along Come Tourists, 02:45–05:30.

Along with the conflict of how to remember the past, the movie stages the everyday life experience of the present-day German generation. This everyday life experience is aesthetically captured through the employment of a subjective handheld camera and gets spatially expanded to the Polish town of Oświęcim and its youth who tries to make a living in proximity to the memorial side of Auschwitz. In one of these scenes Sven is entering a rock concert somewhere in the town. Sven is depicted as enjoying the relaxed atmosphere and rebellious tunes of the rock concert. When the singer of the group addresses him as a possible agent of a record company, the conversation soon turns direction, where Sven's presence will be identified with the German past in Auschwitz. The singer mocks Sven's work at the education center as the return of a "German civil army" in Auschwitz.[20] Obviously the Polish and German youngsters are not on good terms. The staging shows a rather restrained reaction by Sven to the rocker's mocking – just disappointedly nursing his beer and shrugging his shoulders. To me this seems quite an accurate depiction of the behavior from an average German middleclass man. The scene illustrates that taking on the blame has become part of a German identity formation for this generation. During the movie we will find some more scenes that identify Sven with the German past. Thus, the second function of Sven's character in the cinematic narration is to represent the situation of being addressed as the heir of historical guilt.

Fig. 2: The Oświęcim train station. An 'everyday life perspective'.
(Foto: X Verleih AG, Berlin, 23/5 Filmpoduktion GmbH)

---

20 And Along Come Tourists, 08:37–10:36.

Both ways of encountering the dreadful past are situated outside the former death camp. I consider this is a big advantage for the film.[21] The narration does not get involved into the usual strategies to authenticate the past and can draw all attention to the presence and how the presence is afflicted by a past, which sometimes falls prey to everyday interests itself. The plot also refrains from referring to Sven's family story. Thus, the narration emphasizes the generational gap without disconnecting Sven's identity from his German origin.

The troublesome German-Polish youth encounter is intensified through Sven's relation with Ania Łanuszewska (Barbara Wysocka). Sven gets to know her through his position at the education center. Ania works as a guide on the memorial side of Oświęcim. For dramaturgical reasons, she happens to be the sister of the band's solo vocalist Krzysztof Łanuszewski (Piotr Rogucki), whom Sven encountered during the concert. In a later part of the movie Sven and Ania will start a love affair. Before that – in one of the film's most remarkable sequences – Sven and Ania are making a bicycle trip in the beautiful landscape of Auschwitz-Birkenau. The director manages to catch something of the uncanny atmosphere of this place and the helplessness of two young adults to come to terms with it.

Fig.3: Sven and Ania. Their romantic bicycle ride along the fence of the death camp. (Foto: X Verleih AG, Berlin, 23/5 Filmpoduktion GmbH)

---

[21] There is one scene, which stages the suitcase exhibition inside the camp. Thalheim stated in an interview that is seemed indispensable for the narration of the movie. Press booklet: Am Ende kommen Touristen, http://www.x-verleih.de/de/presse/null/dateien/AM-ENDE-KOM-MEN-TOURISTEN (accessed October 20, 2013). Of course it is well known that it is very difficult to get permission to film inside the extermination camps of Auschwitz. Even Steven Spielberg did not get it for Schindler's List.

After cycling through the village of Monowice, which was the site where the IG-Farben concern used forced laborers for the building of a chemical plant, Sven and Ania take a break at a little lake. Sven, who is obviously moved by the presence of the thinly-covered past, tries to start a conversation about it. He asks Ania how she manages to live in such a place, where 'humanity's biggest atrocity took place.' Ania evades a clear answer and stresses the fact that for her Oświęcim is simply the place she grew up in. She returns the challenging question by asking Sven "You are living here now, too. How do you feel about it? You are German." Sven does not find words to reply to the question and the question is finally thwarted by Ania's remark that she does not understand its meaning. The youngsters get up and cycle back, but the camera insists on the question. Not only do we see a lengthy scene when they cycle along the fence of the camp, but also the long shot at the lake holds some aesthetical reading possibilities.[22]

We know from Greek mythology, especially from Ovid's Pan and Syrinx in his *Metamorphoses* that people under pressure might change their shape. Every piece of reed in the lake that fills the background of this scene could be the disguise of a person murdered in Auschwitz. The German and Polish characters in this scene seem to feel their absent presence but do not find a way to include these feeling in their twenty-first century European life.

Another element of the plot is the depiction of an instrumental twist in German memorial culture. A German chemical company which has relocated its operations in Oświęcim uses the Polish survivor for its public image as a historically-sensitive company. Sven is appalled by the behavior of the representatives, which serves as a first turning point in developing a more profound attitude to the past and brings him closer to the Polish survivor Krzemiński in particular. There are two major sequences which stage this instrumental attitude. The first sequence deals with the arrogance of a German engineer, who complains about the bad conditions of the plant as a result of low Polish working standards and a scene in which Krzemiński testifies to the apprentices of the company. The apprentices do not show a deeper interest in his account but want to see the tattooed number on his arm out of morbid curiosity.[23] In the second of these sequences Sven and Ania have already become a couple and are in a good mood on the way to the inauguration of a memorial in Monowice. Both are on duty. Sven is driving the car in his capacity as assistance to Krzemiński and Ania will serve as a translator of Krzemiński's opening speech for the representatives of the Polish community. During this scene the public relation manager of the company, Andrea Schneider (Lena Stolze) interrupts the speech of the survivor because she

---

22 And Along Come Tourists, 45:03–49:08.
23 And Along Come Tourists, 25:17–28:20.

thinks that the weather conditions are not suitable for the occasion. Krzemiński is appalled by the rude behavior and refuses to join a photo together with the representatives of the company and the director of the education center Herold.[24]

In this sequence the narration offers some kind of mute socio-economical criticism as well. The allusion to the German chemical plant clearly carries echoes of the former IG-Farben Trust and a continuity of German economical domination. I do not want to pursue this line of the narration, although it certainly serves to portray an ongoing social divide in modern Europe.

The cinematic narration combines four interrelated storylines: Sven and Krzemiński, Sven's relation to Ania and her brother who works at the chemical plant, the works of the education center and the preservation department and finally the German chemical company, which wants to relocate in Oświęcim. All of them are connected through their relation to the past or – to be more precise – through a conflict between everyday life challenges and representations of the past. The Holocaust is acknowledged as cultural trauma but its meaning on the level of everyday life is rather arbitrary. This is the space the movie exposes and explores.

Fig. 4: Krzemiński and Sven. The 'everyday life' approach.
(Foto: X Verleih AG, Berlin, 23/5 Filmpoduktion GmbH)

After the interrupted inauguration speech, Sven's develops his own interpretation of the "special sensitivity"[25], which the environment requires. Sven keeps supplying Krzemiński with suitcases from the preservation department although

---

24 And Along Come Tourists, 55:54–59:38.
25 And Along Come Tourists, 1:11:15.

the Polish professionals do not want to accept Krzemińskis outdated restoration methods any more. The conservators inform Herold, and Sven gets scolded by him in front of Krzemiński. For Krzemiński it becomes clear that his restoration skills are no longer wanted. In a rather prosaic scene he tells Sven about the promise to deported people at the ramp of Auschwitz to return the suitcases to them, and requests that Sven leave him alone. This last scene with the Polish survivor seems to suggest that he will follow the advice of his sister to move into her place, a house in the remote and quiet countryside.

Sven's private life also reaches a turning point. Ania decides to leave Oświęcim and in ending the relationship with Sven, she explains to him that the job offer in Brussels she received will be her only chance to leave the town; otherwise she might get stuck there like most of her female friends around her.

Fig.5: Ania tells Sven near the train station that they have to separate.
(Foto: X Verleih AG, Berlin, 23/5 Filmpoduktion GmbH)

After being dropped by his lover and frustrated by his work in the education center Sven is resolved to leave Oświęcim for good. The last scene offers an open-ended turning point. Sven is already at the train station of Oświęcim, when a German school class with its teacher arrives. The disoriented group does not know how to get to the memorial site. Again, the narration emphasizes the difficulties of everyday life problems against the background of great educational messages that seem to come from the horrible past. Sven decides to accompany the group and is clipping their tickets while the teacher lectures him about German history and responsibility. The scene displays an inversion of the teacher-pupil relationship, the relations between second- and third-generation Germans, because

Sven is performing a kind of responsibility the teacher is only talking about. The scene stages the difficulty of combining the 'Never Again' master narrative of the second generation with the non-heroic everyday life experience of the third or fourth generation in present-day Europe. I read this final scene as an insight into the kind of struggle that is involved in taking on historical responsibility with a non-heroic attitude. Thus, it can be understood as the staging of a generational appropriation of those contents of the public memory that were mentioned earlier in this chapter. I see it as an attempt to give life to an invented cultural trauma in German memory politics. The most iconic Holocaust images such as trains and suitcases take on another layer of meaning. They link the present, not only to the past as we are used to see them in cinematic narratives, but also connect the past to a present-day generation which tries to make sense for themselves. When Sven is on the way with his wheeled suitcases to the train station in Oświęcim it is clear that these iconic objects refer not only to the past but also to the future of the young German, a double-metaphor – for the 'baggage' they carry and the opportunities they have. The suitcases in particular are a kind of transitional objects which were repaired by Krzemiński to keep them usable for people who will not return, iconic items for the exhibition in the Auschwitz memorial site, while they serve equally an everyday life purpose today. The present is not suspended by the past, while the past remains an object in its own right.

Of course other readings are possible: As I could observe in my academic teaching at Ben-Gurion University quite a few Israeli students were rather irritated by the narrative of the movie. A young non-Jewish German and a Pole discuss the heritage of Auschwitz without including explicitly a Jewish perspective. The question arises – whether the position of the 'Jewish other' has to be addressed in such a narration or not. When I worked at the Fritz Bauer Institute in Frankfurt, we discussed a similar question about the movie. The film-scholar Ronny Loewy argued that a film, which takes place in Auschwitz, has to include a Jewish perspective in his narration and claimed it was missing here. I did not quite agree: Every film that is situated at this location and its vicinity already has Jewish history in its backpack. Thalheim knows this and avoids the redundancy that we usually encounter when we are confronted with the icons of Auschwitz. He chooses to quote them from the everyday life perspective of a third German and Polish generation.[26] Through this narrative strategy the historical perspective is reversed. The past is depicted through the presence of the young adults and through their everyday life problems against the background of a well-established memorial culture. Therefore, the narration does not only *acknowledge*

---

26 Thalheim confirmed to prefer such a cinematic and historic approach in an interview, Gansera, in: Süddeutsche Zeitung, Mai 17, 2010.

the Holocaust as a cultural trauma in German memorial culture; it *expresses* the challenges in the identity formation of the current German generation, and generations to come. Thalheim's film offers a different approach to encounter the German past. The approach provides some potential for rebuilding trust between non-Jewish Germans and Jews because it dares to take on responsibility for this past, unprotected by a melodramatic inclusion of Jewish otherness. Mutual trust relies very much on the certainty to know where the other side is standing.

Another aspect of Ronny Loewy's criticism was that Oświęcim was not only a concentration and extermination camp, but also a Polish town with a large Jewish population.[27] This aspect is indeed neglected in the film, and here I completely agree with Loewy's criticism. Especially since the director decided to tell his story from everyday life perspective, the everyday life and what is missing in it could have become part of the plot. The emphasis on the German-Polish perspective is – from a narrative point of view – by no means excluding the Jewish experience. Still the barriers between the collective memories remain difficult to overcome.

References

Alexander, Jeffrey C. *Trauma. A Social Theory*. Cambridge: Polity Press, 2012.
Elm, Michael. Man, Demon, Icon: Hitler's Image between Cinematic Representation and Historical Reality. In *Hitler – Films from Germany: History, Cinema and Politics since 1945*, Karolin Machtans, Martin A. Ruehl (eds.), pp. 151–167. London: Palgrave, 2012.
Elm, Michael, Kobi Kabalek, Julia B. Köhne (eds.). *The Horrors of Trauma in Cinema: Violence Void Visualization*. Newcastle upon Tyne: Cambridge Scholars Publishing, 2014.
Gansera, Rainer. "Zur Disko am Lagerzaun vorbei," *Süddeutsche Zeitung*, Mai 17, 2010. http://sz.de/1.256149 (accessed January 10, 2013).
Giesen, Bernhard. The Trauma of Perpetrators: The Holocaust as the Traumatic Reference of German National Identity. In *Cultural Trauma and Collective Identity*, Jeffrey C. Alexander, Ron Eyerman, Bernhard Giesen, Neil J. Smelser, and Piotr Sztompka (eds.), pp. 112–154. Berkeley, Los Angeles, London: University of California Press, 2004.
Habermas, Jürgen. Von den Weltbildern zur Lebenswelt. In: Jürgen Habermas, *Nachmetaphysisches Denken II. Aufsätze und Repliken*, pp. 19–53. Berlin: Suhrkamp, 2012.
Halbwachs, Maurice. *The Collective Memory*. New York: Harper & Row, 1980.
Hückmann, Dania. Vengeful Fiction: (Re-)Presenting Trauma in *Inglourious Basterds*. In *The Horrors of Trauma in Cinema: Violence Void Visualization*, Michael Elm, Kobi Kabalek, and Julia B. Köhne (eds.), pp. 90–107. Newcastle upon Tyne: Cambridge Scholars Publishing, 2014.

---

[27] For a more detailed account on the history of Oświęcim and its Jewish population see: http://oshpitzin.pl/between-the-wars/ (accessed June 17, 2014). My thanks for this link go to the English editor of this article, Daniella Ashkenazy.

Kohlberg, Lawrence. *Die Psychologie der Moralentwicklung*. Frankfurt a. M.: Suhrkamp, 1996.
Machtans, Karolin, Martin A. Ruehl (eds.). *Hitler – Films from Germany: History, Cinema and Politics since 1945*. London: Palgrave, 2012.
Olick, Jeffrey. What Does It Mean To Normalize The Past? In *States of Memory: Continuities, Conflicts and Transformations in National Retrospection*, Jeffrey Olick (ed.), pp. 259–288. Durham: Duke University Press, 2003.
Reichel, Peter. *Erfundene Erinnerung. Weltkrieg und Judenmord in Film und Theater*. Munich, Wien: Carl Hanser, 2004.
Schulz, Sonja M: *Der Nationalsozialismus im Film. Von "Triumph des Willens" bis "Inglourious Basterds."* Berlin: Berz + Fischer, 2012.

Filmography

Am grünen Strand der Spree – Große Geschichten. 5 DVDs. Directed by Fritz Umgelter, 1960; Köln: Westdeutscher Rundfunk, Studio Hamburg Enterprises, 2014.
And Along Come Tourists (Am Ende kommen Touristen). DVD. Directed by Robert Thalheim, 2007; Berlin: X-Verleih, 2008.
Inglourious Basterds. DVD. Directed by Quentin Tarantino, 2009; Los Angeles, CA: Universal Pictures, 2009.
My Führer – The Really Truest Truth about Adolf Hitler (Mein Führer – Die wirklich wahrste Wahrheit über Hitler). DVD. Directed by Oliver Hirschbiegl, 2007; Berlin, Warner Home Video, 2007.
The Downfall (Der Untergang). DVD. Directed by Oliver Hirschbiegel, 2004; München: Constantin Film, 2004.
The Devil's General (Des Teufels General). DVD. Directed by Helmut Käutner, 1955; Hamburg: Real-Film GmbH, ARTHAUS Collection, 2009.
Stalingrad. Dogs, Do You Want to Live Forever? (Hunde, wollt ihr ewig leben?). DVD. Directed by Frank Wisbar, 1959; München: Bayrischer Rundfunk, Studiocanal, 2001.
Land of Destruction (Land der Vernichtung). Mini DVD. Directed by Romuald Karmakar, 2004; Berlin, Pantera Film, 2004.

Julius H. Schoeps
Saving the German-Jewish Legacy?
On Jewish and Non-Jewish Attempts of Reconstructing a Lost World

Germany's Jews and their numerous subgroups until the early 1930s had a comparatively clear idea about their own roots, their own tradition, and their own place in the center of Europe. This had a lot to do with a self-confidence that had matured over the centuries, and a minority history, which was closely interconnected, to the development of the German nation and its culture since the Enlightenment.[1] In other words: at least to a certain degree, Jews felt at home between the Baltic Sea and the Alps, between the Rhine valley and River Elbe.

Before 1933, German Jews derived their self-image from their own religion and traditions on the one hand, and from the language and culture of the German majority society on the other. Many felt such a close connection to their surroundings that they frequently named their children after former German emperors, mythical figures, and heroes of the time, especially in the Wilhelminian era.[2] A German Jew, to put it succinctly, was someone who stood by their Jewish heritage, while at the same time being at home in the German language and literature, someone who 'thought German' and was not significantly different in behavior and appearance from others in surrounding society. If a survey had been taken amongst the German Jews before 1933 asking them how they define themselves, as a group, such a question would have been met with uncomprehending shrugs. It is also likely that several names of German-Jewish role models would have been mentioned, certain to include Enlightenment philosopher Moses Mendelssohn, as well as politicians such as Gabriel Riesser and Johann Jacoby, writers of the stature of Ludwig Börne and Heinrich Heine, and most likely renowned composers such as Giacomo Meyerbeer and Felix Mendelssohn Bartholdy, as well.

---

1 Elon, The Pity of It All, 2004.
2 Wolffsohn / Brechenmacher, Deutschland, jüdisch Heimatland, 2008.

The German-Jewish Legacy as a Legitimate Part of German Heritage

As we know, the German Nazis destroyed in the most brutal way possible the former dream of the "German-Jewish symbiosis." Although a few small Jewish communities formed shortly after the end of the war in 1945, ones which represented some German Jews, as well, once flourishing German Jewry associated with names such as Liebermann, Einstein, and Buber had been irretrievably erased from German soil. After the remarkable growth in the Jewish communities in Germany during the 1990s, as an outcome of Jewish immigration from the former Soviet Union, the question as to what exactly German Jewry was, once again becomes relevant. What cultural and traditional remains of this Jewry, so unmistakable and rich, and what should be documented, preserved – even refreshed?

Some of the new immigrants from the CIS who today make up 90 percent of the membership in Germany's local Jewish communities, are indeed interested in the German-Jewish legacy, yet this does not necessarily have anything to do with their own sense of identity. Many Eastern European Jews are familiar with great German minds such as Goethe, Heine, and Kant, but this is not necessarily the case with German-Jewish greats such as Börne, Einstein, Meyerbeer, and Mendelssohn Bartholdy.

This is easy to understand: Why should the 'new Jews' in Germany be forced to identify with a legacy that is even farther from their experience than that of Sholem Aleichem, Joseph Brodsky, or Pasternak? *Cultural* Jewish continuity in Germany cannot be artificially reconstructed even 70 years after the Holocaust. One decisive question remains, however: Whether the German-Jewish legacy will remain of *historical* interest for future generations. This, in turn, will only be possible if the Jewish legacy proves able to be integrated into the *common German* cultural legacy.

Will it be possible to have writers such as Börne, composers such as Mendelssohn Bartholdy, and philosophers such as Horkheimer incorporated into the German cultural legacy and the public consciousness in the same way their non-Jewish counterparts are? Only when this legacy is not seen as 'something foreign,' when it will be recognized as something integral to 'Germanity' will there be a chance for the German-Jewish cultural tradition to continue to survive in Germany in at least a rudimentary form and be given its due respect.

A sober accounting quickly leads to the conclusion that in the future as well, the nurturing of the German-Jewish legacy will remain reliant on the German-speaking cultural sphere. It is illusory to suggest this could happen somewhere else. Things had, admittedly, seemed different, at least during the 1930s when approximately 240,000 Jews fled Nazi Germany and settled all over the world – particularly in Palestine and in the United States, where at least for a while, in certain places, they were able to maintain something similar to a German-Jewish milieu. At this point in time people were still convinced that the German-Jewish legacy had a realistic future outside of the German-speaking world, as well. The founders of the Leo Baeck Institute in New York, London, and Jerusalem thought at the time that studying German-Jewish history could never happen again in Germany, but would only be possible abroad.

Take a look at Palestine/Israel for a moment as an example. There were 50,000 *Yeckes* (the mocking-derisive term at the time for the stereotypical German Jew) who were able to immigrate to Palestine and created a new home for themselves where many continued to lovingly maintain their own cultural legacy to a remarkable degree in salons, concert halls, newspapers, and lecture series. They did this, and continue to do so today as well as they can, albeit cognizant that the culture in which they grew up and brought with themselves is a dying culture. Still, at least the first generation of *Yeckes* continued to adhere to their own culture; it was an inherent part of their own identity.

Things developed in a similar manner in the United States, although the adaptation process to the surrounding society for Jews coming from Germany proceeded much faster and was less problematic than in Palestine, or later in Israel. Their German background often just played a lesser role; acceptance of American citizenship after a period of time resulted in those possessing a U.S. passport considering themselves to be first and foremost Americans, not exile-Germans or refugees. The memories of Germany and of their own background faded significantly faster here.

Yet despite all this, the German-Jewish cultural legacy could soon be felt in particularly prominent ways. This is not only true for the film industry, but also several renowned universities where refugees from Germany transplanted entire scientific disciplines. In the 1930s, Renaissance research, for example – formerly at home in Germany – found a safe harbor in the United States and experienced a new prime. Another significant example is Jewish sociologists, including those from the Frankfurt School, who founded their own Institute of Social Research at Columbia University in New York and had a crucial influence on the New School in New York. Nevertheless, these are 'remnants' – cultural islands and regional phenomena. An authentic, historically-matured German Jewry as it existed among the Mendelssohns, Oppenheims, Wolffsohns, and Wertheimers – a coherent tradition that unites German culture and enlightened with open-minded Judaism – is as good as non-existent in Germany. German Jewry was, for all practical purposes, completely obliterated by the Hitler dictatorship and the

Holocaust, and that which we call 'the German-Jewish legacy' has been struggling with a 'stigma of homelessness' ever since. This can be viewed with regret and a source of grievance, nothing can change the fact that the German-Jewish legacy remains in limbo, no longer with a place to be attached to.

There have been, without question, a few respectable attempts in recent decades to reclaim and integrate the German-Jewish cultural legacy (insofar as this is possible and conceivable), the very least, to make it part of the common German cultural and historical consciousness. This can be illustrated by two concrete examples: Ludwig Börne and Heinrich Heine. These two men are no longer the "homeless journeymen" they were disdainfully referred to in the past by anti-semites of all stripes. Quite to the contrary: The non-Jewish majority society has begun to reexamine their works, even to identify with them. Furthermore, Düsseldorf named their university (albeit belatedly in 1988, 22 years after its founding) after the city's most illustrious native son, Heinrich Heine. Recognition did not stop there. There is now a Heinrich Heine Institute, several collected editions of his writings and letters have been published, and a society with local chapters in different cities carries Heine's name. The city of Düsseldorf also arranged naming a boulevard after the poet. The city also established the Heinrich Heine Prize, which is awarded once every two years to individuals who exemplify Heine's legacy with its emphasis on individual freedom and human rights, social and political progress, and the unity of humankind. It can justifiably be said that Heinrich Heine has finally 'arrived' in Düsseldorf am Rhein.

Something similar can be said for Ludwig Börne, who had been born in the ghetto of the city of Frankfurt. Here as well, his native city named a school after Börne in the center of the city, and every year the Ludwig Börne Prize is awarded to a German-speaking political journalist in the St. Paul's Church. The speeches delivered on these occasions try to commemorate the 'other Germany' – the democratic Germany which had always existed, which is unfortunately all too often forgotten.

Another example of the rediscovery and reevaluation of the German-Jewish cultural legacy is the composer Felix Mendelssohn Bartholdy. Indeed, Richard Wagners trivialization of Mendelssohn Bartholdy and his works (in Wagner's vitriolic essay *Jewishness in Music*, published soon after Mendelsohn's death) led, among other things, to Mendelssohn Bartholdy, a popular and influential figure in the music world prior to his death, being relegated second-rate status, his works rarely performed, then labeled during the Nazi period as works polluted with a 'degenerative Jewish influence.' Mendelssohn's Romantic compositions and his *Songs without Words* (previously maligned as "trivial music") are again enjoying a level of popularity in Germany, after being banned by the Nazis. Today the oratorios *Paulus* and *Elias* even belong to the standard repertoire of German sacred music.

There are also visible signs of progress in science, the media, and in commemorative work concerning the rediscovery and preservation of the German-Jewish legacy. Since the end of the 1980s a whole series of research institutions have arisen dedicated to the history of German-Jewish or European-Jewish relations in Duisburg, Hamburg, Frankfurt, Potsdam, and Leipzig, among others.

At the same time, a number of Jewish museums have opened, for example in Frankfurt am Main, Munich, Augsburg, Halberstadt, Hohenems, Vienna, and especially Berlin. The number of visitors to these museums is more than respectable. There are commemorative works that have been integrated into everyday life and the public space in an utterly 'simple' yet effective way. The *Stolpersteine* (stumbling blocks) by Cologne artist Gunter Demnig, which bear the names of murdered German Jews, inlaid in the street or on the pavement in front of their former homes all over Germany should be mentioned in this respect. What has been undertaken in terms of *local* initiatives and projects that seek to maintain at least a part of the German-Jewish legacy, is indeed remarkable. Nevertheless, as a phenomenon, it has a fragmentary character and unfortunately is not proceding systematically – a necessity if the German-Jewish legacy is to be anchor in the collective memory.

The Imperative to Consolidate the German-Jewish Legacy

Another shortcoming of endeavors to reposition Jews' roles in the history of German society is that until now, there has been no systematic overview or compilation of what historical material on German Jewry exists and where it is, whether it has been archived in Germany or abroad. This does not suggest there is a need for construction of additional research institutions and museums; there are enough of these. What is needed is to secure relevant archives, bequests, estates, and papers of all kinds worldwide which are privately or publicly-owned, often unknown even to professional scholars. The Leo Baeck Institute in New York with its branch offices in London and Jerusalem has thankfully taken on this task in the last few decades. Today, however, the Institute is challenged by generational change and shifting priorities: The refugees from Germany who founded the Institute are largely no longer with us and their descendants in the United States, England, and Israel increasingly have problems devoting so much time and energy to this objective and identifying with the German-Jewish legacy handed down to them.

Under such circumstances what can still be done? There is a vital need to rapidly take stock of the 'inventory' – a priority that has also been recognized by the political echelons in Germany. The Mendelssohn Center is currently working on a project under the direction of Elke V. Kotowski to create a 'handbook' and to establish a data bank that can provide the first comprehensive overview of sources and studies worldwide on the German-Jewish cultural legacy.

For example, in the mid-1990's, the Arnold Schönberg Archive was to be moved from Los Angeles to Europe. The University of Southern California apparently no longer had any use for it. At the time, Berlin and Vienna were competing to receive it. Both cities believed that they could make a legitimate claim to the archive. Vienna ultimately won. As founding director of the Jewish Museum of the City of Vienna, I was involved in the complicated negotiations at the time. On the one hand, the Schönberg family had to be convinced and their consent received, on the other hand, a workable acquisition concept needed to be developed. The decision was finally made in favor of Vienna, not least of all because the city agreed to make available a prestigious venue for the collection and, as a 'cherry on the top' – to create an Arnold Schönberg professorship. Berlin was simply unable to compete with this offer. The 'winning acquisition model' in the Schönberg case (if I may call it that), could certainly be applied to other cases, for example, the personal papers of the famous theatre director Max Reinhardt, presently archived at the University of Binghampton in New York State. It should be returned to where it really belongs, either to Berlin or Vienna.

Naturally, proposals of this nature demand utmost sensitivity. Complex sensibilities continue to exist, but it is at least worth a try to bring them back home to Germany. Discussion and negotiation of such a move can be flexible, and could be consummated via a host of arrangements ranging from outright purchase to long-term loan and exchange programs. Other archival estates that deserve similar discussion include Jewish holdings in the Center for Preservation of Historico-Documentary Collections (formerly, the Special Archives) in Moscow where the papers of Walther Rathenau are located, and where the 1869–1938 records of the Central Association of German Citizens of the Jewish Faith (*Centralverein deutscher Staatsbürger jüdischen Glaubens*) – one of the most important reservoirs of German-Jewish history – were hidden after they were transferred to Moscow among the archival booty seized by the Soviet Union in 1946 (which only resurfaced 45 years later).[3]

---

3 http://www.research.co.il/moscow.html (accessed March 26, 2015).

Countless Judaica objects that are unmistakable connected with German Jewry's legacy, scattered about in collections worldwide, should also be taken into account. Those that come to mind include Judaica collections in major museums in Jerusalem, New York, Los Angeles, and San Francisco, as well as the relatively small art museum such as the one in Raleigh, North Carolina, which all include manuscripts and Jewish ritual objects such as Torah breastplates or crowns (*ketarim*) and finials (*rimonim*), and spice boxes. Their stories – their origins and how they came to be part of each collection – would be of historical interest, as well. Experts are aware that many of the objects displayed in the cases of these important museums originally came from the German-speaking areas. If these manuscripts, ritual items and objects reflecting the daily life of Jewish families in Germany can no longer be returned to their places of origin in German-speaking lands (no one seriously expects this to happen), the least that could be done is to catalogue them and preserve the information in a data bank.

Not only Judaica collections should be documented, but also the libraries that Jews from Germany took with them to Palestine, South America, and the United States. A first attempt in this direction has been made by the staff of the Moses Mendelssohn Center which is documenting the whereabouts of some of these libraries. The libraries of Walter Boehlich, Alex Bein, Ludwig Geiger, Ernst Simon, and other prominent Jews reconstructed in the Mendelssohn Center are thus important not only to pay homage to exceptional minds; they also reflect a pinnacle of German-Jewish cultural history of the past.

There is also an urgent need to systematically record and document paintings and other objects of art that were once the property of Jewish private collectors in Germany, that today are scattered throughout the world. It is unacceptable that there are paintings on display of established museums, and other art stored away in the vaults of such institutions whose history and ownership, how they came to be in the museum's possession, remain unexplained. Proof of origin – which is not viewed as a matter of course everywhere – should be made obligatory for all museums.

An incident that makes it crystal clear why we all must hurry to secure the remains of the German-Jewish legacy in Germany and abroad occurred at the beginning of the 1990s. While preparing the exhibit *Patterns of Jewish Life* in the Gropius Bau in Berlin, we learned of a German-Jewish couple who had been able to save all of their belongings and take them with them when they exited Germany: Literally *all* their apartment furnishings – from furniture and pictures to wallpaper. In San Francisco, where the couple ultimately settled, they took an apartment and decorated it exactly as it had been in Germany, down to the location of each article of furniture – a tangible attempt to retain *an exact replica* of a piece of their lost home. Suffice it to say, our team was electrified by this extraordinary 'time capsule' and immediately embarked for San Francisco to visit the address given. Unfortunately, we no longer were able to meet the couple. As we learned, they had recently died. The biggest shock, however, was the news that the apartment had been cleaned out a few weeks before our arrival and the furnishings had all landed in the trash! Our hunt for a slice of German-Jewish living culture which had survived for decades abroad, had disappeared overnight, without a trace. Thus, studying the past presents unique experiences such as the above, but time is short.

Passing on and Discoursing the Jewish-German Legacy

Exploring the German-Jewish past and cultural legacy should never be limited to an intellectual exercise alone. There is already sufficient impetus for passing on and discussing Jewish history in today's Germany, as the impressive attendance figures at the Jewish Museum in Berlin illustrate. An arena has emerged where non-Jews not only have begun to take an interest in Jewish culture; one even encounters a form of 'mimicry' where gentiles have begun to engage in Jewish culture themselves.[4] There has also been much fruitful, public dialogue where Jews and non-Jews can come together to reconstruct a dramatic history of convergence and divergence. As a result of this dialogue, suddenly, more and more ordinary Germans have begun to recognize the enormous regional and national contributions to the visual arts, medicine, science, music, philosophy, the humanities, the economy, and philanthropy made by German Jews, primarily in the eighteenth, nineteenth and twentieth centuries. It is a journey marked by a broken history. The history of Jews in Germany is an uneven, at times convoluted path – at the same time, impressive and shocking. Jews no longer remain outside the public discourse, and some now participate intensely in it. As a result, some members of the younger generation of Jews in Germany have begun to strongly identify with mainstream society. These young Jews do not ignore the trauma of the Holocaust, but they believe that the present *they* experience reflects a different reality – the emergence of a new society which is drawing lessons from the

---

[4] See: Bodemann, The Return of European Jewish Diaspora. In: Schoeps / Glöckner (eds.), A Road to Nowhere, 2011, p. 183.

past, emphasizing cultural tolerance and seeking to address current problems of ethnic and religious minorities in this spirit.[5]

Dealing with the German-Jewish legacy is a major challenge for historians, journalists, educators and other professionals. What does this mean for those Jews currently building their own new communities, and how does the German-Jewish legacy impact on them?

The overwhelming majority of the Jewish communities of Germany today are Russian-speakers. A series of studies on Russian Jews who settled in Germany during the 1990s and early 2000s have shown that most identify with the history of *Eastern European* Jewry, although, some are proud to be descendants of those Jews who originally came from Central Europe and Germany in the late Middle Ages. In a certain sense, they even perceive themselves as part of a 'return' by their coming to Germany. At the same time, many see their German legacy in more contemporary and personal terms with a distinct 'Russian' orientation: As carriers of the heroic legacy of hundreds of thousands of veterans or offspring-'heirs' of the Red Army who share the ethos of the Great Patriotic War in which, at a horrific cost, the Soviet Union ultimately defeated Hitler and liberated Europe from the Nazis. This is why Russian Jews in Germany are less inclined to mark anniversaries such as November 9 (*Kristallmacht* or the "Night of Broken Glass" in 1938) or January 27 (Day of Liberation of Auschwitz in 1945) which constitute landmark events in the lives of German or Polish Jews who have been living in the country for decades. Instead, Russians émigrés celebrate Victory Day on May 9 with a passion – the day in the spring of 1945 when Berlin fell and the Third Reich unconditionally surrendered to Allied forces. Naturally, they have brought along more than their war medals, the feeling of kinship with the glorious liberators, to Germany. They also act as ambassadors – cultural agents of Russian art, music, and literature – indeed, the 'voice' of the intelligentsia. Even during 70 years of repressive communist dictatorship, some Soviet Jews remained eager to emphasize their Jewish *and* Russian cultural roots.[6] On the other hand, many nearly lost

---

[5] Glöckner quotes a young Jewish historian from Odessa, now living in Berlin, when asked about his feelings living in the country of perpetrators of the Holocaust: "Yes, it afflicts me. On the other hand, I see and feel that this population has undergone tremendous societal changes during the last decades. Especially since the 1960s, German society has proven its ability to deal honestly and critically with its own past. Also, I do not have the impression that current memorial events are pure exercises in political correctness. I feel that there are serious debates on the Nazi regime and all its crimes, especially among young people." Glöckner, Immigrated Russian Jewish Elites, 2011, p. 216.

[6] For example, the Russian-Jewish publicist Rafael Nudelman, who later immigrated to Israel and served as editor-in-chief of the literature magazine "*22*" reflected: "They say that we are Jews by nationality but Russians by culture. Are culture and nationality like an outfit on a mannequin

their ties to Jewish culture, religion, and heritage completely under communism. One of the crucial questions in Jewish community life today is: what are the main concerns of Germany's 'new Jews'? Perhaps the second generation of these immigrants will develop a strong interest in reconstructing local Jewish history and develop a closeness to German-Jewish cultural heritage as their own inheritance.

Next to the Russian Jews, a large number of Israeli and American Jews have found their way to unified Germany, with most opting to live in metropolitan centers such as Berlin, Frankfurt, and Munich. Some are descendants of the former *Yeckes*, and it will be very interesting to see how all these different groups of Jews will constitute a *new* German Jewry. Meanwhile, some elements of the original German Jewish *religious* tradition have returned from across the Atlantic. Starting in the Cold War, military rabbis and other personnel at American military bases in West Germany have established ties with local Jewish communities and became quite active members. Some have even remained, and others arrived later in unified Germany. These American Jews are hallmarked by their interest and involvement in Liberal and Reform Jewry who were attracted by the foundation of the Union of Progressive Judaism in Germany (UPJ) in 1997, some even becoming community leaders. Today, the UPJ is part of the World Union for Progressive Judaism (WUPJ), which was founded in London in 1926, but whose center of gravity was Germany: WUPJ's first convention was held in Berlin in 1928 and in its formative years, the Reform movement was led by German rabbi Leo Baeck. The strong German-Jewish impact on the early development of the WUPJ was anything but accidental. The first seeds of Liberal Judaism developed over a period of 200 years in Germany, beginning with people such as David Friedländer,[7] who in the nineteenth century championed Jewish emancipation, modernization of Jewish ritual, and establishment of interfaith ties with Christians, then flourishing in the Wilhelminian Germany, continuing in the Weimar Republic. Landmark educational and religious institutions were founded, for example, the Institute for the Scientific Study of Judaism (*Hochschule für die Wissenschaft des Judentums*) in Berlin in 1872 and the Free Jewish School (*Freies Jüdisches Lehrhaus*) in Frankfurt in 1920, which pioneered innovative philosophical, liturgical, and cultural contributions to the emergence of a modern Jewry. Without a doubt, the traditions, liturgies, and ideas of the Liberal Jewish movement in Germany have strongly

---

or water in a glass? When a mighty press drives one metal into another, it is then impossible to separate them, even by slicing them? We were put under enormous pressure for decades. My national feelings have no other expression than through my culture. [...] If you divide me up, I should like to know, which cells of my soul are colored in Russian, which in a Jewish color?", quoted in: Epstein / Kheimets, Immigrant Intelligentsija, 2000, p. 469.

[7] See: Schoeps, David Friedländer, 2012.

and decisively affected non-Orthodox Judaism worldwide, and modern American Jewish life in particular. The WUPJ, today serves approximately 1.8 million Jews in 45 countries. While today, the center of gravity of the Liberal Jewish movement is in North America, at least some of its spiritual and intellectual orientation is 'returning-reverting' to Germany. Nonetheless, those Jews organized in local Jewish congregations who define themselves as Liberal ones still form a small minority in Germany,[8] and it remains an open question whether the philosophical and theological ideas of Martin Buber, Franz Rosenzweig, or Gershom Scholem will again assume a leading role, and whether the liturgical music by German-Jewish composers such as Louis Lewandowski will witness a revival.

Since the late 1940s, Jewish community life in Germany has been dominated by Jewish traditions from Poland and other Eastern European countries introduced by Holocaust survivors who decided to stay and settle in Germany. Of course, in the years and decades following the Second World War significant differences appeared between 'Easterners' and 'Westerners' but their unique situation and the small size of the community forced all sectors to join together in Unified Communities (*Einheitsgemeinden*). This unique German historic construct – which required Jews in each and every locality to operate under one 'roof' that would incorporate all sectors of the community and administer all community needs and would represent the Jewish community vis-à-vis authorities – is still preferred by some of the Jewish elites even today.

Independent liberal Judaism was possible only after the downfall of the Iron Curtain and German unification. Today, the Abraham Geiger Kolleg (AGK), a rabbinical school founded in Postdam in 1999, constitutes a flagship of non-Orthodoxy dedicated to training future Liberal clergy not only for Germany, but for all of Europe.[9] Interestingly, many of the rabbinical students come from Jewish families of Eastern Europe background (for example Russian, Ukrainian, or Hungarian). On the other hand, many local Jewish communities still favor Orthodox rabbis and Orthodox rituals, at least for prayer services.[10] This is the general pattern 25 years after the advent of Russian Jewish immigration into Germany. Such trends may rightly be viewed as part of a process of differentiation and pluralization developing amongst Germany's new Jews. Despite the demographic growth in

---

8 According to its own data, today, the Union of Progressive Jews has 22 local Jewish congregations with almost 5,000 registered members. The most active has been founded in Hannover, the capital of the federal state of Lower Saxony, the *Liberale Jüdische Gemeinde Hannover*. The Community includes Jews from 10 different countries and it is led mainly by German Jews, among them many women. See: http://www.ljgh.de/ (accessed August 22, 2013).
9 See the article by Rabbi Walter Homolka in this Volume.
10 For example, all seven local Jewish communities in the federal state of Brandenburg, which surrounds Berlin, call themselves Orthodox, including the Jewish community of Potsdam.

Jewish communities during the 1990s and all of the dynamic change seen across the generations, one should not discount the possibility of rebuilding the vibrant and diverse structure that once typified German Jewish life in the nineteenth and early twentieth century. Germany's 500,000 Jews not only had prestigious synagogues, well-attended schools, strong political organizations such as the Central Association of German Citizens of the Jewish Faith, and an efficient social welfare network headed by the Central Welfare Agency for Jews in Germany (*Zentralwohlfahrtsstelle der deutschen Juden*)[11], but they also had extensive networks of Jewish associations connected to the synagogues in the medium-sized towns and big cities.

Finally, from an historical perspective, prominent and wealthy German Jews of all different backgrounds and professions have been eager to co-found and run associations, foundations, and institutions that promote their members' social interests and needs, providing for culture needs and mutual economic aid.[12] For example, members of the Mendelssohn, Oppenheimer, and Friedländer families were very engaged as philanthropists, art collectors[13], patrons of academic projects, and sponsors of health institutions, or recreational centers. They viewed such public-spirited activities as a sign of their patriotism for Germany; this stance remained popular until the 1930s but the dream of a "German-Jewish symbiosis" was extinguished in the gas chambers of Auschwitz and Treblinka. Decades passed before Jews in Germany were willing or able to again take part in public discourse or raise their voice in any social or political context. Nevertheless, three features have come to characterize those Jews who were willing to speak out as Jews in (West) Germany: strong support behind combating neo-Nazism or racism in any form, and upholding human rights in Germany; a commitment to a 'politics of remembrance' for victims of the Holocaust and others; and, finally, more or less unconditional solidarity with Israel. While all these activities remain necessary and commendable, they are not really associated with the original core heritage of the German Jewry before 1933.

---

11 The Central Welfare Board of German Jews was founded in 1917 as the umbrella organization of the various Jewish social welfare institutions and organizations. The famous Austrian feminist Bertha Pappenheim (1859–1936) was a strong influence. The Welfare Board was closed by the Nazis in 1939.
12 One of the famous examples in Berlin was the Society of Friends (*Gesellschaft der Freunde*) founded in 1792 and closed by the Nazis in 1935. It was originally an intellectual club for young Jewish men, but later turned into an important cultural center led by Jewish professional elites and closely connected with the Berlin Jewish community. At the turn of the twentieth century, the Society also served as an informal network for the well-to-do and was commonly frequented by non-Jews as well. See: Panwitz, Die Gesellschaft der Freunde 1792–1935, 2007.
13 See: Ludewig / Schoeps / Sonder (eds.), Aufbruch in die Moderne, 2012.

Are there signs of a 'healing process' in German-Jewish relations? It is interesting to note that a few years ago there was an internal debate whether to the name of the Central Council of Jews *in Germany* should be changed to the Central Council of *German Jews*.[14] The unresolved debate seems to indicate that at least some of Germany's Jews indeed 'feel German' today. Of course, this says little about their distinctive self-image and identity towards the German-Jewish heritage of the past, or other forms of Jewish heritage for that matter. Even for those Jews who are descendants of German Jewish families, it is extremely difficult in today's Germany to reconnect with their former heritage. This is the crux of the core question that remains hanging about the future of Jews in Germany: How will the general Jewish population in Germany understand itself in the long run? Perhaps the next generation of Jews in Germany will reflect interaction among the community's disparate parts, fueling a new identity or new identities that will be the product of a cross-fertilization of worldviews and practices of Russian, American, Israeli, and 'indigenous' German Jews – an identity that perhaps will be able to embrace former German-Jewish culture, parallel to self-confidence and pride as equal European citizens.

For older Jews in Germany, including the second generation after the Holocaust (children of survivors), this might be impossible, not only due to the disruption and destruction of the Jewish world of their parents from before 1933, but also because of their own exposure to stigmatization by their non-Jewish surroundings in the postwar years. My own father, who returned from Sweden where he found refuge during the Nazi period, received a chair at the University of Erlangen, however, he was the recipient of countless letters of latent and open anti-semitism, enough 'material' to fill a book... I think it was even more painful for him that well-meaning friends never ceased asking him – "Why have you re-migrated to Germany of all places?" We know from recent sociological studies that Russian Jewish immigrants from the 1990s were asked the same question. As long as this question remains significant in the dialogue between non-Jews and Jews in Germany, normalcy will remain a distant prospect. In the meantime, the 'stigma of homelessness' continues, and the hour for 'a new German Jewry' has yet to arrive.

---

14 The discussion was even promoted by Charlotte Knobloch, President of the Central Council of Jews in Germany from 2006 till 2010, but ultimately ended with no results, see: Herzinger, in: Die Welt, August 22, 2009.

References

Bodemann, Michal Y. The Return of European Jewish Diaspora. New Ethno-National Constellations since 1989. In: *A Road to Nowhere? Jewish Experiences in Unifying Europe*, Julius H. Schoeps, Olaf Glöckner (eds.), pp. 179–217. Leiden, Boston: Brill, 2011.

Elon, Amos. *The Pity of It All. A Portrait of Jews in Germany 1743–1933*. London: Penguin, 2004.

Epstein, Alek, Nina Kheimets. Immigrant Intelligentsia and its Second Generation. Cultural Segregation as a Road to Social Integration? *Journal of International Migration and Integration* 1 (2000): pp. 461–476.

Glöckner, Olaf. Immigrated Russian Jewish Elites in Israel and Germany after 1990 – their Integration, Self Image and Role in Community Building. Potsdam: Potsdamer Universitätsverlag, 2011. http://opus.kobv.de/ubp/volltexte/2011/5036/pdf/gloeckner_diss.pdf (accessed August 22, 2013).

Herzinger, Richard. "Zentralrat der Juden zerstritten über Umbenennung," *Die Welt*, August 22, 2009. http://www.welt.de/politik/deutschland/article4377717/Zentralrat-der-Juden-zerstritten-ueber-Umbenennung.html (accessed August 25, 2013).

Ludewig, Anna-Dorothea, Julius H. Schoeps, and Ines Sonder (eds.). *Aufbruch in die Moderne. Sammler, Mäzene und Kunsthändler in Berlin 1880-1933*. Cologne: Dumont, 2012.

Panwitz, Sebastian. *Die Gesellschaft der Freunde 1792–1935. Berliner Juden zwischen Aufklärung und Hochfinanz*. Hildesheim: Olms, 2007.

Schoeps, Julius H. *David Friedländer, Freund und Schüler Moses Mendelssohns*. Hildesheim: Olms 2012.

Schoeps, Julius H., Glöckner Olaf (eds.). *A Road to Nowhere? Jewish Experiences in Unifying Europe*. Leiden, Boston: Brill, 2011.

Wolffsohn, Michael, Thomas Brechenmacher. *Deutschland, jüdisch Heimatland. Die Geschichte der deutschen Juden vom Kaiserreich bis heute*. Munich: Pieper, 2008.

Migration as the Driving Factor of Jewish Revival in Re-Unified Germany

Eliezer Ben-Rafael
Germany's Russian-speaking Jews
Between Original, Present and Affective Homelands

A Three-branch National Identification

An important segment of the Jewish exodus from the Former Soviet Union settled in Germany in the 1990s.[1] Russian-speaking Jews who integrated into Israel's Jewish national society formed a new ethnocultural entity; those who immigrated to the United States joined the existing Jewish community becoming a new component of American Jewry's position as a major minority culture in the American mosaic. The circumstances of Russian-speaking Jewish émigrés who settled in Germany was diametrically different: There was, in essence, genuine Jewish community of any kind in Germany when Russian Jews began arriving in Germany, and today they constitute the overwhelming majority (90 percent) of the Jewish population of the country. One could say that on the ashes of Germany's notorious Nazi years, Russian Jews built a renewed Jewish community, although prior to their arrival during decades under a Marxist-Leninist political and social system they themselves had lost most of their Jewish heritage, arriving with no experience in Jewish communal life, but nevertheless clinging to 'Jewishness by identification.'[2]

Whatever the reasons they choose Germany as their destination, once established there they constitute, a population torn between three very different poles of national identification: One pole is, of course, Germany where they now live, to whose language and culture they have progressively acculturated, eventually becoming full-fledge German citizens. A second pole is the 'old country' – Russia, the Ukraine or another former Soviet republic where they may still have friends or relatives whose language and culture they carry and continue as cultural baggage. A third pole is Israel, which many view as the genuine 'land of the Jew' and where the largest Russian-speaking Jewish population in the world now resides; as a result, Israel engenders strong feelings of affinity and a source of solidarity.

The purpose of this paper is to examine, based on empirical research, how each of these poles is viewed and related to by Germany's Russian-speaking Jews

---

[1] Ben-Rafael / Lyubansky / Glöckner / Harris / Israel / Jasper / Schoeps (eds.), Building a Diaspora, 2006; Remennick, Idealists Headed to Israel, 2005.
[2] Gitelman (ed.), Jewish Life after the USSR, 2003.

and how this impacts on their lives as Jews and shapes the nature of this present-day Diaspora community.

Migration, Transnationalism and Russian-speaking Jews

Russian-speaking Jews constitute but one example of a larger phenomenon: how globalization as a worldwide phenomenon is reshaping immigrant communities[3] that has been marked by the formation of transnational diasporas.[4] Consequently, in many contemporary societies – especially in the West, one now speaks of 'insertion' instead of 'integration'; the change in terminology reflects new realities, where many migrating groups no longer seek to integrate the dominant culture, but to enter new societies without abandoning allegiance to their native cultures and motherlands.

Such developments beg the question: How then do people define their collective allegiance or allegiances to the collective when the components that formulate or give substance to the allegiance(s) are not necessarily uniform, and do not appeal to everyone to the same degree?[5] The pluralistic nature of contemporary Jewishness is a good example of such divergences in identity formulation. What seems to still hold such varied forms together as a 'collective' rests primarily on the fact that Jews worldwide still roughly refer to the same people when they speak of 'Jews' and the diverse forms they have developed-chosen to adopt as signifying their Jewishness in terms of identification and practice, draw many of their symbols from the same reservoir or repertoires, notwithstanding different interpretations that often are, to a large degree, 'situational' – reflecting the particular community, class, or the social milieu where Jews happen to reside. Members of the world Jewish community nowadays, indeed, live in very different cultural contexts and are subject to an immense variety of influences. In many Western societies, Jewish life has evolved and been shaped in environments driven by individualism where the density of community life is often tenuous. As a result, their collective identity as Jews is grounded primarily on personal choice while meaning and practice vary from person-to-person.

This is especially true of Russian-speaking Jews in Germany, whose experience under Communist regimes has left few anchors to cling to as signifiers

---

[3] Castles, Migration and Community Formation, 2002.
[4] Soysal, Citizenship and identity, 2000.
[5] Ben-Rafael, Ethnicity, Sociology of, 2002.

of their Jewishness. What they found in Germany, moreover, could not entirely structure their new existence as a Jewish community. Only a small cohort of less than 15,000 old-timers who had remained in the country after 1945 or had previously migrated to Germany welcomed them.[6] Some of this small Jewish population had settled in East Germany (German Democratic Republic) driven by empathy for Communism while the others formed the entity that was referred to by Jewish institutions, officially-recognized by the State.[7] The sudden collapse of the USSR followed by the reunification of Germany, sparked an unexpected mass immigration of Russian-speaking Jews into Germany in the 1990s – a migration that was welcome by German authorities. As a consequence, Russian-speaking Jews became *the* Judaism of Germany: The number of Jews in Germany rose to approximately 200,000 (from 15,000) and the number of Jewish communities jumped from a handful to 130. Germany's Jews became one of Europe's largest Jewish communities – third in size after France and Britain. Assistance from a host of Jewish organizations outside Germany – ultra-orthodox, orthodox, non-orthodox, liberal, or secular (each with its own agenda to shape the face of the emerging Jewish community still in its formative years) provided fresh stimulus for communal growth.[8]

The research discussed in the following asked about the internal dynamics of this German Jewish community: Can and do these new Jews in Germany hold the keys to the resurgence of Germany's historic Jewish community? As immigrants in an era of globalization, how do they look back on their native homelands? How involved or concerned with Israel are they – the place that they probably have always perceived as 'the land of the Jews,' irrespective of their own personal choice to settle elsewhere?

In brief, the research investigated to what extent and along what lines Russian-speaking Jews in Germany are creating a new Jewish community with its own unique Jewish *problématique*.

The Nature of the Research Sample

The research was conducted in 2008–2009, based on a questionnaire designed to poll a representative sample of Jews living in Germany. The sample population was comprised of 1,200 subjects – 90 percent (1,018 respondents) Russian-speaking Jews, and

---

[6] Gidal, Jews in Germany, 1998.
[7] Schoeps (ed.), Neues Lexikon des Judentums, 1998.
[8] Hasidic Chabad, the Lauder Foundation, the World Union for Progressive Judaism among many others.

10 percent 'veteran' German Jews. The Russian-speaking Jews who are the subject of this chapter, were located initially by contacting individuals on lists of the parents of Jewish schoolchildren, members of Jewish clubs and student organizations; snowballing techniques were then used to expand the sample. While the sampling procedure was not random, we believe that the large size of the sample population (and the wide distribution found among the actual participants on a host of indexes that indicate our sample reflects the nature of the community) adequately compensate for this shortcoming. Indeed, respondents encompass registered members of community bodies and non-members, participants in Jewish frameworks and unaffiliated persons, and age cohorts were representative. Geographically, the researchers ensured that participants would be recruited from a large number of cities throughout Germany. The sample was also gender-balanced. The 20-to-25 minute-long questionnaire was written in both German and Russian, and respondents could choose their preferred language. The questionnaire polled attitudes toward significant of issues – such as satisfaction with life in Germany, attitudes toward different collective identities, and concerns regarding their children's future. The input was statistically analyzed to reveal attitudinal patterns and significant correlations with sociological variables (socioeconomic status, education, religiosity, age, gender, place of residence). This chapter discusses only the most interesting findings that clearly reflect the character and mindset of the Russian-speaking Jews in Germany.

At the outset, it is important to be cognizant of the special demographic make up of Russian-speaking Jews in Germany: 60 percent immigrated after the age of eight had resided in Germany for less than ten years at the time the questionnaires were gathered. 29 percent arrived after the age of eight, and had been in Germany between eleven and fifteen years, and 11 percent had been in Germany for more than 15 years. On the other hand, the German Jewish community is relatively old. 42 percent are over the age of sixty; 26 percent are between 41 and 60 years of age, and only 32 percent are under 40. In addition, 60 percent live with a spouse or a partner and two-thirds of the couples (66.3 percent) have children. Interestingly enough, a full 63 percent have post-secondary academic education.

Insertion in Society

Before addressing the issues of allegiances, it is important to clarify briefly the issue of social insertion of Russian-speaking Jews in German society. We speak here of 'insertion' since 'integration' generally assumes that a given group has become a part of society by acculturation and assimilation, and is thus perceived by others. Insertion, by contrast, hinges on differing degrees of commitment to the host society set by the immigrants themselves, and the manner and degree of engagement of the host society on the newcomers' own terms.

Yet, the degree of engagement for Russian-speaking Jews is surely affected by their status in the workplace, or marked absence as the case may be. Responses to the questionnaire show that nearly a fifth (18.6 percent) are students and 12.6 percent are salaried laborers or employees, and only 9.7 percent are professionals or business people. A most salient feature of Russian-speaking Jews is that over a third (34.1 percent) are unemployed and live on social welfare, and another 25 percent are retired. This pattern – where nearly 60 percent of the community is outside the labor market places is not only indicative of the difficulty of converting human capital acquired elsewhere into locally-relevant job qualifications. Such a state of affairs places most of this population on the margins of society – both in terms of isolation from mainstream society and standard of living. Hence, a majority (59 percent) estimates that one's income is below the national average, an additional barrier to being 'seduced' by the new society. Less than half (45.3 percent) describe their insertion in society as 'very satisfactory' or 'just satisfactory' and only a half feel genuinely 'at home.'

Another relevant aspect to collective identification is religiosity: Only a small minority (13.2 percent) of the respondents feel close to orthodoxy while a fifth (22.3 percent) is closer to liberal (Reform or Conservative) Judaism. One of every three respondents defines themselves as 'somehow traditional' and another third as 'secular.' It is significant to note that 25 percent of the respondents come from families where one parent is not Jewish, and 38 percent of those who have a family of their own live with a spouse or partner who is not Jewish according to Orthodox standards of Jewish law (*Halakha*).

As is characteristic among migrant group, differences exist among respondents according to age and length of residence in Germany. Age impacts on a variety of counts – but especially language mastery. Three quarters of the subjects under age 40, for example, evaluate their German as 'good' or 'quite good' while such responses among seniors (above age 61) is much lower. In the family or among friends (who often are Russian-speaking Jews themselves) the language of discourse remains Russian.

Length of stay is a decisive factor in linguistic engagement: Among those who have been in Germany longer, German is used more extensively in a variety of situations, and nearly 60 percent of the sample evaluate their command of the language as 'good 'or 'quite good' while the figure for those who are less years in the country drops to 25 percent. Moreover, longer residence is also linked to more positive attitudes toward society, in their evaluation of their social integration and the degree to which they 'feel at home' in Germany. Not surprisingly, the use of German, in all areas of activity investigated, gains ground among the young, and they are more attached to German society and describe their integration in society as more satisfactory than their elders. Furthermore, in contrast with older immigrants, they report that the memory of the Holocaust does not seriously impede their engagement with German society.

The levels and types of religiosity among Jews create divisions when related to the question of social insertion.

Responses in Table 1 reveal that command of German is an indicator of the respondents' readiness to invest efforts into social integration. The degree to which Holocaust memory plays a role and is perceived as 'problematic' for living as a Jew in Germany, is a function of acculturation, access to and appreciation of German culture. Awareness of this possible relation led us to ask respondents about their aspirations for their children and perceptions of their chances to achieve and succeed in society, as indicators of how far Germany is viewed as open and fair by respondents.

Table 1: Russian-speaking Jews' Integration into German society*

Secular	Traditional	Liberal	Orthodox	
1.1 Knowledge of German (N=861)				
36.9	29.6	30.1	18.3	Poor
32.2	36.5	37.7	29.8	Somewhat
14.3	19.6	21.3	32.7	Quite good
16.6	14.2	10.9	19.2	Good
100.0	100.0	100.0	100.0	Total
1.2 In the context of the past, is living as a Jew in Germany (N=878)				
10.5	3.4	5.9	9.1	Very problematic
31.4	44.5	39.4	50.0	Problematic
58.1	52.1	54.8	40.9	Not problematic
100.0	100.0	100.0	100.0	Total
1.3 Importance of children's adopting German culture (N=718 ;%; γ^2=0)				
11.5	10.2	11.5	27.9	Not at all
6.7	14.4	9.1	20.9	A little
49.6	49.3	46.1	27.9	Moderately
32.1	26.0	33.3	23.3	Very much so
100.0	100.0	100.0	100.0	Total

We divided respondents into four categories of religiosity: *orthodox religiosity* (modern orthodox and ultra-orthodox), *non-orthodox religiosity* or liberal

Judaism (Reform or Conservative approaches), *traditional orientation* (meaning observance of some customs out of collective solidarity and respect for the Jewish heritage) and *secular Jewishness* (i.e., freedom from any religious or traditional obligation).

The data indicates that mastery of German is still difficult for respondents; that mixed feelings prevail regarding the problematic character of living as Jews in post-Holocaust Germany, and acculturating to German culture is only moderately endorsed. Yet, a large majority is convinced that growing up in Germany holds out promise for their children. This reflects an 'instrumental' perspective towards German society but also hopes for children.

Interesting enough, in terms of religiosity of the participant, orthodox respondents' evaluation of their mastery of German is higher than secular Jews (with moderately-observant participants falling between the two). On the other hand, the data shows that orthodox Russian-speaking Jews tend to be younger than secular Jews – and probably the dependent variable for German mastery is age-related exposure to the language at an early age, not religiosity. The same variable – age – probably explains the fact that half the orthodox respondents' friends are not Russian-speaking, while the corresponding figure for secular Jews is 25 percent. Thus, it appears that religiosity has no direct effect on language-learning or integration in society. At the same time, the secular appear to attach less importance to the memory of the Holocaust in their insertion in society and assigned more importance to their children acculturating to German culture. Put succinctly, religiosity or secularism has no significant impact on individuals' ambitions regarding their new national society.

It is also reasonable to hypothesize that intermarriage (endogamous vs. exogamous couples) would influence how individuals integrate, or insert themselves in society – that is, mixed couples would tend to be less insular than families where both spouses are Jews. The differences were less marked than expected. The main finding regarded social relations of mixed couples involved friendship patterns: Among those whose marriage partners are Jewish 41 percent have close friends who are exclusively Jewish, but this is also true of a full 25 percent of those living with a non-Jewish partner. Thus, exogamy does lead to more openness to contact with non-Jews, but distinctively different patterns were not found: Whether assimilated or not, the majority of Russian-speaking Jews do not seem to involve themselves in German society – at least at this stage.

Building Community

To what extent are the newcomers joining the Jewish community in Germany and participating in building community?

Most respondents are members of local Jewish communities (see Table 2) but only a quarter describe contacts with these communities as continuous. The vast majority attends synagogue services only occasionally. Yet, many respondents have either only Jewish friends (Russian-speaking Jews as a rule) or both Jewish and non-Jewish ones. A few have only non-Jewish friends. Hence, one can speak of a pattern of both 'Jewish' and 'mixed milieus.'

Table 2: Attitudes toward the Community by Religiosity

Secular	Traditional	Liberal Judaism	Orthodox	
2.1 Synagogue attendance (N=881)				
23.3	4.9	7.5	1.8	Never
49.4	31.6	38.5	26.4	Rarely
19.5	33	25.1	24.5	Several times a year
7.9	29.3	28.9	47.3	Frequently
100.0	100.0	100.0	100.0	Total
2.2 Closest friends in Germany (mostly) (N=877)				
29.1	38.5	31.9	50.0	Jewish
0.9	1.1	2.1	2.8	Non-Jewish
69.9	60.4	66.0	47.2	Both
100.0	100.0	100.0	100.0	Total
2.3 Russian-speaking friends (mostly) (N=881)				
31.3	42.3	34.6	50.0	Jewish
0.6	0.4	2.1	3.6	Non-Jewish
68.0	57.3	63.3	46.4	Both
100.0	100.0	100.0	100.0	Total

Religiosity was found to be a significant factor in the intensity of synagogue attendance. Not surprisingly, Orthodox respondents demonstrated stronger ties to the synagogue than others. They are also more exposed to Jewish media and socialize more with Jews in general and Russian-speaking Jews in particular. Hence, orthodox Jews – although they are a small minority among Russian-speaking Jews – are actually the most active segment of the Jewish community. The liberal and the traditional segments of the Jewish community are less involved, and the secular appear to be the least involved. On the other hand, age is a strongly-significant factor in community involvement, as well: It is the *youngest* age group (under 40) that shows the strongest involvement in the community: three quarters attend synagogue at least several times a year (i.e. the figure for those over 60 is also high, nearly 60 percent). Similarly, length of time in Germany is also a significant factor: Attachment to Jews and Jewry is stronger among longer-term residents (more than 16 years in Germany): This seems to indicate that many Russian-speaking Jews – who did not have any experience in Jewish community life in their countries of origin – find conditions in Germany favorable for building a Jewish community environment.

Nevertheless, degree of religiosity, age, and length of residence in Germany only reveal half the story of community building: An additional factor is intermarriage. As could be expected, indeed, respondents in mixed marriages (and offspring of mixed marriages) show weaker attachment to the Jewish community, are less often affiliated with Jewish organizations, and attend synagogue in smaller numbers. Hence three-fourth of the respondents where both spouses are Jewish are affiliated with Jewish organizations in Germany, compared to 52 percent among respondents in mixed marriages (and offspring of mixed marriages). In short, Russian-speaking Jews who live with a non-Jewish partner are less attached to Jewry than those living with a Jewish partner – both in terms of their contacts with Jewish institutions and patterns of socializing among others. Yet, intermarriage and being raised in a mixed family does not necessarily lead to a rupture of ties with Jewish life and community.

Thus the research shows that communities in Germany to which Russian-speaking Jews have greatly contributed or have played a role in their renewal in recent years still revolve around the synagogue – that is – 'community' rests on a religious institution above all. At the same time, Russian-speaking Jews also form Jewish milieus that include religious and non-religious people and people who are Jewish under Jewish law and those who are not. This is a community that is by no means an enclave, let alone a ghetto, yet still has its own distinct structure.

Collective and National Identifications

The above traits serve as the backdrop to the main bulk of our data and the core questions we sought to investigate: Respondents' national identifications.

Russian-speaking Jews have many options for self-definition: Russian-speaking Jews were classified as Jews under the Soviet system whether they identified with the ascription or not, and regardless of what form, if any, this Jewishness took. In fact, expressing solidarity with Israel was often seen by Soviet Jews as an act of defiance – an 'unauthorized' expression of Jewishness, liberated from state-sponsored ascription imposed by the dominating regime. In Germany, Russian-speaking Jews could also define themselves culturally and linguistically as a mixture of Jewishness and Russianness. They even could perceive themselves as Jews whose allegiance to their Jewishness had been colored by their presence in Germany – a 'German Jewishness' that in the subtext expressed aspirations to 'normalize' their status as an ethnic sub-grouping in their new society. The option to consider themselves mainly as Russian-speakers existed, however. It would express solidarity with non-Jewish ethnic Germans who resettled in Germany in large number and who, like them, carry with them the cultural baggage of the Russian language and culture. Table 3 shows how respondents related to the variety of options open to them – orientations none of which was found to be irrelevant or mutually exclusive.

Table 3: Feeling Part of/Solidarity with/Give Collective Allegiances to (%)

Feeling part of	Much	Some	A Little	Not at all	Index*	Total	N
The Jewish people	47	35	14	4	0.37	100	867
Israel	62	23	10	5	0.36	100	957
The Russian-speaking Jewish community	29	39	24	8	0.32	100	930
Russian-speaking community	17	40	23	20	0.30	100	854
Nation of origin	12	32	28	28	0.25	100	932
German nation**	3	20	31	46	0.16	100	946

*Index calculated by giving numerical increasing values to each answer (the smaller the numerical value, the smaller the strength of solidarity expressed in respondents' answers), multiplying by the number of respondents who choose this value and dividing the sum obtained by the general number of respondents in the given category: (A*4+B*3+C*2+D)/ N.

**On this count, there may be a positive skew since in the original sample, no differentiation was made between Russian-speaking Jews and veteran non-Russian-speaking Jews.

Affinity with the Jewish people is undeniably the strongest allegiance among Russian-speaking Jews and it is closely followed by solidarity with Israel and then by Russian-speaking Jews relating to themselves as a community – reflecting a collective consciousness as a distinct entity. By contrast, feelings of belonging to Russian-speakers in Germany ranks only fourth place, above the sense of belonging to their country of origin. German nation engenders the weakest sense of self-ascription.

What Defines 'Jewishness' for Russian-speaking Jews in Germany?

By what terms do Russian-speaking Jews define their 'Jewishness'? The data show clearly that religion is the primary axis of Jewishness for a slight majority (51 percent). This is followed by culture which was cited by a very significant minority (43 percent). Ethnicity ranked third place (30 percent), and group solidarity fourth with only a quarter of the respondents citing this component. Thus, religious affiliation remains the primary defining principle – despite the fact that the majority of Russian-speaking Jews in Germany are not observant: Only a minority feels close to orthodox Judaism and the same holds for adherents to more liberal streams of Jewish observance.

Not surprisingly, Orthodox respondents show stronger attachment to Judaism and the Jewish people than secular respondents. This is further confirmed by levels of aspirations to give children a Jewish education and exposure to Jewish media. Table 4 also shows that a majority of those who describe themselves as secular Jews have no objection to their offspring marrying a non-Jew. Less clear is why a substantial minority of the Orthodox shares the same attitude; this may reflect the impact of the open and liberal atmosphere that prevails in German society. On the other hand, as expected, many orthodox respondents conceive of Judaism and 'who is a Jew' in terms of Jewish law, contrary to the secular who emphasize cultural and educational practices as defining factors.

Despite high identification with Israel as a component in their Jewishness, other data show low membership in Zionist or pro-Israel organizations: Even membership of the Orthodox in Zionist or pro-Israel organizations (17 percent) is low, although substantially higher than that of the secular's (5.6 percent). Also noteworthy is that while respondents under 40 years of age express a desire to offer the children a Jewish education, this is even stronger among those over 60 years of age – a cohort that also scores highest in a sense of belonging to the Jewish people and membership in Jewish organizations and Russian-speaking Jews frameworks.

A closer review of trends reflected in Table 4 shows that Russian-speaking Jews are nearly unanimous in their attachment to Jewishness and solidarity with Israel, despite fluctuations correlated to age, duration living in Germany, and even religiosity. By contrast there is less unanimity in attitudes toward their country of origin and, even less so, regarding their new homeland – Germany. Here, let us add, age again plays a role: the over-60 respondents maintain stronger contacts than the younger generation with their former country and visit family and friends more frequently. In a same vein, Russian-speaking Jews who have resided in Germany for 16 years or more, also retain less contacts with their country of origin than those who came later: half of those who have lived in Germany ten years or less visit their country of origin twice as frequently (i.e. at least once every two years) than those who have lived in Germany for 16 or more years.

Table 4: Kind of Religiosity and Attitudes toward Markers of Jewish identities

Secular	Somewhat traditional	Liberal Judaism	Orthodox Ultra-Orthodox	
4.1 Importance of children receiving a Jewish education (n=760 ;%; γ^2=0)				
44.9	19.7	22.3	7.5	Not at all
30.8	23.1	24.6	20.4	A little
19.0	29.7	34.3	15.1	Moderately
5.3	27.5	18.9	57.0	Very much so
100.0	100.0	100.0	100.0	Total
4.2 Feeling about child marrying a non-Jew (n=814; %; γ^2=0)				
8.0	18.5	14.3	43.3	Opposed
33.4	45.2	43.4	32.0	Not enthusiastic but supports
58.5	36.3	42.3	24.7	No opposition at all
100.0	100.0	100.0	100.0	Total
4.3 Child of non-Jewish man and Jewish woman (n=873 ;%; γ^2=0)				
27.5	39.5	42.6	67.9	A regular Jew
19.2	17.1	11.2	10.1	Like a Jew
3.5	4.2	4.3	2.8	A regular non-Jew
49.8	39.2	42.0	19.3	Depends on home
100.0	100.0	100.0	100.0	Total
4.4 Child of non-Jewish woman and Jewish man (n=871 ;%; γ^2=0)				
11.0	6.0	4.8	7.3	A regular Jew
18.2	15.8	19.6	11.0	Like a Jew
14.0	23.8	25.4	54.1	A regular non-Jew
56.8	54.3	50.3	27.5	Depends on home
100.0	100.0	100.0	100.0	Total

One should also underscore here that, as shown in Table 6 (below, discussed in detail) respondents from heterogeneous families refrain from cutting off their relations with relatives or friends who remained in their country of birth and continue to share feelings for the country from which they came to Germany. This complements the findings of Table 4, which show that Russian-speaking Jews feel a sense of belonging as a particular population, but not in an exclusive manner. Multiple allegiances are not particular only to Russian-speaking Jews; like other groups, they constitute a 'transnational diaspora' – possessing a strong allegiance to the Jewish world, but at the same time not alienated from other intersecting identities.

The Allegiances of Jewish Couples and Mixed Couples

At this point, investigation of the behavior and feelings of individuals who originate from mixed parentage where only one parent is Jewish is of particular interest. Where do they stand in this intermingling of allegiances, when compared with Jews who grew up in homogeneous Jewish families?

Table 5 shows that individuals from ethnically mixed families feel less a part of the Jewish people, feel less solidarity with Israel, and relate more strongly to their nations of origin (Russia, Ukraine or other ex-Soviet republics). Yet, the data in the table also indicates that to be of heterogeneous family origin does not, necessarily, cut off individuals from Jewishness and relating to Israel: only small minorities are insensitive to Jewishness or Israel, and the difference compared to respondents of homogeneous families is by no means drastic. Nevertheless, it is also undeniable that such individuals are more attached to the former country's nation. Yet, this is not sharply in contrast to respondents of homogeneous origin, who may also retain some feelings for the 'old country.'

Table 5: Jewish Identity and Mixed Family Origin

	Family of origin of respondent*	
	Heterogeneous (N=267)	Homogeneous (N=683)
5.1 Feeling part of the Jewish people (%)		
Not at all	12.0	1.5
A little	24.4	10.9
Moderately	38.0	35.3
Much so	25.6	52.3
Total	100.0	100.0
5.2 Feeling solidarity with Israel (%)		
Not at all	4.5	2.3
A little	14.8	6.8
Moderately	33.3	24.4
Much so	47.3	66.5
Total	100.0	100
5.3 Feeling part of former country's nation (%)		
Not at all	20.9	31.3
A little	25.6	28.3
Moderately	36.2	30.8
Much so	17.3	9.6
Total	100	100

*The N values represent the average number of respondents to the diverse questions.

To complete the analysis, Table 6 examined three important criteria and compared responses among participants brought up in homogeneous and heterogeneous families, and whether their own marriage partners are Jewish or not. The data shows that both homogeneous Jewish origin and practice of endogamy ('marrying within the faith') are strongly associated with considering Jewish education as at least moderately important; respondents who are of heterogeneous origin or have non-Jewish partners are markedly less concerned in this respect. Nevertheless, a good third of those raised in mixed marriages and married to non-Jewish partners still assigned some importance to Jewish education and a majority supported Jewish education at least 'a little.' A similar gap between 'Jewish households' and 'mixed households' appears with respect to the feelings of respondents regarding the possibility that their child would marry a non-Jew. Yet, as with the previous data, again, we find that a significant minority – a third – of 'mixed households' do not embrace this possibility with unanimity.

Table 6: Exogamy and Jewishness – Selected Items

	Family of origin of respondent		Respondent's partner	
	Heterogeneous (N=267)	Homogeneous (N=683)	Non-Jewish (N=259)	Jewish (N=670)
6.1 Importance that children get Jewish education (%)				
not at all	39.3	26.9	42.6	24.1
a little	22.2	26.4	24.3	25.4
Moderately	20.9	25.2	18.7	28.5
much so	17.6	21.6	14.5	22.0
Total	100.0	100.0	100.0	100.0
6.2 Feeling about child marrying a non-Jew (%)				
Opposed	10.4	17.5	6.1	21.1
Unenthusiastic support	25.7	43.0	31.7	43.5
No opposition	63.9	39.6	62.2	35.4
Total	100	100	100	100
6.3 Synagogue attendance (%)				
Never	23.5	8.0	19.5	8.6
Rarely	35.1	41.3	41.4	40.6
Several times a year	21.6	27.3	22.6	28.6
Frequently	19.8	23.5	16.5	22.2
Total	100	100	100	100

The differences between 'Jewish households' and 'mixed households' tend to fade away when it comes to synagogue attendance: in all categories, the 'never' and the 'rarely' attend constitute a majority or near-majority of all the answers. On the other hand, the data show that the number of 'mixed households' who 'never' attend synagogue is triple the (low) non-attendance of more Jewish households. In brief, we find large percentages of individuals of mixed backgrounds (including current marital status) who even though they are still a minority, contribute to a fluidity of the meanings of attachment to Judaism among Russian-speaking Jews but by no means stand on the sidelines or cross the line where Jewishness is totally irrelevant to their lives.

Deeper investigation of the most crucial of those three criteria for Jewish continuity – attitudes towards Jewish education for children – reveals quite unexpected findings when the variables religiosity, age, and length of residence in Germany are examined. The favorable majority among the secular is smaller, increasing substantially in all other religiosity categories, but on the whole, for most of respondents, Jewish education is important. On the other hand, besides the Orthodox, the strongest support for Jewish education was registered by younger cohorts: 80 percent of respondents below age 40 and 62 percent among those ages 41+. Length of stay in Germany also emerged as a dependent variable: more veteran Russian-speaking Jewish residents (77 percent among those residing in Germany 11 years or more, compared to 67 percent among more recent arrivals) support Jewish education. Hence, notwithstanding the differences of opinions over what 'Jewishness' means and how it should be expressed, and despite the fact that respondents had no opportunity for such an education when growing up in the Soviet Union, Russian-speaking Jews – especially the younger generation –, are most anxious to provide such an education.

Thus the findings indicate that settling in Germany strengthens allegiance to Judaism and the feeling that Jewish education for children is a 'must.' Secondly, the data indicates that the younger Russian-speaking Jews who received at least a part of their education in Germany are more sensitive than their fathers or elder brothers and sisters to the importance of Jewishness for their children. This, we may conclude, indicates that they feel this importance for themselves, as well.

Conclusion

We have seen that Russian-speaking Jews insert themselves in the German society with undeniable difficulties, but that this process becomes smoother with the passing of time and the emergence of young generations. At the same time, Russian-speaking Jews are also attached to the building of a community and formation of milieus where they recognize themselves. What fuels these dynamics is the feeling of belonging to the Jewish people that goes hand in hand with solidarity with Israel. These two components of identification are most marked, nay even *the* most prominent allegiances among our respondents. Allegiance to Jewishness is primarily linked to religious principles, despite the fact that most respondents do not identify with Orthodox Judaism and quite a few define themselves as 'secular.' While a majority do attend synagogue from time to time, respondents seem to mix designations based on Jewish law, and educational criteria when defining Jewish identity, while displaying a markedly permissive outlook and inclusive attitude toward exogamy.

It appears that for many Russian-speaking Jews Germany provides the conditions to re-attach themselves to Jewishness – and as a corollary to Israel as a focus of all-Jewish solidarity – even among the sons or daughters of mixed families and those who live with non-Jewish partners (although attachments are, not surprisingly, more ambiguous among them).

Furthermore, our research reveals additional features singular to Russian-speaking Jews' collective and national allegiances. It reveals a population that has entered the Jewish world without abandoning use of its native tongue and culture. In this way Russian-speaking Jews in Germany form a part of a wider and dispersed entity – a transnational diaspora of its own – that is now one of the major components of global Jewry. On the other hand, and this is particularly relevant to the case of Germany, Russian-speaking Jews may also see themselves as a part of the Russian-speaking population (i.e. the *Aussiedler* who were ethnic Germans in the Former Soviet Union). Besides these identities, Russian-speaking Jews cannot be discounted as part of Germany's social fabric, and will, sooner or later, become 'Germans.' (Although this identity still arouses the weakest enthusiasm at present).

These multiple influences raise questions about the future of Russian-speaking Jews in Germany. Bodemann[9] forecasts Russian-speaking Jews' assimilation into the German society, the product of their 'empty Judaism' (the wording is ours). This assumption, is not, however, substantiated by our findings that show Russian-speaking Jews, in fact, tend to adopt stronger markers of Jewishness the longer they are in Germany. Bodemann also contends that Russian-speaking Jews have experienced Nazism less dramatically than other Jewish populations and therefore are less reluctant to integrate the German society. This too is not supported by our data that show an awareness of the respondents to the problematics of Jewish life in Germany.

A more optimistic hypothesis has been presented by Pinto[10] who forecasts that Russian-speaking Jews – in Germany as well as elsewhere in Europe – are now able to contribute to the re-emergence of a European Jewish Jewry that will constitute a third axis of the Jewish world, between Israeli and American Jewries. Several factors shed doubt on this projection: The absence of a common European language and the numerical weakness of the total Jewish population in Europe, compared to Israel and the United States. Realization of such a projection hinges, perhaps, on further 'Jewish maturation' of Russian-speaking Jews – a process that seems to be well in progress when one considers Russian-speaking Jews' present-day activism. Numerous Russian-speaking Jewish figures are already playing prominent roles as rabbis and community leaders, heads of clubs and cultural centers, while journalists have set up a new press.

---

[9] Bodemann, New German Jewry, 2008.
[10] Pinto, Can one Reconcile the Jewish World in Europe. In: Bodemann (ed.), The New German Jewry, 2008.

Russian-speaking Jews in Germany also participate in transnational-diaspora structures, which bind them to their counterparts in Jerusalem, Moscow, and New York. Germany's Russian-speaking Jews, who are now the bulk of this country's Jewry, are neither a continuation of past German Jewry, nor its transformation or metamorphosis. They are a transplant that anchors itself in a new soil and develop new roots. It is but another sequence of a long history of Jewish migrations.[11] In line with this legacy, Russian-speaking Jews, whatever their hesitancies regarding what 'Jewishness' means, rely on Jewish education to transmit to the young what should make Jewish life meaningful.

References

Ben-Rafael, Eliezer, Michail Lyubansky, Olaf Glöckner, Paul Harris, Yael Israel, Willi Jasper, and Julius H. Schoeps (eds.). *Building a Diaspora: Russian Jews in Israel, Germany and the USA*. Leiden, Boston: Brill, 2006.

Ben-Rafael, Eliezer. Ethnicity, Sociology of. In *International Encyclopedia of the Social and Behavioral Sciences*, Vol. 7, Neil J. Smelser, Paul B. Baltes (eds.), pp. 4838–4842. London: Elsevier, 2002.

Bodemann, Michal Y. (ed.). *The New German Jewry and the European Context. The Return of the European Jewish Diaspora*. New York: Palgrave, 2008.

Castles, Stephen: Migration and Community Formation under Conditions of Globalization. *International Migration Review* 36 (2002): pp. 1143–1168.

Cohen, Steven M., Arnold Eisen. *The Jew Within. Self, Family, and Community in America*. Bloomington: Indiana University Press, 2000.

Gidal, Nachum T. *Jews in Germany. From Roman Times to the Weimar Republic*. Cologne: Konemann, 1998.

Gitelman, Zvi (ed.). *Jewish Life after the USSR*. Bloomington: Indiana University Press, 2003.

Pinto, Diana. Can one Reconcile the Jewish World in Europe. In *The New German Jewry and the European Context. The Return of the European Jewish Diaspora*, Michal Y. Bodemann (ed.), pp. 13–32. New York: Palgrave, 2008.

Remennick, Larissa. Idealists Headed to Israel, Pragmatics Chose Europe: Identity Dilemmas and Social Incorporation among Former Soviet Jews who Migrated to Germany *Immigrants & Minorities* 23 (2005), pp. 30–58.

Schoeps, Julius (ed.). *Neues Lexikon des Judentums*. Munich: C. H. Beck, 1998.

Soysal, Yasemin N. Citizenship and identity: Living in diasporas in post-war Europe? *Ethnic and Racial Studies* 23 (2000), pp. 1–2.

---

11 Cohen / Eisen, The Jew Within, 2000.

Julia Bernstein
Russian Food Stores and their Meaning for Jewish Migrants in Germany and Israel

Honor and 'Nostalgia'

This article deals with the special meaning of food practices in the migration process taking as a prism of Russian food stores which have turned out to be very popular among ex-Soviet Jewish migrants in Israel and Germany. Fieldwork in the German context was conducted in parallel periods between 2002 and 2004 substantiated earlier findings. The Israeli case study was conducted in 2006–2008. The researcher and participants had extensive and intensive contact in both contexts. Three additional frameworks for data-gathering proved to be informative in the German context. First, I participated in and observed activities within the Jewish community in Germany that play an active role in the lives of the Jewish immigrants. Second, I conducted regular participant-observations in different centers and churches where several participants received free food rations. Third, I visited official agencies with participants on a regular basis and observed their interaction with public servants – serving as their translator from Russian to German on a number of occasions, helping participants communicate with representatives of official organizations. In the course of this, participants generously shared information with me about their lives. In addition, I collected, catalogued, and categorized numerous artifacts of the packaging of food products sold in the Russian food stores over the last ten years in Israel and the last six years in Germany. Indeed, many of these exemplars were actually given to me by participants who concluded that this was my own unusual hobby. The total collection consists of thousands of artifacts organized in four thick binders, which represent a multitude of images and product affiliations. This collection proved very rich, interesting, and useful in two ways: First, the artifacts provided relevant topics for discussion during the observations and interviews. In particular, trends in and cultural messages on the packaging were discussed with participants in both settings. This enabled me to understand the participants' perceptions of these products and especially the contradictory, often politically laden messages found on the packaging. Second, the collection was a rich resource for content analyses.

The research population selected consisted of 30 families (comprised of 55 persons) in Israel and 30 families (consisting of 57 individuals) in Germany, all of whom were 48–65 years of age or older, although most were above 50 years of age. This made it possible to view the sample population as one generation and assume that they share common memories. All the participants in the case study held university degrees in technology or the humanities and immigrated from the big cities of Russia and the Ukraine. Most of the interviewees were not employed in their original professions, made their living in jobs that did not require extensive education, and, consequently, were overqualified for their jobs.

Food and Identity

Food practices encoding information about communication systems are an integral part of a person's relationship with different social groups and can be seen as "a physical as well as a social event."[1] Various kinds of food, when used in different social contexts, signal an economic and political status and are codes to the individual's concepts and behavior, which need to be deciphered in terms of defining group boundaries, social status, and economic class.

Some food choices can define success, ethnic association, or spiritual values. In this way people can aspire to certain foods on the one hand and limit themselves to certain foods on the other. Food and drink are often used by different groups to recall memories, demonstrate identities, or construct "their own sense of nostalgia for customary sociability."[2] Not only is cuisine a product of 'double orality' – taste, and talk;[3] consumption of food can be linked symbolically to multiple identity affiliations where the consumer is prompted to buy a product by different visual images, names, and statements displayed on packages. In doing so, food functions along a spectrum between two poles: Nationalization of food that is presumed 'to belong to us' versus post-modern Western consumer societies in which everyday mobility requires open-mindedness, culinary cosmopolitanism, and authenticity.[4] Clifford described this as "travelling in dwelling, dwelling-in-travelling."[5]

The packaging of commodities is particularly characteristic and is a key to understanding the connection between food and identity. Herzfeld referred to "packaging [as the] poetics of authenticity,"[6] and Grasseni argued that it also symbolizes the "shift toward a marked commodification of taste."[7]

---

1 Douglas, Food in the Social Order, 1984, p. 15.
2 Miller, Consumption and Commodities, 1995.
3 Ray, Nation and Cuisine, 2008.
4 Ching, Beyond 'Authenticity'. In: Döring / Heide / Mühleisen (eds.), Eating culture, 2003.
5 Clifford cited by Döring / Heide / Mühleisen (eds.), Eating culture, 2003
6 Herzfeld cited by Grasseni, Slow Food, Fast Genes, 2005.
7 Grasseni, 2005.

Food and Homeland

Some researchers described the meaning certain food products carry as creating a sense of home in the migration process, for example Ayse S. Cargal in her research of Döner Kebap among Turkish migrants in Germany;[8] Mankekar Purnima in her investigation of "India shopping" among migrants in the United States;[9] and Tsili Dolve Gandelman's findings about the meaning of *injera* among Ethiopian Jewish women in Israel.[10] In my study I investigated Russian food stores as a creative scene manifesting identities and 'images of belonging' for ex-Soviet Jews in Israel and Germany.

In order to understand this and other different product images, symbolic manifestations, and meanings of Russian food stores for ex-Soviet Jewish migrants in Israel and Germany it is necessary to understand the tensions surrounding self-images and statuses with which ex-Soviet Jewish participants of the study have to cope. Participants do not 'burn their bridges' with the original society as it was often assumed; rather, as active, creative social agents they maintain intensive networks and develop creative transnational spaces. In this context the question of loyalty has proved to be particularly relevant, as it has become most doubtful that transmigrants demonstrate exclusive loyalty towards one national state.[11] In this respect several status conflicts arise in the lives of participants in my study:

1. The subjects' high professional qualifications, the product of decades of university education, credentials gained during their professional careers, and social recognition accrued in the former Soviet Union proved irrelevant and inappropriate, and remained unrecognized in Germany. In Israel the majority of participants failed to find jobs in their original professions, which were reduced to/transformed into status signifiers in/from a "previous life" (as some participants formulated it). Uprooting placed them in terms of socioeconomic status at the lower end of the social hierarchy in Germany and Israel where the discrepancy clashed with the transported self-image of highly qualified professionals, a contradiction that was very transparent. This became very apparent during of my field research, talking with the subjects in private conversations at home around the table in Israel or while waiting in

---

8 Caglar, McKebap. In: Lentz (ed.), Changing Food Habits, 1999.
9 Mankekar, India Shopping. In: Watson / Caldwell (eds.), Cultural Politics of Food and Eating, 2005.
10 Dolve-Gandelman, Ethiopia as a Lost Imaginary Space. In: MacCannell (ed.), Other Perspective, 1990.
11 Cohen, Sociological Analysis. In: Gordis / Ben-Horin / The / Wikstei (eds.), Jewish Identitiy in America, 1991.

line for free food rations allotted by a German church, about the importance of the professional positions they had held in the former Soviet Union.

2. Their affiliation with the Soviet *intelligentsia* engendered little interest among non-Russian-speaking groups in Israel or Germany. Their command of the beautiful literary Russian language – a source of pride and social recognition in the former Soviet Union – did not contribute to social participation in either absorbing societies. Quite the opposite; the migrants linguistic insecurity often becomes noticeable as *existential insecurity* in the self-perception and behavioral patterns of migrants.[12] Their deep ties with Russian culture have a positive connotation in the eyes of the migrants and while many try to continue to take pride in their Russian culture, the same attribute stigmatizes them and labels them as 'Russians' (without the cultural capital this carries for and among Russians).

3. Their pride in belonging to the European cultural *habitus* (within a Russian context, particularly compared to Asian republics), was not reciprocated once they moved to the West where such status was even highly questioned in both contexts, but especially in Germany where suddenly they were often seen as 'half Asian.'[13] The host's view stems from the long history of juxtaposing Eastern and Western European affiliations, as well as socialization to negative perceptions of the totalitarian regime of Soviet European republics, such as Russia and Ukraine.

4. Another key source for collective pride for the migrants was pride of being part of one of the world's superpowers – socio-political capital that dissolved with the fall of the Soviet Union. The dismantling of the Soviet Union was viewed from a 'Western perspective' in Israel and Germany as evidence of the failure of the socialist system. Ironically, the dream maintained over decades – of material wealth in communism, was only symbolically realized in the 'capitalistic West' within the German but also the Israeli case.

5. Affiliation and identification with the collective 'winners of the Second World War' shifted significantly from being a source of pride and strong support, to being but another 'narrative of Otherness' – in their case, assuming the role of victims reserved for Jews. For Jews already residing in Germany for some time, the essential 'Jewish contribution of the migrants' to the Soviet victory was pushed into the background (i.e. treated with scepticism or questioned due to Soviet policy of withholding the truth about the Holocaust).

---

[12] *Ehlich quoted by Reitemeier*, Gute Gründe für schlechte Gesprächsverläufe. In: Chirly dos Santos-Stubbe (ed.), Interkulturelle Soziale Arbeit in der Theorie und Praxis, 2005.
[13] Stölting, The East of Europe. In: Breckner / Kalekin-Fishman / Miethe (eds.), Biographies and the Division of Europe, 2000.

6. The migrants' identification as 'being Jewish' – an affiliation that involved much pain and difficulties in the Soviet Union – was perceived to be a fabrication or at best flimsy by resident groups in both new contexts. Indeed, attitudes towards their 'Jewishness' was often patronizing, reflected in statements that the veteran Jewish community "must make them real Jews."[14] In this context, the migrants' experience of anti-Semitism was viewed insufficient as a badge of being 'genuinely Jewish.' Although many Jewish migrants were interested in Jewish religion and history, many participants reported that they are again being 'punished' for suppression of Jewish culture in the Soviet Union that led to a lack of knowledge of Jewish religion and culture, while the parts of the Russian-Soviet *habitus* they had internalized were transformed into a 'liability' in the eyes of veteran members of the Jewish community – as evidence of 'not being Jewish.'

Codes and Nostalgia

Loss of feeling at *home* on different levels combined with subjective memories, motivated the participants to long for the *real, original, authentic, same*, but also *'the right* stuff' and *'that* taste.' Such yearnings for warm and familiar tuft were based on idealized, images of *home* with a positive connotation and "rosy recollections"[15] of past experiences. In analyzing the concept 'nostalgia,' Boym found that nostalgia places different emphases on restorative and reflective components, namely on *nostos* and *algia*: "Restorative nostalgia puts emphasis on *nostos* and proposes to rebuild the lost home and patch up the memory gaps. Reflective nostalgia dwells in *algia*, in longing and loss, the imperfect process of remembering."[16] Both of these components are present within Russian food stores and in the participants' consumption patterns in Israel and Germany.

Migrants immigrating to Israel encountered a milieu rife with hegemonic nationalist messages extolling the Jewish homeland that at times appeared in tandem with images extolling the Russian motherland. This can be seen when one compares labeling in Russian versus labeling in Hebrew on the same product, available in Russian food stores. For example, the Russian brand name on a package of mushrooms – *Domik v Derevne* ('Little House in the Country' in Russian – is accompanied by depiction of a house that is likely to arouse asso-

---

[14] Riebsamen, in: Frankfurter Allgemeine Zeitung, November 11, 2006.
[15] Lupton, Food, the Body, and the Self, 1996, p. 50.
[16] Boym, The Future of Nostalgia, 2001, p. 41.

ciations with a Russian *dacha* for consumers. However, the Hebrew label states *kafri ve beiti* ('My Country Village' and 'My House' in Hebrew), associated with the Zionist idea of a home in the native (Israeli) *homeland* (A second meaning of this label can be understood as meaning 'country-baked' and 'home-baked.') Similarly, the plastic bag packaging bread baked by the Angel Bakery in Jerusalem states *Rodnoe Selo* ('Native Country Village' in Russian) accompanied by a picture

Fig. 1: Brand name for special bread: "Rodnoe Selo" (Native Country Village). Foto: Bernstein.

of a field with harvested yellow sheaves associated with vast Soviet expanses, along side the Hebrew *HaKfar Sheli* ('My Village' in Hebrew) which appeals to Jewish consumers. Thus, a Russian-speaking consumer whose eye is likely to perceive the Russian text first and then the Hebrew receives two conflicting messages from the product's packaging – with different ideological content, the Soviet versus the Zionist *national home*. Such commercial messages are hardly compatible as the nationalist terminology is absolute and each demands loyalty to the 'correct' national home.

Fig. 2: Nostalgic Signifier: Rye Bread of the Past. Foto: Bernstein.

Fig. 3: Harvester gathering an abundant wheat harvest. Picture from the Soviet Food Encyclopedia, published by Igor Sivalop: "Kniga o Vkusnoi i Zdorovoi Pishche" [The Tasty and Healthy Food Book], USSR Ministry of Food Industry, Moscow 1952.

Similarly, the packaging of the Israeli *Pa'am* Rye Bread ('once-upon-a-time' in Hebrew or 'old-style rye bread' like the Russian 'rye bread of the past' – in Hebrew, a shortened version of the Hebrew expression *im ta'am shel pa'am* – 'with the taste of yesteryear' – an expression used as a nostalgic signifier of 'the the good old days' – not only for food) depicts a field of rye with a huge combine harvester gathering the yield from the soil of the Jewish homeland. The bread's bakery is called *Ahdut* ('Unity' in Hebrew), a word associated with the concept of *ahdut ha'am* ('unity of the Jewish people' in Hebrew). However, the Russian statement on the same package is "rye bread of the past".

Thus, even if Russian consumers understood the reference to the Zionist value embedded in the Hebrew text, they are more likely to associate it to the promises of communism in the Soviet Union and one of its central symbols – the harvester gathering an abundant wheat harvest, as depicted on one of the first pages of the Soviet-era 'food encyclopaedia' entitled *On the Tasty and Healthy Food Book*.

In the Israeli context, Russian-speaking Jewish migrants are also exposed to additional commercialized nationalistic nostalgia – for example, the six-pointed Star of David, use of a blue-and-white color scheme (similar to the Israeli flag), or Jewish religious symbols such as the menorah, candles, or certain food products connected with particular holidays. Collectively, these symbols are integral to and representative of the hegemonic Jewish-national political narrative which is reinforced by its appearance on consumption products encountered daily by Israelis in the course of their lives.

During the 1920s, consumption of local food products by Jews distributed under the label *Totzeret Ha'aretz* (literally, products of the Land [of Israel] in Hebrew), but this ideologically-driven labeling refers to products from the Jewish economic sector only of Mandate Palestine and buying *Totzeret Ha'aretz* was considered 'a patriotic act'[17] and this value played an important role in the promotion of products. Although not in the scale of the 1920s, there are still many products today that incorporate symbols of politically-loaded images related to the centrality of the Jewish homeland. For example, in honor of the sixtieth jubilee anniversary of the establishment of the State of Israel in 2008, special marketing strategies employing national symbols appeared in regular Israeli supermarkets to attract Jewish consumers, such as a package of regular Elite Turkish coffee that prominently displayed an Israeli flag along with the statement about the producer – signifying Elite was part of the 'founding generation': "Roasted and ground Turkish coffee – 60 years of coffee roasting in Israel."

Images of Paradise

In fact, the *esprit de corps* of the unconquerable Soviet empire narrative with its fifteen republics led by Russia continues to be salient in the Russian-speaking

---

17 Raviv, National identity on a plate, 2001/2002.

enclave. Even if the powerful empire no longer exists physically, symbolic and often stereotypic revival serves as active signifiers for ex-Soviet citizens abroad. This is apparent in the food products consumers purchase – adorned with images of the powerful Soviet empire and "patriotic gigantomania."[18] Here, the symbolic emphasis on the richness and power of the Soviet empire serve a compensatory role for migrants who are usually perceived to be a marginal minority by the absorbing society and lack political, social, and economic resources. Thus, one encounters the phrase "one sixth of the land" – referring to the richness, expansion, and power of the Soviet empire that at its height spanned one-sixth of the land mass of planet earth – a term frequently used by Russian and non-Russian-speaking entrepreneurs, as it is assumed to have a positive connotation for ex-Soviet emigrants.

Russian food stores made it possible to realize, for the first time, the opulent "spread on the table" depicted in illustrious Russian fairlytales with its powerful and magical ability to produce the desired abundance of dishes, wines, fruits, and gourmet delicacies. Through symbolic realization of the ideal image of the proper home and hearth in the communist food paradise in the Soviet homeland, migrants could participate in its imaginary political power, and richness – albeit in the Western 'here and now.' Highly politicized in the Soviet Union, food retained many of its characteristics after emigration.

In comparison to their lives in the Soviet Union, the participants in both Germany and Israel acknowledged and 'celebrated' the improvement in their material state, evidenced in their everyday diet and occasional luxurious festive settings. It seemed that a visit to the Russian food store was more than a means to acquire commodities. In fact, as described by participants, it was more like an adventure involving a 'hunt' for a variety of symbols of a wealthy, powerful, and rich life often dreamt of but seldom realized in the Soviet Union. The pictures used in advertisements and displays of Russian food stores were identical to or very similar to illustrations in the original, politically-laden version of the Soviet book. In some cases pictures on tins of food products were almost identical to pictures in the book: For example, "Glory Chocolate"[19] from *On the Tasty and Healthy Food Book* is very similar to the same chocolate sold in Russian food stores in Israel Products mentioned in the famous Soviet recipe books as well as products commonly known to be hard to find in the Soviet Union 'back then' – such as sturgeon, beluga, carp, mackerel, calamari, crayfish, shrimp, catfish, squid, trout, and especially cod-liver, pink salmon, and sprat – are available in

---

18 Genis / Vail, Poteryannyi rai, 2003.
19 The Russian word *slava* can also be translated in English as 'honor', which conjures up associations with military honor.

numerous variations in Russian food stores in both Germany and in Israel. As there is no universal consensus about expensive and prestigious food, some of the food products mentioned above did not necessarily carry high status in the local dominant market in Israel or Germany and were for the most part affordable and even cheap, however, within the framework of the Russian food stores, they remain prestigious and special.

Fig. 4: "Glory"-Chocolate, once a beloved delicacy in the USSR, is a fast seller in Israeli Shops, too. Picture from: Igor Sivalop, "Kniga o Vkusnoi i Zdorovoi Pishche"

Fig. 5: "Glory Chocolate" with Israeli price tag. Foto: Bernstein.

Western affluence is expressed in the Russian food stores by groceries imported from Russia or the Ukraine such as the attraction of chocolates produced by confectioners whose brand names sound paradoxical in the new reality: "Red October", "Bolshevik," "Karl Marx," "Krupskaya" (Lenin's wife).

Gastronomic Slavophilism

Two parallel processes are involved in these phenomena. The first, the newly nationalized Russian mobilization of shared symbols of national pride taken from the Soviet period. The second, introduction of new images from old Russian traditions including symbols from Slavic folklore and Eastern Orthodox Christianity; crests of nobility and feudal markings; portrates of Russian tsars and empresses; motifs from old Russian fairytales; and legends about Russian heroes conquering foreign enemies (such as Tatars and Mongols) and saving the Russian motherland. Among them one can encounter *Vivat Russia!* Chocolates depicting Catherine I (the first Russian empress); *Lyubite Rus Vodka!* ('Love Russia,' where "Russia" appears in pre-revolutionary version *Rus*); and Motherland Vodka which is sold together with Jewish vodka in Russian food stores in Germany. Interestingly, some but not all of the motifs and marketing initiatives promoting Russian nationalist feelings are not local; for example, the logo "*Rossiya shedraya dusha*" ('Russia Generous Soul' in Russia) is found on chocolates in Israel and Germany produced by a Swiss firm in Russia – Nestle-Russia Yet, independent of where *Russianness* was produced, "Russia shopping" undertaken abroad is perceived by consumers differently from consumers of similar products in the Russian Federation. In particular, the findings suggest that the act of "tasting/savoring nationalism"[20] from abroad was significantly limited, smoothed over, and relativized due to the physical distance of participants from their former national borders, as well as through the very act of voluntary emigration which in national terms could raise questions vis-à-vis their patriotism and loyalty to their land of origin. Consuming such manifestations of *Russianness* from abroad while independent of the Russian system allows participants the opportunity to distance themselves from it and to criticize the system. Thus, construction of *Russian motherland* as a total signifier appears to have lost its totalizing nature, post-emigration. Furthermore, in looking for the *authentic* and the *Russian*, the participants often overlooked or neglected national-nationalistic Russian signs, perceiving only the fragmentary image of *Russianness* offered in the stores and, in particular stereotypic, all-encompassing signifiers of their collective cultural affiliation – exported to and designed to appeal to and preserve the identity of Russian émigrés in Israel or Germany. Thus, direct manifestation of *Russianness*, even if nurtured by contemporary Russian nationalized symbols, are employed by ex-Soviet Jewish participants abroad as an empirical category as a 'was bought, and served' – served in every sense – as a 'badge of affiliation,' even if it became a stereotypic, homogenized cultural marker of immigrants. Furthermore, in the German case, symbols of nationalized Russianness may signify an imaginary homeland with which the émigré consumer – who for the most part continue to hold Russian citizenship – can partially express their affiliation; this is in contrast with their counterparts in Israel who hold Israeli citizenship and therefore are more open to 'trying out' the national Israeli narrative about the new homeland – identification that Israel actively seeks to inculcate among its immigrants.

"You Are What You Eat"?

Whereas for outsiders, Russian political images seem to be the total signifier of a particular commodity's image, for many migrants this dimension is *only one of several dimensions* that a box of chocolates can possess, encompassing an entire 'social world.' There are several connotations: The prestigious box of chocolate conjures up personal experiences in Russia. Moreover, it affirms the migrant consumers' enhanced status as 'part' of the well-to-do in Soviet society. This would seem to be an interesting application of the well-known adage "You are what you eat." To what degree is this adage 'valid' here? To clarify this question I would like

---

[20] Caldwell, The Taste of Nationalism, 2002.

to note a very provocative example that clearly contradicts this notion, with no impact on the self-image of the participants.

Fig. 6: Chocolat Brand "Vecherniy Kiev" (Kiev at Night) with monument of Bogdan Khmelnicki. Foto: Bernstein.

The box of chocolates *Vecherniy Kiev* ('Kiev at Night' in Russian) which can be found in Russian food stores in Israel as well as in Germany, is appreciated by many migrants (particularly from the Ukraine) mainly because of the quality of the chocolate. The package boasts a key spot in the Ukrainian capital where a monument to the Cossak leader Bogdan Khmelnicki – a venerated figure for Ukrainians – stands. During the seventeenth century however, Khmelnicki was personally responsible for the massacre of many thousand Jews (some historians speak of 300,000 Jews) – a fact well-known to many Russian-speaking Jewish migrants. Yet, the product remains popular, *despite* the 'negative icon' for Jews (employed by the manufacturers as a positive branding enhancement within local markets in the Ukraine). Likewise, images of Cossacks decorate the packaging of *pelmeni* with meat and cheese filling; the cossacks' notoriety as anti-Semites and as perpetrators of pogroms does not seem to annoy Jewish consumers at the Russian food stores. When I mentioned during the interviews the 'symbolic dimension' – the dissonance between the packaging and Jewish history – the explanation that I received all the time was that these food stuffs tasted good, and the linkage with the oppression of the Jews was artificial/a more superficial one.

This is well articulated in the response of Katia, a history teacher who lives in Germany:

> We buy the taste, you know. And when such associations [with oppression of the Jews] turn up, you try to get away from them, to extinguish them and to shift them [points to her stomach] deep down, as far away as possible.

It is important to add some biographical information about the speaker and her 'Jewish side.' Katia goes to the synagogue regularly, she fasts on Yom Kippur, lights Sabbath candles, and says that she has pangs of conscience when she eats pork. She has been to Israel four times already, where she has many family members. Although consumption of such symbolisms takes place, the interview leaves no doubt that ex-Soviet Jews do not identify with the resurgence of nationalism in Russia and the Ukraine reflected in the packaging, and even cite increasing anti-semitism as a reason for emigration.

The above example shows that 'rewriting history' and exchanging one dominant Russian or Ukrainian group for another does not mean that the new version of history will, automatically, reflect the history of minorities living (or previously living) in these territories. Indeed, the very elements being cultivated in the emerging new Russian public discourse and selected to be depicted on packaging have been problematic or controversial in relation to historic representation of Jewish life in Russia. Indeed, some of the images and narratives revived by dominant Russian groups correspond – coincidentally and in some cases directly in contradiction to the historical facts of Jewish participation in the Russian or Ukrainian national narrative. Indeed, reviving any historic events as part of nationalizing processes would be 'problematic' from the Jewish standpoint since this history was characterized by undeniably strong discrimination against Jews.

Realization of Dreams

Russian food stores enabled immigrants to *taste capitalism* on 'familiar turf' based upon past experiences in the Soviet Union, especially through the essential process of 'procuring and getting' desired food items. Furthermore, certain aspects of the abundance they once dreamed of attaining are realized in Russian food stores in Germany and Israel. This includes food products that were highly desired and prestigious in the Soviet Union that most participants might never or may very rarely have been able to afford when living in the Soviet Union. Thus, paradoxically, it was only after emigration to a capitalist society that certain food products that exemplified communism's dream – as expounded in the *On the Tasty and Healthy Food Book*, – became available, affordable, and are purchased regularly by migrants at Russian food stores.

Indeed, shopping itself became a very pleasurable activity, particularly because in doing so the migrants are able to satisfy desires and realize dreams that were impossible to achieve when living in the Soviet Union. Applying the analysis of Jackson and Holbrook,[21] the participants allow themselves to be self-indulgent and to splurge on delicacies and fancy foods, especially when this allowed them to 'treat' family members. Furthermore, attaining exemplars of abundance enables participants to consume "cultural tales"[22] including the dreams of the opulent *spread on the table* and the *taste of life abroad*, referred to previously. Such food consumption epitomizes the materialization/actualization of the desires of those who opted to emigrate to Israel and Germany for economic reasons (i.e. pursuit of the 'land of milk of honey' in the literal sense). Thus overall, one major outcome of these processes has been that all participants in both contexts claim that their post-immigration diet had improved significantly, even though most participants believe that their social status had declined since their arrival in Israel or Germany.

Different images of products purchased in Russian food stores are inextricably linked to a projection of social status. To restate this through the terms employed by Douglas[23], the act of consumption can be conceived to be an "act of social attachment" in two key ways: First, in the sense of marking group borders in the new society; second (and no less important), in the sense of performing a respectable, past action associated with the social status that is recognizable through common cultural terms shared by participants, who in this case belong to the educated intelligentsia stratum. This atmosphere of support and solidarity helps preserve dignity and recreate lost social status disrupted in the migration process through 'changing the environment' by those who recognized this status in the past.

One particularly interesting characteristic of the Russian food stores observed during the fieldwork was that people who came to the shops often talk about their past and present experiences. Some customers explained that they have a routine of coming to the shop on a set day in the week so that their conversations were

---

[21] Jackson / Holbrook, Multiple Meanings, 1995, pp. 1919-1921.
[22] Appadurai, How to Make a National Cuisine, 1988.
[23] Douglas, Purity and Danger, 1966; Douglas, Deciphering a Meal, 1975; Douglas, Standard Social Uses of Food. In: Douglas (ed.), 1984.

ongoing, and in some cases they did not even purchase anything. Here, Slava (Israel) explained his reasons for going to a Russian shop he frequents regularly: "Simply to meet acquaintances and to enjoy an informal atmosphere with nice educated people."

Visitors to the Russian shops also exchange information and recommendations on a wide range of topics. They reported to me, for example, recommending names of Russian-speaking doctors and sharing information about new books, films in the Russian language, interesting TV programs, worthwhile activities or clubs for children, Russian-speaking guided tours, and stores offering good discounts. People shared anecdotes and news about themselves and children attending university; gave one another advice regarding difficulties or problems they encountered; and discussed cultural or political events, or newspapers articles in Russian, They also come to post or to view personal announcements on the shop's bulletin board.

It would be mistake to claim that these *imaginary homes* and *homelands* in the shops are a kind of vacuum in which the participants reproduce and live in a hazy past, unconnected to contemporary events. On the contrary, local events in Israel and Germany as well as those taking place in the contemporary Commonwealth of Independent States (CIS) are discussed intensively in the Russian food store social club and, accordingly, new forms of reference are created. This was especially the case in the Israeli context as significantly different national images and contemporary Slavophil Russia and Zionist, Jewish, Israeli nationalized narratives are simultaneously consumed and re-activated in Russian food stores in Israel.

An emotional dimension – closeness and the sense of community – have developed and characterize the service provided by Russian-speaking clerks – ambiance that offers a different local level of kinship and empathy. Such an atmosphere has been preferred by participants to a visit of the regular supermarket. This preference substantiates Gold's findings in his study of Russian-speaking migrants in the USA.[24] This finding is reflected by the statement of a clerk in an Israeli Russian food stores when describing what his work entails, given the social atmosphere created in the store by consumers and staff alike:

> People come here to talk. To remember. They share with us what is happening to them, tell us about themselves: Whose child is in the army. Who has left on vacation. Who is working where. They talk about their problems. It really is not like it was in the Soviet stores... you do remember!? [i.e. referring to the unpleasant nature of service in the Soviet store and the stressful struggle involved in 'attaining' everything]. People come here even if they don't want to buy anything.

---

[24] Gold, Community Formation. In: Lewin-Epstein / Roi / Ritterband (eds.), Russian Jews on Three Continents, 1997, p. *264.*

Similar to other studies, the clerks in Russian food store function as "cultural ethnic brokers"[25] and as communication sources who can interpret 'intercultural' issues.[26] Moreover, it seems that these clerks have served an additional role as surrogate social workers or demi-psychologists for migrants. I observed that they were ready to listen to various and often endless accounts of problems and difficulties encountered by new and regular customers, and to offer their advice. For example, when I stated my amazement that a clerk (in Israel) knew my name after my first visit, he explained:

> My function is to know all these things, not only the products' prices – such as names of customers' relatives, phone numbers of different institutions – for example *Misrad Haklita* or *Bituach Leumi* [The Ministry of Absorption or The National Insurance Institute, interjecting this Russian with the Hebrew names of these key institutions] because people ask me. I am trying to create a home atmosphere here. So, I have to know all these things.

Imaginary 'Homes'

Russian food stores should not be considered to be a unique or isolated 'self-contained phenomenon'; rather, they are part of an evolving and growing Russian-speaking enclave comprised of different institutions where participants meet and create their communal life. As found in studies conducted among other such migrant communities,[27] the decision to frequent a Russian store does not mean that consumers intend to go back to the original society. Rather, by participating in the institutional life of the enclave they are involved in creating and sharing a new symbiosis with different *home* and *homelands* narratives that evolve continuously and gain legitimacy in the multicultural society.

It was interesting to note that the criterion of 'healthy food' often claimed to be one of the most important criteria in Western food consumption does not play even a secondary role in the purchases of consumers in Russian food stores. One encounters consumption of festive salads traditionally prepared with liberal quantities of mayonnaise, as well as preference for the 'right' sour cream (i.e., with at least 30 percent fat content). The choice of canned meat and fish products is wide both in Germany and Israel. Particularly noteworthy in terms of health one encounters products from Russia but especially from the Ukraine – ranging from unrefined sunflower oil to chocolates made by certain companies – that are

---

25 Darieva, Russkii Berlin, 2004.
26 Mankekar, 2005.
27 Mankekar, 2005.

produced in areas (particularly Pripyat and Gomel) located very near Chernobyl. Customers overlooked the source in all the cases I observed. Furthermore, when I inquired if they knew where the product was produced, the question was met with humor: For example, several participants argued that I had emigrated too long ago and consequently had distanced myself from what is "natural" for them and as a result I pay attention to other "strange" things. It was obvious that the desirable 'images of home' these products carries is much more important to the consumers than calorie content, cholesterol, or even possible radiation.

Russian food stores present what Kunow labels a "proxy for home"[28] by offering multiple narratives and *home scenarios* on the packaging of products for sale in these shops. I would argue, however, that this remains a kind of *imaginary* home. In this sense, Russian food stores' *real praxis* is, above all, a "place-making practice"[29] – performed by displaying different food images of imaginary *homes* and *homelands*. The physical walls of Russian food stores create a special microcosm where customers can feel comfortable, embraced, and safe in a home that symbolically replaces the migrants' prevailing sense of *homelessness* felt on a host of levels in their current lives as new immigrants.

Conclusions

Food practices in the migration process obviously contribute to "living memories"[30] – yet they do much more: They also "make a place" for a virtual home that preserves social status and stabilizes the self-esteem of customers who frequent Russian product stores – confirming, modifying, and, manifesting self-images; marking-symbolizing group belonging; and creating an illusion of objective reality and immediate supportive environment taken for granted.

Naturalization of the given order[31] or naturalization of basic ideas about questions such as – How does society operate? How can I find my way around? – Along with preserving the *habitus* of people from highly educated social strata, are fundamentally challenged by the crisis of the migration experience. For migrants, both 'recovering'/retrieving the *habitus* and 'doing things as one is used to' seem to take place with the help of common symbolic codes inherent in food practices shared by Russian-speaking Jews abroad. Food consumption in the migration process seems to promote contouring collective 'we' identities or in

---

28 Kunow, Eating Indian(s). In: Döring / Heide / Mühleisen (eds.), Eating Culture, 2003, p. 158.
29 Ray, The Migrant's Table, 2004.
30 Bernstein, Food for Thought, 2010.
31 Bourdieu, Distinction, 1984.

the case of ex-Soviet Jews in Israel and Germany – 'doing-being *nashi*' ('our own' in Russian) or *nashi*zation if you wish.

Addressing different images of food items enables me to reveal the multilayered and dynamic processes of coping with different forms (at times contested forms) of affiliation – such as doing-being *nashi* or *nashi*zation as fluid key-symbol category for the group under investigation. *Nashi* 'doers' were those who aspire to find and achieve a new *home* within the framework of Russian food stores in Israel and Germany, albeit in different way. All these manifestations of *nashi* affiliation among those who participate in it, symbolically participate in realization of the Soviet paradise abroad. This is not void of contradictions: These symbolic acts are often performed by individuals who on one hand cultivate Russian elite culture but simultaneously purchase proletarian food as the ultimate stamp of authentic 'Russianess.' The badge of *nashi* identity is, thus, often 'purchased' along with food products imported from the Commonwealth of Independent States. In doing so, it has been strongly influenced by the politics of nationalization and *nashi*ization processes afoot in Russia, where recently this key symbol of collective national affiliation has become even more pronounced.

References

Appadurai, Arjun. How to Make a National Cuisine: Cookbooks in Contemporary India. *Comparative Studies in Society and History* 30 (1988): pp. 3–24.
Bernstein Julia. *Food for Thought. Transnational Contested Identities and Food Practices of Russian-Speaking Jewish Migrants in Israel and Germany*. Frankfurt a. M., New York: Campus, 2010.
Bourdieu, Pierre. *Distinction: A Social Critique of the Judgment of Taste*. Cambridge: Harvard University Press, 1984.
Boym, Svetlana. *The Future of Nostalgia*. New York: Basic Books, 2001.
Caldwell, Melissa L. The Taste of Nationalism: Food Politics in Postsocialist Moscow. *Ethos* 67 (2002): pp. 295–319.
Caglar, Ayse S. McKebap: Döner Kebap and the social positioning struggle of German Turks. In *Changing Food Habits: Case Studies from Africa, South America and Europe*, Carola Lentz (ed.), pp. 263–285. Newark: Gardon & Breach, 1999.
Ching, Lin Pang. Beyond 'Authenticity:' Reinterpreting Chinese Immigrant Food in Belgium. In *Eating Culture. The Poetics and Politics of Food*, Tobias Döring, Markus Heide, and Susanne Mühleisen (eds.), pp. 53–70. Heidelberg: Winter, 2003.
Cohen, Steven M. Sociological Analysis of Jewish Identity. In *Jewish Identity in America* Gordis Davide, Yoav Ben-Horin, Susan The, and David Wikstei (eds.), pp. 27–29. Los Angeles: Ktav, 1991.

Dolve-Gandelman, Tsili. Ethiopia as a Lost Imaginary Space: The Role of Ethiopian Jewish Women in Producing the Ethnic Identity of their Immigrant Group in Israel. In *The Other Perspective in Gender and Culture*, Juillet MacCannell (ed.), pp. 242–257. New York: Columbia University Press, 1990.

Döring, Tobias, Markus Heide, and Susanne Mühleisen (eds.). *Eating Culture. The Poetics and Politics of Food*. Heidelberg: Winter, 2003.

Douglas, Mary. *Purity and Danger: An Analysis of the Concepts of Pollution and Taboo*. London: Routledge, 1966.

Douglas, Mary. Deciphering a Meal. *Daedalus* 101 (1975): pp. 61–81.

Douglas, Mary (ed.). *Food in the Social Order: Studies of Food and Festivities in Three American Communities*. New York: Russell Sage Foundation, 1984.

Douglas, Mary. Standard Social Uses of Food: Introduction. In *Food in the Social Order: Studies of Food and Festivities in Three American Communities*, Mary Douglas (ed.), pp. 1–39. New York: Russell Sage Foundation, 1984.

Genis, Alexander, Peter Vail. *Poteryannyi rai. Emigraziya: popytka avtoportreta.* (Lost Paradise). Ekaterinburg: U-Faktoria, 2003 [1983].

Gold, Steven J. Community Formation among Jews from the Former Soviet Union in the United States. In *Russian Jews on Three Continents. Migration and Resettlement* Noah Lewin-Epstein, Yaacov Roi, and Raul Ritterband (eds.), pp. 261–284. London: Routledge, 1997.

Grasseni, Cristina. Slow Food, Fast Genes: Timescapes of Authenticity and Innovation in the Anthropology of Food. *Cambridge Anthropology* 25 (2005): pp. 79–94.

Jackson, Peter, Beverley Holbrook. Multiple Meanings: Shopping and the Cultural Politics of Identity. *Environment and Planning* 27 (1995), pp. 1913–1930.

Kunow, Rüdiger. Eating Indian(s): Food, Representation, and the Indian Diaspora in the United States. In *Eating Culture. The Poetics and Politics of Food*, Tobias Döring, Markus Heide, and Susanne Mühleisen (eds.), pp: 151–177. Heidelberg: Winter, 2003.

Lupton, Deborah. *Food, the Body, and the Self*. London/New Delhi: SAGE, 1996.

Mankekar, Purnima. India Shopping. Indian Grocery Stores and Transnational Configuration of Belonging. In *The Cultural Politics of Food and Eating. A Reader*, James L. Watson, Melissa L. Caldwell (eds.), pp. 197–214. Malden/Oxford: Wiley-Blackwell, 2005.

Miller, Daniel Consumption and Commodities. *Annual Review Anthropology* 24 (1995): pp. 141–161.

Raviv, Yael. National identity on a plate. *Palestine-Israel Journal* 8 and 9 (2001–2002). http://pij.org/details.php?id=805 (accessed March 28, 2015).

Ray, Krishnendu. *The Migrant's Table: Meals and Memories in Bengali-American Households*. Philadelphia: Temple University Press, 2004

Ray, Krishnendu. Nation and Cuisine: The Evidence from American Newspapers ca. 1830–2003. *Food and Foodways* 16 (2008): pp. 1–39.

Reitemeier, Ulrich. Gute Gründe für schlechte Gesprächsverläufe. SozialarbeiterInnen in der Kommunikation mit Migranten. In *Interkulturelle Soziale Arbeit in der Theorie und Praxis*, Chirly dos Santos-Stubbe (ed.), pp. 83–104. Aachen: Shaker, 2005.

Riebsamen, Hans. "Kleine jüdische Wunder," *Frankfurter Allgemeine Zeitung*, November 10, 2006. http://www.faz.net/aktuell/politik/leitartikel-kleine-juedische-wunder-1380079.html (accessed March 26, 2015).

Stölting, Erhard. The East of Europe: A Historical Construction. In *Biographies and the Division of Europe*, Roswitha Breckner, Deborah Kalekin-Fishman, and Ingrid Miethe (eds.), pp. 139–158. Opladen: Leske & Budrich, 2000.

Tsypylma, Darieva. *Russkii Berlin: Migrants and Media in Berlin and London*. Münster: LIT, 2004.

Elke-Vera Kotowski
Moving from the Present via the Past to Look toward the Future

Jewish Life in Germany Today

In the course of my recent research I have been confronted with two seemingly contradictory phenomena; Jewish emigration *from* Germany in the 1930s and immigration *to* Germany in the 1990s.[1] Throughout the 1930s, Jews had to leave Germany, a country, which many of them had loved and even adored. More than 300,000 men, women, and children searched worldwide for a refuge, narrowly escaping from a regime that planned the Final Solution for all of Europe. Surprisingly, 70 years later, Germany itself has become a refuge and destination of choice for Jewish émigrés who have left the crumbling Soviet Union and its successor states. Are there any links connecting those Jews who lost their homes during the Nazi period in Germany, and those Jews who are searching for a new beginning in Germany today?

Members of the first group continue to dwell on the trauma of their hasty escape and the loss of German culture. Members of the second are entering virgin territory, left to decipher German culture and society (including veteran Jewish communities) from their own perspective as Eastern European refugees. My recent research as a German scholar from Potsdam has presented me with some exciting opportunities to travel between these different worlds, to speak with émigrés from then and now and meet Jewish migrants from all different walks of life. Initially, I was puzzled as to what those exiled German Jews and those who are expected to build a new Germany Jewry could have in common. Yet, the longer I spoke with people, the more similarities I discovered. Although on the face of it, it would seem almost impossible to bring together the Jewish expatriates from the 1930s and the Jewish arrivals in the twenty-first century, I will try to do so in the context of this chapter. Such an exercise requires careful consideration of which Jewish traditions, cultural values, religious (or secular) self-understandings and the social experiences each carries.

The first thing both groups have in common is the idea of the 'packed suitcase.' Not only for Jews under German Nazi rule could it be life-saving to have

---

[1] Here I would like to take the opportunity to thank my colleague Olaf Glöckner for his valuable input and suggestions regarding current sociological studies on the integration of Russian-Jewish immigrants in Germany.

already packed one's suitcases in time. What about unpacking after emigration? How long did German Jewish refugees struggle with this quandary? How long did they harbor the idea of returning, despite the unthinkable crimes perpetrated by the Germans in the Second World War? Could Jews from the former Soviet Union have been conflicted with similar quandaries when they arrived to find refuge in Germany, at a time when Right-wing extremism was on the rise? Undoubtedly, the early 1990s were restless years in recently unified Germany, at least for newcomers from abroad.

How long did Jews in the DP camps after 1945 who were waiting to leave, but wound up staying in Germany after all, keep their suitcases packed? How about the few German Jews who survived in hiding or returned to Germany after emigrating – what about their 'suitcases'? What about those Russian Jews who came to the West after 1989, taking their first steps with unpacked suitcases in Berlin, Frankfurt, or Munich? Maintaining the suitcase metaphor – what exactly was or is in the suitcases anyway?

When German-speaking Jews left their homeland following Hitler's rise to power in 1933, along with photo albums and starched white tablecloths, their suitcases were filled with the works of Goethe, Schiller, or Eichendorff – books perceived capable of giving them a 'piece of home' far away. What did those DPs from Eastern Europe, who saw Germany only as a stopover on their way to America or Israel, but nevertheless ended up staying, having children, and at some point making homes for themselves, who still kept their suitcases packed and always in sight – what did they have in their bags? Finally, what was in those suitcases packed in Odessa, Volgograd, or Moscow to be taken along to Berlin, Frankfurt, or Munich? If there were books among their belongings, who were the authors and what were the topics?

Where do all of these people position themselves? Which identity is their own? Which sense of self defines them? What do they associate with home and what culture do they feel at home in? Is there an element that connects the estimated 200,000 to 300,000 Jews living in Germany today, of which about 110,000 are members of the Jewish community? They are the descendants of the different groups, which represent Jewish life after 1945.

The first groups are prewar German Jews – those who survived in Germany in hiding (ca. 3,000) or as a 'non-Aryan' spouse (ca. 12,000), and those who survived the concentration camps (ca. 8,000). They were augmented by former emigrants who chose to return to Germany after the war (estimated to be five percent of those Jews who fled Germany) – whether fueled by political considerations or due to homesickness. These two groups have constituted the minority of Jews in Germany since the 1950s. A much larger group was the Eastern European DPs who had survived the concentration camps, often as the only member of their families. The majority originated from Poland and Hungary. Their traumatic experiences during the Holocaust encumbered their view of postwar Germany, exacerbating the difficulties of adjusting to a foreign country, dealing with a more or less hostile environment, and navigating a foreign language and foreign culture in daily life. Robbed of their youth, having lost their family, and often without a school education or professional training, a new beginning seemed almost hopeless, yet the will to continue to survive was unbroken despite all of the barriers and obstacles. Even the harsh criticism they faced from Jews all over the world ('How can a Jew live in the land of the perpetrators after the Holocaust?!') did not stop this first postwar generation of Eastern European DPs and those returning from exile from building lives for themselves in postwar Germany. They had children and built a Jewish community and Jewish institutions in defiance of all of the negative predictions, but what did the decision taken by the parents' generation mean for their children? The burden on the 'second generation,' that their parents' decision meant that they had to accept living in Germany, was immense for no small number of such offspring. Paul Spiegel, who served as chair of the Central Council of Jews in Germany from 2002–2006, once remarked as a representative of this second generation: "I'll admit that if I had been 25 or maybe 30 at the end of the war and not 8, I would not have returned to Germany."[2] It is completely understandable that many members of the second generation have an ambivalent, if not troubled relationship to Germany, the land of their childhood and therefore of their socialization. This begs the question, whether some semblance of 'a cultural home' and sense of identity of any kind whatsoever could develop within this generation. If so, is it the same for *all* groups – that is, for both the children of 'native' German Jews, as well as the offspring of immigrant Jews in Germany of Polish, Baltic, Galician, or Hungarian origin who are considered German Jewry? This question is further complicated by the fact that both groups are lumped together under *one* Central Council of the Jews in Germany – deemed to be representative of Germany Jewry.

Already in 1952, there were a hundred newly-founded Jewish communities and two newly-built synagogues (in Saarbrücken and Stuttgart) in West Germany. Community centers like the one opened in 1959 on the Fasanenstraße in Berlin, built on the site of a former synagogue, outwardly attested to the beginnings of consolidation, but this did not reflect realities, and even masked internal weaknesses. The so-called "unified community model" which places every Jewish 'denomination' from Orthodoxy to Reform in one community often offered the only chance for an organized Jewish community to continue to exist locally. The system for social welfare and senior care was expanded, a growing need as the

---

[2] Interview with Paul Spiegel, see: Richarz, Leben in einem gezeichneten Land, 2007, p. 243.

Jewish population aged, but otherwise the community remained stagnant. Establishment of a few youth centers and Jewish adult education centers could not hide the fact that demographically, decades after the Holocaust, the days of organized Jewry in Germany were, in essence, numbered. At the dedication ceremony for the community center in Frankfurt am Main, completed in 1986, the architect and later Vice chair of the Central Council of Jews in Germany, Salomon Korn, claimed optimistically: "He who builds a house, wants to stay."[3] Nevertheless, the question remained hanging in the air: Who would fill the building and how – particularly in the long term?

On closer examination, it was shown that many Jewish community members were losing interest in the Jewish religion and only fragments of Jewish tradition and culture were being handed down to the next generation. Similar to many Christian communities, attendance at worship services was limited to the High Holy Days, and religious rites were practiced more out of a sense of attachment to tradition than out of religious conviction. Only a small minority of Jews lived and continues to live in accordance to Jewish religious laws. The common denominator of 'Jewishness' has become the memory of Nazi persecution and the Holocaust, combating new forms of anti-semitism and racism, and a strong feeling of solidarity with Israel.

Still, some internal Jewish dissimilarities vis-à-vis religious outlook and practices continue. While the majority of German Jews before 1933 identified with the Liberal stream of Judaism and were affiliated with the Reform community, most of the newly-founded 'unified communities' founded after 1945 were affiliated with the Orthodox stream. This also led to conflicts within the communities, as the Orthodox standards of ritual observance were introduced by rabbis who, without exception, came from abroad. The departure of Leo Baeck, Gunther Plaunt, and other Liberal leaders with the rise of Nazism, left a void and after 1945 there were no institutions for training Liberal rabbis in Germany. Liberal streams initially viewed the Jewish life that took shape in postwar Germany with some reservation; only in the late 1990s was the prewar link to Liberal Judaism reestablished with the renewal of training for non-Orthodox rabbis in Germany – a milestone that reflected both the growing need for non-Orthodox rabbis and the growth of religious pluralism within the Germany Jewish communities.

The unification of Germany also ushered in a complete transformation of Jewish life. This does not refer to the new generation of leaders in the Jewish communities in both East and West, nor to a collective relocation of the some 400 Jews who had previously been spread out over eight Jewish communities in East Germany. Rather, it was the fall of the Iron Curtain and not the fall of the Berlin

---

3 See: Korn, Geteilte Erinnerung, 2001, p. 14.

Wall that sparked the transformation of Jewish life in Germany, leading to the migration into Germany of more than 200,000 Jews and their non-Jewish relatives from the former Soviet Union. Within a very short time, new Jewish communities sprang up in regions of Germany that previously lacked any kind of Jewish infrastructure, while in existing Jewish communities such as in Berlin, Frankfurt, and Munich, membership multiplied, and new synagogues and Jewish community centers were being built all over the country.

The influx of 'Russian Jews' indeed saved Judaism in Germany from demographic collapse, at least for a few decades. Consequently, it is not surprising that those Jews who had been living in Germany viewed this immigration as a great opportunity, which was also specifically welcomed by parts of the non-Jewish public. In the initial euphoria, Jewish communities had not registered that a successful integration of the newcomers would require an enormous amount of inter-cultural acceptance, a comprehensive familiarization process and mutual understanding. As we now know, the Jews from the former USSR (a significant percentage with non-Jewish spouses and dependants) came to Germany, Israel, and the United States with very different expectations and worldviews. Their level of secularization was much greater than that amongst Jews in Western and Central Europe. Many, to this day, do not see this as a real problem; rather, they define their Jewishness as an ethnic affiliation, a sense of self-definition further amplified by anti-semitism, epitomized by pronounced intellectualism coupled with heightened interest in Jewish history and philosophy, and a lifestyle marked by a mixture of Jewish and Russian culture.

During the 1990s, when the Russian Jews in Germany became a pronounced demographic majority in most local Jewish communities, many were concerned primarily with elementary questions of social integration into German society. The older immigrants often felt that they would not be able to master the German language and mostly kept to themselves out of necessity. In large cities like Berlin, however, many were able to find support and social outlets in independent networks and circles which the Berlin sociologist Judith Kessler described as a kind of "Russian colony" in the 1990s. However, the middle generation of the Russian Jews, at least those already in their forties, also frequently experienced social marginalization, primarily sparked by a major loss in professional status. Were these people – respected doctors, professors or men and women of letters in Odessa, Volgograd or Vilnius – who found themselves standing in line at the unemployment agency considered difficult to place. In addition (as was shown in Israel Studies as well) there were serious cultural differences from the host society that set them apart – from the preferred language, literature, music, theater, fashion to educational methods. Mutual frictions resulted. Interestingly, almost none of the Russian-Jewish immigrants felt the need to sacrifice, or even deny, their native culture to gain faster social integration. This demonstrates a strong collective self-consciousness in general that can also be felt in the dynamics of the Jewish communities. Russian Jews also often consider themselves to be a part of a "transnational diaspora", with kindred spirits living on at least three different continents.

With the immigration of Russian Jews to Germany, the Jewish community in Germany has not only significantly grown numerically; it has also witnessed a sharp increase in diversity. This can and should be understood as an opportunity, doing so, however, should not be taken for granted.

Is Jewish culture in Germany generating new identities? Is this question only germane regarding the inner-perspective, or is there an inherent outer perspective as well? Also, are we only talking about members of the Jewish communities, or even perhaps, only those who keep Jewish law? Or does the question also relate to unaffiliated Jews who do not belong to a community? Is the 'new identities' question germane for all those with a Jewish background, regardless whether they are religious, non-religious or indifferent?

In any case, we have seen a growing religious, as well as cultural, differentiation within the Jewish communities in Germany since the late 1990s, without the unified community model seriously being called into question. Having said that, today there are a number of independent Liberal communities, once again the beginnings of Conservative Judaism (*Masorti* – mainly in Berlin), and there are even dynamic innovations on the observant Orthodox side – albeit in the form of rather small communities. More secular-oriented Jews are building networks in Jewish cultural and educational associations, theater and music festivals, and sometimes in political initiatives and projects, as well. There are Russian Jews along with local Jews in all of these groups, as well. Today, two decades after the advent of large-scale Russian-Jewish immigration, questions of collective and individual identity, positioning of self, and cultural orientation have once again significantly grown in importance. If we allow ourselves a look back in history, by comparison we encounter the startling fact that Germany's Jews who fled their country during the 1930s, also, in effect, took their German-Jewish heritage with them.

Russian Jews experienced a gradual, systematic destruction of their institutions and traditions over the course of seventy years of Soviet dictatorship. Shortly after the Bolshevik Revolution, Hebrew was forbidden; Stalin largely destroyed Yiddish culture. In the last few decades of the Soviet Union, religious community life was limited to a few synagogues; also in this regard, Gorbachev's liberalization came too late. Nevertheless, many Jews from the Soviet Union did not forget or negate their Jewishness. The second generation of Jews from the former Soviet Union must now decide how they will handle their heritage in the long run, and this decision will have a crucial impact on Jewish life in Germany. However, it seems unlikely that the Russian Jews in Germany will look to connect to local tradition as found, for example, in the works of Moses Mendelssohn, Leo Baeck, Martin Buber, or Bertha Pappenheim. This raises a fascinating question: To what extent will the second generation of Russian Jews develop a common cultural and/or religious identity with the children of Jews who have been living in Germany longer, and what role can descendants of 'indigenous' German Jews still remaining in Germany (the *Yeckes*) be expected to play in the future? Where will the continuities emerge in the Jewish religion, and if any, what will be their preferences? What kind of identity do Jewish communities develop when faced with a growing number of secular members? Where can secular Jews 'connect' outside of the communities? These questions are axiomatic when contemplating the positioning of Jews in Germany, their identities (and possible changes in identity), and what they attribute to themselves as Jews and what is ascribed to them as Jews by others.

No discussion of the diverse fabric of German Jewry would be complete without mentioning the surprising and growing number of Israelis living in Germany either long-term or permanently. Today, there are an estimated 15,000 to 20,000 Israelis living in Berlin alone. Berlin has become a magnet for young people from Israel since German unification, by no means just for students, but increasingly for artists, businesspeople, academics, and others, as well. All of these groups, the 'locals,' the DPs, the Russians and of late also the Israelis do not form a homogenous whole. Their religious, political, or cultural creeds are just as diverse as their individual experiences and values. Once again, the question arises – How do they live and define themselves as Jews in Germany? Do they consciously gravitate toward the above-mentioned sub-cultures and societies-within-society, or are they forced into them by surrounding society? Do some wish to become integrated into the majority mainstream society or do they prefer a parallel society? And the purely rhetorical question remains: Will we ever be able to speak of a common identity for Jews in Germany?

This last and cardinal question can be examined by returning to the suitcase metaphor: What was in the suitcases that these immigrants – regardless whether after 1933, after 1945 or after 1989 – took with them to begin a new life, and in essence, to construct a new identity – beyond the basics (personal documents, clothes, and so forth)?

In 2012, I was in Buenos Aires, where one of the largest Jewish communities outside of Israel is located, with all of the attending similar conflicts within and among its own individual communities. In the course of my sojourn, I visited Roberto Schopflocher, who fled Germany with his parents in 1937 at age 14. As a guest, it was inappropriate to ask directly where he would place himself, and no doubt such a question would not be easy to answer in any case, however, an attempt was made on both scores when I asked him – "How would you describe yourself? As an Argentinean Jew, as an Argentinean Jew with German roots, as a German Jew in Argentina?" My host gave me a prompt and heartfelt answer, but did so in a very special, deeply culturally rooted manner: His answer was to share with me a poem he had composed about ten years ago, long before he began writing his autobiography, which was published in 2010 in Germany under the title *Weit von Wo – mein Leben zwischen drei Welten* ('Far from there – my life between three worlds').[4] Roberto Schopflocher's "Confession" as he called his poem is, in the subtext, an avowal and a clear statement of his identity.

GESTÄNDNIS (Robert Schopflocher)	CONFESSION
Seit über sechzig Jahren	In Argentina
in Argentinien,	for more than sixty years
aber beim Wort ‚Baum'	but the word "tree"
fällt mir zunächst und noch immer	still means to me first and always
die Dorflinde Rannas ein,	the village linden in Ranna
in der Fränkischen Schweiz,	in Franconian Switzerland
gelegentlich auch eine Eiche	sometimes an oak tree as well
oder ein deutscher Tannenbaum;	or a German pine
nie dagegen oder doch nur selten	but never or hardly ever
ein Ombú der Pampa,	an ombú from the pampa
ein Paraíso in Entre Ríos	a paraíso in Entre Ríos
ein Ñandubay, Lapacho, oder ein Algarrobo,	Ñandubay, Lapacho, or Algarrobo
wie sich's doch geziemen würde	when it would be the thing to do
schon aus Dankbarkeit	just out of gratitude
dem lebensrettenden Land gegenüber.	to the country that saved our lives.
Aber ‚Frühling' bedeutet mir noch immer	But "spring" still means to me
Mörikes blau flatterndes Band.	Mörike's blue waving ribbon.
Schiller, Goethe und die Romantik,	Schiller, Goethe and Romanticism,
Jugendstil, Bauhaus und Expressionismus,	Art Nouveau, Bauhaus and Expressionism
prägten mir ihren Siegel auf,	impressed their stamp on me
nicht weniger wie der deutsche Wald,	no less than the German forest,
der deutsche Professor	the German professor
oder der jüdische Religionsunterricht –	or the Jewish religion lessons-
wohlgemerkt: der der letzten Zwanziger-,	please note: those of the late 20's
der ersten Dreißigerjahre.	the first years of the 30's.
Ja, selbst der fragwürdige Struwwelpeter	Yes, even the dubious Struwwelpeter
Karl May Hauff die Grimm'schen Märchen	Karl May Hauff Grimm's fairy tales
oder Max und Moritz, diese beiden,	or Max and Moritz, these two,
rumoren weiter in mir	are still knocking around in me
und lassen sich nicht ausrotten.	and won't be exterminated.
Nun ja: Leider! Trotz alledem.	And so – it's a shame. Despite everything.
Oder etwa Gottseidank?	Or maybe thank God?
Und wo liegt es nun, mein Vaterland?[5]	Any where is it anyway, my homeland?

---

4 Schopflocher, Weit von Wo, 2010.
5 Schopflocher, Hintergedanken, 2012, p. 33.

Why am I presenting this 'confession' or 'avowal' of Schopflocher's? He has been living in Argentina for more than 75 years, married there to a Jewish woman of German background, had two sons he raised in three cultures – the Argentinean, the Jewish, and the German. He actively participates in Jewish community life in Buenos Aires (in a Liberal German-speaking community it should be noted, where up until a few years ago, the services were conducted in German) and yet he still seems to be living in three worlds and has not found his home in 'just one.'

Are there not parallels to be found between Schopflocher's experience and the histories and life plans of those Jews living in Germany today? Schopflocher's cultural as well as his religious socialization took place in Germany, he came to Argentina as a teenager, became fluent in Spanish, went to university and then, due to external circumstances, worked in a profession that did not suit him very well (in agriculture). He lived in a political system that did not correspond to his convictions and still, he adapted himself to this life, this country which offered him and his family shelter and also offered him the possibility to shape his life for himself, where he could find and keep his disparate identities. Yet herein may lie the crux of a parallel between Schopflocher and a Ukrainian, Latvian, Muscovite, or Leningrader of the same age. They both define themselves over the course of their lives through different horizons of experience, which are reflected in their different perceptions and cultural codes. Take, for example, the commemorative realm of memorial culture: While Roberto Schopflocher thinks of November 9, 1938 (*Kristallnacht*) as one of the most significant dates in German-Jewish relations, for Ukrainian, Russian or Lithuanian Jews in Berlin, Leipzig or Munich the most significant date is May 9, 1945 ('Victory Day' in the Soviet Union or VE Day in the west, marking the unconditional surrender of Germany, ending the Second World War in Europe) – a date celebrated annually in Russia and among Russian émigrés elsewhere – even in Germany, with veterans proudly wearing their Red Army campaign medals and decorations.

What insights about the complexities of self-ascription and collective memory can we derive from the above? How is personal and collective memory constructed? Jan Assmann wrote: "When a person – and a society - is only able to remember that in the past which can be reconstructed within the frame of reference of the present at hand, then exactly that will be forgotten, which no longer has a frame of reference in that present."[6]

Assmann's definition above (of the hypothesis formulated by the sociologist Maurice Halbwachs already in 1925) suggests we have different memories based on different frames of reference and horizons of experience which stand next to one another, but are mutually almost incomprehensible. Only with great diffi-

---

6 Assmann, Das kulturelle Gedächtnis, 2007, p. 36.

culty can a common, collective memory be created from this mix. Therefore, what is important here is that all sides are willing to accept the frame of reference of the others and not to exclude or discount it.

Jews from the former Soviet Union make no secret of their unique view on Jewish history and heritage, linked closely to the experiences of their own families. They are fully aware of the fact that Eastern European Jewry, at the end of the ninteenth century still the largest Jewish center worldwide, has been constantly eroded over the past 130 years.[7] Regardless of their suffering under the Tsar, the Bolshevik revolution, the civil war that followed and decades of Communist suppression, at least some Russian Jews never separated themselves from non-Jewish Russian culture. On the contrary, some years ago, Michail Rumer-Sarajew, second editor-in-chief of the Russian language monthly *Evreyskaya Gazeta* (Jewish Paper) in Berlin, reflected this when he described "the wedlock between the Jewish intellectual passion and articulateness and the Russian spiritual peculiarity has developed – in its best variants – into a bond of mighty power and exquisite potential."[8] In other words, for Rumer-Sarajew and his relatives and friends, there is a bonus in continuing to live in several cultures – a Jewish and a Russian legacy. In Germany, their chosen country of destination, a third culture with its own codes, priorities and values is introduced to the equation, but the already internalized 'home cultures' persevered and imparted through the family, is not abandoned. Sociologists speak here not only of "cultural self-assertion", but also of the formulation of "additive identities". Moreover, some Russian-Jewish immigrants understand integration not just as one-sided efforts of acculturation or even an *obligation* to assimilate; rather, they view it as a mutual cultural learning process.

This includes the imparting of one's own cultural experiences to the German public space and non-Russian audiences. For example, in several German cities where Russian Jews have settled in great numbers, émigrés have established open amateur theaters – much in the way the Gesher Theater in Tel Aviv-Yaffo operates, albeit rarely with the same professional success as the Israeli endeavor: These theatres perform bilingual (i.e. with simultaneous translation) dramas and comedies, targeting a Jewish and non-Jewish, Russian and German audience at the same time. A prime example is the Rossiskaya Aktyorskaya Shkola, founded in 1995 on the campus of Bremen University by the former Muscovite theatrical director Semjon Arkadjevitsch Barkan (born in 1916). At the time, Barkan was

---

[7] At the end of the ninteenth century the Jewish population in Eastern Europe (especially Poland and Russia) numbered about five million, see: Gitelman, A Century of Ambivalence, 1988, p. 3. Today, less than a tenth of this former Jewish population lives there.

[8] Rumer-Sarajew, Evreyskaya Gazeta, 2005, p. 188.

already 79 years old. The theater successfully performed classic Russian plays and Jewish dramas and brought together amateur actors from the Jewish community, German ethnic repatriates (*Aussiedler*) and German students. The Bremen Jewish Community, realizing the significance and advantages of Barkan's work, provided rooms for performances, food for rehearsal breaks and for trips, and sometimes even organized actors' costumes. Without a doubt, the Rossiskaya Aktyorskaya Shkola makes integration a living reality.

Some historians and sociologists compare today's Russian Jewish émigrés – regardless whether they immigrated to Israel, North America, or Germany, and the German Jews (*Yeckes*) who emigrated to Palestine throughout the 1930s. Both hold a deep belief in the superiority of 'their' own culture, doggedly maintaining Russian/German in private conversation and émigré print media, upholding and promoting outstanding Russian/German artistic heritage (literature, music) and strengthening their own informal networks. Such structures of opportunity are, of course, viable only where Jews (and/or other migrant groups) resettle in greater numbers.

The question remains how the émigrés will affect Jewish life in their countries of destination? Within our research project "German Jewish Cultural Heritage Worldwide" we often note how exiled German Jews of the 1930s who were religious or strongly connected to Jewish tradition, often were eager to join or even to establish *Liberal* (i.e. Reform) Jewish communities. In other words, they not only brought with them their dresses and 'signature' suit jackets (*yecke* in German), their books shelves, gramophones and musical instruments, but also their prayers and ideas on how Jewish liturgy should be shaped.

For today's Russian Jewish immigrants, finding their individual connection to Jewish religion and tradition appears to be a much greater challenge. Many of the middle-aged and elderly appreciate community life, and love to see their kids and grandchildren in the synagogue. Nevertheless, they find it difficult to reconnect with the roots of Judaism themselves. A distinct minority describe themselves as religious, in larger towns often joining new Orthodox centers affiliated with Chabad and of the Lauder Foundation. Others have long been reaching out to other population groups in Germany. For example, Gregori Pantijelew, a former Russian musicologist, is busy as a lecturer on Eastern European music history and sometimes conducts music in Bremen, as well. He has also initiated an intercultural working group that brings together non-Jewish Germans, German Jews, and immigrants devoted to overcoming mutual (cultural) prejudices and enhancing acceptance of otherness, but also reworking the past. As Pantijelew stresses, this involves "deal[ing] with the German history – and that's why the participation of descendants of former offenders and former victims [under the Nazis] is so important. We mainly work according to the TRT [To-Reflect-and-Trust] method of Israeli psychology professor Dan Bar-On."[9]

Not only the German-Jewish émigrés from the 1930s but also Russian-Jewish newcomers from the 1990s have unpacked their suitcases. Very few return to their former homeland or have opted in favour of a second emigration. It seems that the second generation of immigrants will be able to participate in Germany's society with great success. Thus, German-born American Michael Blumenthal, head of the Jewish Museum in Berlin, prophesized that one must take the long view regarding the future for this new group of immigrants:

> I am convinced that the young generation of Russian Jews – those who are studying now – will go their way in Germany. In 10 to 15 years, some of them will have a seat in the Bundestag [the German parliament], others will be university professors, others successful entrepreneurs and artists. But I think it still needs a little bit of time.[10]

A much more intriguing issue is how the young Russian Jews will adopt and *live* German, Russian, and Jewish culture and what this will mean for the future of the Jewish communities in the long run. In any case, some of these young writers, artists, and intellectuals are *already* dealing with their Jewish heritage parallel to becoming involved in general social issues, understanding themselves as part of Germany's increasingly multicultural society. Thus, there are startling examples of a cultural synthesis – particularly among young Jews, who meanwhile belong to the fourth generation. For example, Lena Gorelik, born in Leningrad (St. Petersburg) in 1981, came with her family to Germany as a Russian-Jewish contingent refugee in 1992. She went to school in Munich and trained to be a journalist at the German School of Journalism before earning a degree in Eastern European Studies at the Ludwig Maximilian University. In 2004, she published her first novel *Meine weißen Nächte* ('My White Nights') and three more novels have followed. In 2013 a collection of essays was released entitled *„Sie können aber gut Deutsch!" Warum ich nicht mehr dankbar sein will, dass ich hier leben darf, und Toleranz nicht weiterhilft* ('"You really speak an excellent German!" Why I no longer want to be grateful for being allowed to live here and why tolerance doesn't help'). The provocative statement within the title is meant to be an answer to the incessantly asked question – How does it feel to be 'Jewish' and 'a refugee' in Germany. In a recent interview Gorelik commented on her "Jewishness":

---

[9] Regarding TRT ("To Reflect-and-Trust") method developed by Dan Bar-On see: Bar-On, Die „Anderen", 2003; regarding the cultural initiatives organized by Gregori Pantijelew see: Glöckner, Immigrated Russian Jewish Elites, 2011, pp. 245 ff.
[10] Blumenthal, in: Jüdische Zeitung, April 2006.

> In Germany it's something that I have to deal with, but not because it's something I want to do, but because I'm made to do it. For me personally, being Jewish is a feeling. This includes a certain sense of humor and takes on life. I'm happy when I hear Jewish music or read Jewish literature. For me it's less something religious.

She emphasizes that she wrote her current book "about people" in Germany:

> about people who live in this country, have some kind of influence on it, enrich it, confuse it, and ultimately make it into what it is. Because, after we have finally discovered several decades too late that we have already been an immigrant nation for a long time, and the debate (because we Germans love debates!) on what it means that we missed that happening and are now really busy inviting 'fellow citizens of Turkish origin who have arrived in society' to political talk shows and integration alliances so that they can finally tell us once and for all how they could integrate themselves and people like them in our non-defined and probably also indefinable German society, we've forgotten that we're really talking about people.[11]

The future will show if in three or four more generations Jews will be living in Germany in one or more worlds, or, as Lena Gorelik has already pointedly defined, whether "those fellow citizens of Turkish origin who have arrived in society" will finally tell "us Germans" how "they and people like them can integrate" into "our" German society.

References

Assmann, Jan. *Das kulturelle Gedächtnis. Schrift, Erinnerung und politische Identität in frühen Hochkulturen*. Munich: C. H. Beck, 2007 [1992].
Bar-On, Dan: *Die 'Anderen' in uns. Dialog als Modell der interkulturellen Konfliktbewältigung*. Hamburg: Edition Körberstiftung, 2003.
Becker, Franziska. *Ankommen in Deutschland. Einwanderungspolitik als biografische Erfahrung im Migrationsprozess russischer Juden*. Berlin: Dietrich Reimer, 2001.
Belkin, Dmitrij, Rafael Gross (ed.). *Ausgerechnet Deutschland! Jüdisch-russische Einwanderung in die Bundesrepublik. Katalog, Jüdisches Museum Frankfurt*. Berlin: Nicolaische Verlagsbuchhandlung, 2010.
Ben-Rafael, Eliezer, Michail Lyubansky, Olaf Glöckner, Paul Harris, Yael Israel, Willi Jasper, and Julius H. Schoeps (eds.). *Building a Diaspora: Russian Jews in Israel, Germany and the USA*. Leiden, Boston: Brill, 2006.
Ben-Rafael, Eliezer, Olaf Glöckner, and Yitzhak Sternberg. *Jews and Jewish Education in Germany Today*. Leiden, Boston: Brill, 2011.

---

11 Gorelik, ‚Sie können aber gut Deutsch!', 2012, p. 12.

Bernstein, Julia. *Food for Thought. Transnational Contested Identities and Food Practices of Russian-Speaking Jewish Migrants in Israel and Germany*. Frankfurt a. M., New York: Campus, 2010.

Bodemann, Michal Y. (ed.). *The New German Jewry and the European Context. The Return of the European Jewish Diaspora*. New York: Palgrave, 2008.

Gitelman, Zvi. *A Century of Ambivalence. The Jews of Russia and the Soviet Union. 1881 to the Present*. New York: Schocken, 1988.

Gundlach, Christine. *Ein bißchen anders bleibt man immer. Jüdische Zuwanderer in Mecklenburg-Vorpommern*. Schwerin: Helms, 2000.

Glöckner, Olaf. *Immigrated Russian Jewish Elites in Israel and Germany*. Saarbrücken: Südwestdeutscher Verlag für Hochschulschriften, 2011.

Gorelik, Lena. *‚Sie können aber gut Deutsch!' Warum ich nicht mehr dankbar sein will, dass ich hier leben darf, und Toleranz nicht weiterhilft*. Munich: Pantheon Verlag, 2012.

Hegner, Victoria. *Gelebte Selbstbilder. Gemeinden russisch-jüdischer Migranten in Chicago und Berlin*. Frankfurt a. M., New York: Campus, 2008.

Herzig, Arno, Cay Rademacher (eds.). *Die Geschichte der Juden in Deutschland*. Hamburg: Ellert & Richter, 2007.

Jebrak, Svetlana, Norbert Reichling (eds.). *Angekommen?! Lebenswege jüdischer Einwanderer*. Berlin: Hentrich & Hentrich, 2010.

Koerber, Karen. Puschkin oder Thora? Der Wandel der jüdischen Gemeinden in Deutschland. *Tel Aviver Jahrbuch für deutsche Geschichte* 37 (2009), pp. 233–254.

Korn, Salomon. *Geteilte Erinnerung. Beiträge zur deutsch-jüdischen Gegenwart*. Berlin: Philo, 2001.

Richarz, Monika: Leben in einem gezeichneten Land: Juden in Deutschland nach 1945. In *Die Geschichte der Juden in Deutschland*, Arno Herzig, Cay Rademacher (eds.), pp. 238–249. Hamburg: Ellert & Richter, 2007

Rumer-Sarajew, Michail. Evreyskaya Gazeta. In *Russische Juden und transnationale Diaspora*, Julius H. Schoeps, Karl E. Grözinger, and Gert Mattenklott (eds.), pp. 183–198. Berlin/Vienna: Philo, 2005.

Schoeps, Julius H., Willi Jasper, and Bernhard Voigt (eds.). *Ein neues Judentum in Deutschland? Fremd- und Eigenbilder der russisch-jüdischen Einwanderer*. Potsdam: Verlag für Berlin-Brandenburg, 1999.

Schoeps, Julius H., Karl E. Grözinger, and Gert Mattenklott (eds.). *Russische Juden und transnationale Diaspora*. Berlin/Vienna: Philo, 2005.

Schopflocher, Robert. *Weit von Wo – mein Leben zwischen drei Welten*. Munich: Langen-Müller, 2010.

Schopflocher, Robert. *Hintergedanken. Gedichte aus zwei Jahrzehnten*. Nuremberg: Spätlese, 2012.

Fania Oz-Salzberger
Israelis and Germany
A Personal Perspective

It was a story of both enchantment and amazement. The enchantment of Israelis, mainly young Israelis who found their way into what was again the capital of the united Federal Republic of Germany in the 1990s and in the 2000s, with Berlin's global and postmodern charms; and the amazement that not only Jews from the former Soviet Union, but also thousands of Israelis, many of them coming from families that had some Holocaust memories and wounds and pains, have chosen to establish their abodes, temporarily permanently, in this new Berlin.

I began writing the travel book *Israelis in Berlin* in the autumn of 1999, during my sabbatical year at The Institute for Advanced Study, Berlin (*Wissenschaftskolleg*). What, I asked, was the secret code that allured thousands of Israelis, Jewish and Arab, most of them young women and men, to the former capital city of the Third Reich? I attempted to dig into the roots of their enchantment, and my own amazement, as well as the novelty of the story itself. For this story was new. It was not a run-of-the-mill narrative of Jews and Germans. It was about Israelis of my generation, or younger, and the city of Berlin, an urban landscape of many layers, already emerging as the globalized mecca for artists, musicians, and sophisticated culture-seekers that it has since become.[1]

The book combined personal experience, scholarship, on-the-ground observation, and many conversations. I interviewed about twenty Israelis who lived in the German capital at the time, from the concertmaster of the Berlin Philarmonic Orchestra, to young clubbers, members of the gay community, a rabbi, businessmen, old communists, academics, women and men who married a German and started a family in Germany, and others. These tags are obviously misleading: Not a single interviewee can be pushed into one slot of identity. All are complex, multifaceted, and if they have any common denominator, it is the awareness and reflection that comes naturally with this most self-conscious of migrations, that of Israelis to Berlin.

The distancing from regular Jewish-German discourse is a main theme of the book. Berlin is a city, not a country, and it is conducting a profound dialog with Tel Aviv, and sometimes with Jerusalem, over the heads of their respective states. Those dialogues are not at all new: Berlin has been paired with Jerusalem since

---
1 Oz-Salzberger, Israelis in Berlin, 2001.

Moses Mendelssohn's philosophical opus *Jerusalem* (1783),[2] and with Tel Aviv at least since Agnon's novella *Ad Hena* (*To This Day*, 1952).[3] Jerusalem had attracted Berlin both as a Christian symbol, from the seventeenth century, and as a target of imperial ambition since the age of Bismarck. Tel Aviv, in its turn, was shaped by Berlin both architecturally, through the Bauhaus school (which extended its touch to art and design), and culturally, with the rich influx of German-Jewish immigrants that helped reshape its art, music, theater, street, and café culture in the 1920s and 1930s. This urban exchange is returning today with new energies and scopes. Berlin and Tel Aviv are an excellent pairing and a fine demonstration that along the routes of creativity, cities can converse in many ways unavailable to countries and officialdoms.

The numerous conversations I had with Israelis in Berlin, then and ever since, can be titled "identity-dialogs." Such dialogs are held not merely between two people, but more poignantly between a person and his or her spheres of belonging. Identities, as I have already suggested, are prone to shallow representation. No young-artistic-liberal-Israeli-Berliner is exactly like the next one, although many of the Israelis currently residing in Berlin can be classed under these tabs. They also tend to be in their twenties and thirties, irreligious, global-minded, and politically critical of Israel's government or society. But their opinions on their homeland, on their Jewish self-definition, and on their personal relationship with their nation's history are far more variegated than this list of common characteristics may suggest.

Not all Israelis are Jews, not all Jews are Israelis: this self-evident truism is, all too often, ignored. Hence, my book had very little interface with Berlin's traditional Jewish establishment, with which Israelis, then and now, had little contact or desire for contact. By interviewing several Arab Israeli citizens residing in Berlin, an interesting perspective on "Israeliness" emerged. Some of them, indeed, felt "Israeli" for the first time when they took their abode in Berlin. One of the most interesting new perspectives I found in those conversations was with an Arab Israeli resident of Berlin whose interview took place in a nightclub. When I asked him the question I put to most of my interlocutors, what Israeli landscape he misses most, he expressed longing for the urban cityscape of Tel Aviv, rather than his native city of Akko (Acre). This was a telling response: cityscapes, real and imagined and longed-for, can pull our emotional strings in ways that transcend national fault lines.

Another interviewee, a Jew, provided a shrewd and unsentimental account of her veteran-Zionist family tree. Indeed, many Israelis in Berlin are vocally critical

---

2 Mendelssohn, Jerusalem, 1783.
3 Agnon, Ad Hena, 1952.

of their homeland's politics, economic situation, or cultural preferences. But her particular narrative blended intimacy, involvement, and critique into a deeper self-distancing, based on ambivalent familiarity. That was when I realized that what I liked most about the Berlin vantage point on Israel is the unique set of vistas that Berlin can provide for us Israelis on our self-image and constructs of identity. It is a mind-boggling prism, challenging preconceptions, offering surprises. An Israeli Arab who longs for Tel Aviv may seem a rarity in Israel, but unexpectedly consistent in a nightclub near Nollendorfplatz. An Israeli Jew critically revisiting her parental legacy may be deemed a cliché in Tel Aviv, while acquiring new layers of complexity when speaking in Berlin.

The sensitive part-overlap of Jewish and Arab Israelis in Berlin, which I have experienced anecdotally, requires further treatment by researchers and by writers and artists. One important aspect, I suggest, is that this expatriate encounter could shed interesting light, and form interesting discussions with Berlin's own fabric of ethnic, religious, and cultural communities. There are meeting points between Israelis of various origins and Turkish-German Berliners. These meeting points are happening on street level (and home, shop, school, and kindergarten level) as well as in the arts and social activism. What new "identity-dialogs," I wonder, are emerging from these encounters?

Clearly, Berlin can tell us something new about Tel Aviv. But Tel Aviv can tell its German visitors and residents something new about Berlin, too: that of the past, especially the first decades of the twentieth century, and about present-day Berlin. This reverse perspective calls for another book by another author, and there is already a bookshelf compiled by Germans in Israel, especially in Tel Aviv.[4] For me, it was enormously refreshing to view Israel and Israelis from Berlin.

These days I am preparing a new edition of *Israelis in Berlin*. Since the time of writing, back in 1990–2000, the floodgates broke open. Several books and dozens of articles, some academic but most in the popular media, have been dedicated to Berlin's Israeli denizens during the last decade. Likewise, dozens of films, both feature films and documentaries, and numerous television and radio reports have focused on the topic. In the Internet, the most flourishing and interactive scene, there are online magazines, chat groups, and Facebook pages, alongside other social media outlets, bringing Israelis in Berlin and their observers closer together than ever before.

Despite this constant rise in numbers and coverage, exact figures are hard to obtain. In 1999 I went to the Israeli Embassy to inquire how many of my fellow-

---

[4] For recent works by Germans visiting or residing in Israel see: Kinet, Israel, 2013; Engelbrecht, Beste Freunde, 2013; Flohr, Wo samstags immer Sonntag ist, 2011; Höftmann, Guten Morgen, Tel Aviv!, 2011.

citizens actually reside in Berlin. The embassy did not know. A cautious estimate put the number at two to four thousand. Today, Israeli officials are still unable to provide reliable figures, since only a fraction of Israelis living abroad actually report their whereabouts to the consulates. But estimates have risen to fifteen to twenty thousand Israeli citizens in Germany, a significant majority of who resides in Berlin.

Today you can hear Hebrew spoken often in Berlin's public spaces, trains, markets, clubs, and concert halls. In the late 1990s it was very unusual to hear my mother tongue in loud exchanges on the streets of Berlin. When *Israelis in Berlin* recounts a Hebrew conversation, at night, on the streets of Charlottenburg, it refers to the year 1915, in Agnon's aforementioned novella *Ad Hena* (*To This Day*). The narrator, ostensibly the young Shmuel Yosef himself, strolls with a group of other Eretz-Israelis, as they were called at the time, along the sleepy streets. They are students or artists, caught in Berlin during the First World War. Ambling aimlessly, they finally head for a bakery to get a cheap loaf of bread. Their Hebrew is first-generation modern Hebrew, spoken by a few thousand young Jews who were already born in, or migrated to, the Ottoman district of Palestine (*Eretz Yisrael*).

But even that early group of Eretz-Israelis already included a sculptor known as "Druzi". Agnon notes that he did not know whether Druzi was Jewish, Syrian, or Lebanese. He was probably a member of the Druze minority. In some sense, this figure – whether Agnon invented or really met him – is the predecessor of Israeli-Palestinians in Berlin today, like some of my interviewees. Moreover, his presence may explain why the conversation took place in Hebrew rather than Russian, or Polish, or Yiddish. This is ironic, but also important for our theme. The presence of 'non-Jewish Israelis' in Berlin is as old as Agnon, and today it once again redefines the boundaries of Israeli identity beyond Israel.

Let us dwell on groups and individuals. The tens of thousands of Israelis living in Berlin today are not clanned together. They do not resemble the old Jewish *Landsmannschaften* of families and congregations hailing from the same town, region, or country. They are tens of thousands of individuals; because what really characterizes Israelis in Berlin is that they are not forming what has been called in the scientific literature an 'expat' community, a close-knit neighborhood or network of expatriates. There are such Israeli communities in Los Angeles, and in Melbourne, in New York, and in other places around the globe. But Berlin caters to individualists. They are young, they are 'alternative,' they are rebellious, they are artists, they belong to various branches of the music scene, to various gay sub-cultures, some of them are hipsters, or at least hype-sters. Yet, they do form a loose federation of micro-communities.

Two currents are of particular interest to me, because of their capacity to form strong communities even among twenty-first century individualists. One of them is the new sphere of digital communities, and the other is the ancient sphere of family life as a factor of regrouping.

Let us look at the social media first. Today there is an Israeli-German radio station, *Kol Berlin*, broadcasting in Hebrew and German. There are several journals, such as *Spitz Magazin*, with online as well as offline publishing and social activities. Several entrepreneurs are offering networking meetings for professionals in search of jobs, career, or business opportunities and, to some degree, social encounters. A series of such meeting has recently been held in the bar Louis Zuckerman in Mitte. Even more recently, a Hebrew library was opened, with its own Facebook page. Other Facebook pages offer a hub for digital socializing, mostly for practical purposes such as sublet hunting and job seeking, alongside bureaucratic advice on visas and administrative regulations. In parallel, and sometimes on the same social media outlets, exchanges on art, culture, and current affairs are on display.

Note, however, that the old impetus bringing immigrants together is at work among Israelis in Berlin, as well. While relatively few families migrate as such from Israel to Berlin, many young families are forming there, with parents of Israeli origin (one of them or even both). Parenthood tends to advance root seeking and a search for belonging. Israeli parents wish to get their children together to speak Hebrew, to celebrate the Jewish holidays together, to exchange Hebrew children's books and DVDs. Some of these parents have turned their back on 'everything Israeli' before starting a family, but wish to share their fondest childhood recollections, as well as their mother tongue, with their offspring born or raised in Berlin. Perhaps parenthood is only one aspect of this process: Rebels in their twenties sometimes become culturally nostalgic in their thirties.

The synagogues are not a popular venue for such realigned congregations. Most Israeli parents seek out the secular aspects of Israeli-Jewish identity, as practiced back in Israel: cultural (rather than religious) holiday celebrations, unorthodox versions of Jewish ceremonies such as bar and bat mitzvahs, and the vast array of cultural goods created in Hebrew, including literature, cinema, and songs.

Seldom is the synagogue part of this new search for identity. Nor is the non-Israeli Jewish community sought by Israelis to cater to such needs. Like many of the Jewish migrants into Germany from the former Soviet Union, these young Israelis are not in dire need of a religious common tent, but their Hebrew roots, rich with culture and ritual, also keep them separate for the time being, from the myriads of 'Russian Jews' in Berlin and elsewhere in Germany.

Thus, my present-day stocktaking suggests that there is no single Israeli community in Berlin; rather, there is an ever-growing network of micro-communities. A cautious, gradual 'normality' – the dispersed normality of twenty-first century metropolitan transnationalism – is setting in. Already, some of the younger or hipper Israelis are complaining that Berlin is not what it used to be ten years ago. This dovetails with the parallel complaint of Germans who loved the old, pre-1989 Berlin, or the "poor and sexy" Berlin of the 1990s. The city has become expensive, middle-class (worse: bourgeois), and unbearably touristy. The 'old' fortresses of alternative culture were either closed down, like the Tacheles compound, or run over by cellphone-clicking tourists, like the Berghain nightclub. Berlin, to the horror of its hipper residents, is becoming gentrified. Some Israeli insiders, like non-Israeli Berlinites of a certain mold, are beginning to wonder which city is going to become the next Berlin: perhaps Warsaw?

In the original introduction of *Israelis in Berlin*, written in 2000, I asked a question that may no longer be relevant. How, I ask, can an Israeli live in Berlin without constantly hearing voices screaming from underneath the pavement stones, from the cellars, from the railway tracks? I thought that Berlin is full of dark secrets and underground ambushes aimed at Israelis like myself. I thought that memory will keep pouncing on us in unexpected moments.

Today I must rephrase this question. Israelis in Berlin do not constantly reflect on their choice to live in the former capital of the Third Reich. Nor can they. Nor should they. And yet, many of the current Hebrew-speaking residents of Berlin whom I have met in recent year, Jews as well as Arabs, are enchanted, fascinated, and sometimes even obsessed with the dark past. Berlin remains problematic for them, and they live their problematic life in it as a matter of choice; because life is not meant to be simple, and because this urban, highly cultured, intense global-polis is not offering its newcomers either harmony or simplicity. It is not part of the deal.

The fascination, of course, is mutual. Many Germans are deeply intrigued with things Jewish and Israeli. Political displeasure is part of this, of course, but older layers of mutual interest are still very strong. And the fields of enquiry that brought so many Israelis to Berlin (and quite a few Germans to Tel Aviv and Jerusalem) – art, culture, literature, and academia – are excellent grounds for exploring the perennial Israeli-German discomfort. Its staying power is enormous. It is not going away any time soon.

Look at Israeli literature. When I began writing *Israelis in Berlin*, in 1999, I had to dig hard for Israeli fiction written *about* Germany, let alone *in* Germany. Unlike the pioneering Hebrew authors of the early twentieth century, for whom Weimar Germany was an important life-station en route to Palestine (alongside Agnon, Leah Goldberg and several others wrote beautiful works about Berlin), the young Israeli writers of the 1950s and 1960s did not turn their gaze to that dark horizon: the Holocaust memory was too raw, and Israel's War of Independence and the subsequent era of state-building, social growth, internal and external conflict, provided sufficient materials. The silence was broken first by the young journalist and essayist Amos Elon, whose famous reportage *BeEretz Redufat HeAvar* (*Journey through a haunted Land: The New Germany*), brought together the poignant articles he wrote as correspondent for *Haaretz* in Bonn. Elon was the only Israeli journalist based in Germany in the 1960s.[5] In the same decade Dan Ben Amotz published his novel *Lizkor veLishkoakh* ('To Remember and to Forget'), whose protagonist has an affair with a German woman in Frankfurt am Main.[6] Berlin had not yet returned to the map of Hebrew fiction.

A. B. Yehoshua devoted one chapter of his novel *Molcho*, in the early 1980s to Berlin, which the book's eponymous hero briefly visits. But once in Berlin, Molcho mostly sits in a hotel room and reflects on his past marriage and his dead wife. This part of Yehoshua's novel is not about Berlin, but about Molcho, with the German city mobilized as the powerful backdrop of inner reflection, turmoil, and transformation.[7] As I have argued elsewhere, Israeli novels have often tended to take their protagonists abroad without allowing 'abroad' – the geographical location – to play out as more than an exotic or foreboding backdrop for an intimate inner plot. Both author and characters remain deeply conversant with themselves, their family, their society, their nation and/or their home country. The host country or city, even Berlin, does not play a substantial part in the story.[8]

But something new has happened. Elsewhere, I have called the new phase of Israeli-German mutual sensitivity, which began in the 1990s, a "new abnormality." The strong, almost physical reflexes against the German language that characterized two generations of postwar Israelis began to weaken. German names, words, manufacturers, products, became acceptable in everyday speech. Thousands of Israelis began traveling, either privately or in groups, to Germany itself and to the central and East European landscapes of wartime horror and prewar remembrance. Yet, at the same time a different, deeper sort of memory was at work. Other strata of the mind became stamped with horror and pain. The skin-deep hypersensitivity gave way to an irremediable inner wound. For many Israelis of my generation, and for younger ones too, the pain about things German is no longer a matter for the eardrum; it is deeper in the guts. It will not disappear in the foreseeable future. Unlike some German contemporaries, we Israelis are not dealing with the question of 'normality' in our relations with Germany, present and past. Rather, we have developed a new abnormality, *eine neue Unnormalität*.[9]

---

5 Elon, Be'eretz Redufat He-avar, 1967.
6 Ben Amotz, Lizkor Ve-lishkoach, 1968.
7 Yehoshua, Molcho, 1987.
8 Oz-Salzberger, Israelis in Berlin. In: Feinberg (ed.), Rück-Blick, 2009.
9 Oz-Salzberger, 2009.

The Federal Republic of Germany is dramatically different today from what it was in 1965. So is the State of Israel. Political borders have shifted. Historical moments have changed the face of geography, politics, and society. Both countries have developed a strong and lasting set of relationships: economic, scientific, and cultural. No other European country has given Israel more international support and full commitment to its existence and prosperity than Germany has done. Let me emphasize: the wounds are not healed. Yet, the new abnormality is not an obstacle for political and human relationship; rather, it is a particularly fruitful and unique field, albeit a tension-field, of international cooperation and cultural interaction. This uniqueness, this strong link established upon deep unhealed wounds, makes the fifty-year history of Israeli-German relations all the more remarkable.

During the last decade and a half, major Israeli works – novels, stories, poetry, memoirs, essays, plays, and scripts – are written not only *about* Germany, and especially Berlin, but also in residence, elsewhere in Germany but mostly in Berlin. Some recent Israeli books about Berlin are biographical or autobiographical, and as such they could have referred to other German cities and towns. The journalist and author Ruvik Rosenthal based his book *Rehov Ha-prachim 22* ('Blumenstrasse 22') on his own family history, stemming from his ancestor, Berlin bookseller Erich Freier, and ending with Rosenthal's own visit to his relatives in East Berlin in the 1970s.[10] In a somewhat similar way, Israeli author Yoram Kaniuk's book *Ha-Berlinai Ha-acharon* (*Der letzte Berliner*) is based upon his own family history and recent travels.[11]

Yet Berlin's role in this book is not just a biographical accident. Despite the fact that Kaniuk's parents grew up in Berlin and fled from it, his book does not home-in on Berlin merely for family reasons. In a plot-within-plot, the narrator (openly identified with the author), an Israeli writer making several trips to Germany in the wake of his translated books, plans to write a novel for young people. It will tell the story of an Israeli-born grandson and his German-born grandfather; "that man", we are told, "probably has to be a Berliner".[12]

And why so? Because the protagonist has inherited a secret map from his grandfather, a mental map based on hyper-accurate memories of Berlin in the 1920s. As he walks up and down the new Berlin, he re-enacts its map like a detective or a medium, raising ghosts from the earth. Not just human ghosts, but also the lost streets and vistas, shops and buildings, the spirits of a lost urban landscape. It is a cartographical *séance* that only Berlin, of all cities, can inspire.

---

10 Rosenthal, Rehov Ha-prachim 22, 2003.
11 Kaniuk, Ha-Berlinai Ha-acharon, 2004.
12 Kaniuk, 2004, p. 22.

Haim Be'er's *Lifney HaMakom* ('Upon a Certain Place')[13] is another case in point. Like many other Israeli writers, Be'er was invited to stay in the Literary Colloquium in Wannsee, a beautiful writers' guesthouse founded in 1963 by Walter Höllerer in a former grand mansion on the shores of the poisoned lake. Its location, a short walk from the villa where the Final Solution came into being, creates a microcosm of Berlin's past and present pain. No other German city has a place like Wannsee. Be'er's complex and painful novel revisits the intellectual depths of Jewish Berlin that were lost and are being rediscovered, while disquietingly registering an Israeli's fear for the future of Israel's own cultural treasures, which face the threat of destruction by war. *Lifney HaMakom* is an untranslatable worldplay: it is a traditional Jewish phrase that means "facing God" of "in the presence of God", but the word *makom* in modern Hebrew means a *place*, a geographic or mental location. The book's English title (as it appears in the book's credits page, since it has not yet been translated into English) is 'Upon a Certain Place.' And Berlin is the place. It is *the* place. The book's dramatic plot and deep layers and reflections hinge upon it. It is no longer a mere backdrop for universal human agonies or for Israeli inner conversations. Berlin has now become – comparably to old Amsterdam, dubbed *Mokum* by its erstwhile Jews and present-day residents – our own *makom*, our place.

I will not speak in detail of the cinematic field of Israeli-German creativity. Several major Israeli works, both feature films and documentaries were shot partially or wholly in Berlin. Then they often revisit Berlin, alongside many other Israeli films, in the annual Film Festival. They include, most famously, Eytan Fox and Gal Uchovsky's *Walk on Water* (2004) and Assaf Bernstein's *The Debt* (2007). In both these films, Israeli men and women visit Berlin to seek justice, to expose or punish perpetrators, and to have Berlin's sins, as it were, revisited upon it. But Berlin draws them into other plots, offering them new understanding of self and other.

For Israelis of my generation and younger, Berlin is no longer taboo. It has been 'de-tabooed.' By the way, this is true for Berlin far more than for Germany, because in such processes cities precede countries. Today's Tel Aviv walks ahead of Israel and today's Berlin walks ahead of Germany in their rich, personalized, informal dialogs. It has very little to do with the official Israel, Jerusalem if you like, or the official Germany, except where funding is involved. But civil-society funding and even governmental funding, in this unique case, mostly aims to serve rather than dictate.

Berlin today is not what it was when I first came there in the summer of 1990s, when parts of the wall were still standing. Nor does it resemble the scene

---

13 Be'er, Lifney HaMakom, 2007.

of *Israelis in Berlin*, completed in 2000. Sometimes I think our task as Israelis in Berlin is to tell Berlin what is happening to it on its fast track, from a halved city to a capital city to a global-polis.

So, the Israeli prism that I can offer, and there are many of them, but I will limit myself to one, is that the alternative Berlin, the poor, sexy and rugged cityscape of the old Kreuzberg, of Prenzlauer Berg before it was gentrified, of the *Tacheles* which has been just shut down and exists no more, this complex of alternative art and life – in this order, art and life – which so attracted young Israelis for the last two decades. The Chancellor's Berlin is slowly but surely pushing out, conquering the rugged Berlin with its quasi-socialist and quasi-revolutionary pretenses. Deep beneath, older Berlins, the sinister and the glorious and the literary and the philosophical, are still lurking. They tell some stories to the Israeli sensitivities, and other stories to other observers. We need to share our particular modes of listening to Berlin.

No less than Berlin, or Tel Aviv, other factors in our complex algorithm have changed dramatically over the years. Migration itself has been transformed. Twenty years ago, we Israelis still spoke, often with reproach, of *yordim*, the down-goers, those emigrating from Israel, as if they were stepping down from the high, from the elevated realm of the Jewish State. Then a more neutral tone emerged, the one used by social scientists, *mehagrim*, migrants. Nowadays scholars and commentators speak of "transnationals", men and women freely roaming the lines between different countries and cultures, and able to be at home in both, or perhaps being at home nowhere at all. They can belong to more than one society and to more than one nation. They commute between them, physically and textually and digitally, with an ease that no previous migrants ever knew.

Some time ago I received an offer of friendship from the new Facebook page of the Ravensbrück concentration camp museum. I was very touched. My mother-in-law had been an inmate there, together with her sister, and their mother was murdered in that camp. Becoming the Facebook friend of the Ravensbrück memorial site is twenty-first century surrealism. Is it horrifying? Is it emblematic of our new abnormality? Is it part of an unimaginable future that we are already living? I do not know. I accepted the friendship request.

References

Agnon, Shmuel Yosef. *Ad Hena*. Jerusalem, Tel Aviv: Schocken, 1952; (English transl. Hillel Halkin, *To This Day*, Jerusalem: Toby Press, 2008).
Be'er, Haim. *Lifney HaMakom*. Tel Aviv: Am Oved. 2007.
Ben Amotz, Dan (Dahn). *Lizkor Ve-lishkoach*. Tel Aviv: Amikam, 1968.

Elon, Amos. *Be'eretz Redufat He-avar*. Tel Aviv: Schocken, 1967; (English transl. Michael Roloff, *Journey Through a Haunted Land: The New Germany*. New York: Rinehart and Winston Holt, 1967).
Engelbrecht, Sebastian. *Beste Freunde. Als Deutscher in Israel*. Berlin, Leipzig: Evangelische Verlagsanstalt, 2013.
Flohr, Markus. *Wo samstags immer Sonntag ist. Ein deutscher Student in Israel*. Berlin: Kindler, 2011.
Höftmann, Katharina. *Guten Morgen, Tel Aviv! Geschichten aus dem Holy Land*. Munich: Heyne, 2011.
Kaniuk, Yoram. *Ha-Berlinai Ha-acharon*. Tel Aviv: Yediot, 2004; (German transl. Felix Roth, *Der letzte Berliner*. Munich: List, 2002).
Kinet, Ruth. *Israel. Ein Länderporträt*. Berlin: Ch. Links, 2013.
Mendelssohn, Moses. *Jerusalem oder über religiöse Macht und Judentum*. Berlin: Friedrich Maurer, 1783.
Oz-Salzberger, Fania. *Israelis in Berlin* (German transl. Ruth Achlama). Frankfurt a. M.: Suhrkamp, 2001.
Oz-Salzberger, Fania. Israelis in Berlin: Ein neues Bücherregal. In *Rück-Blick auf Deutschland: Ansichten hebräischsprachiger Autoren*, Anat Feinberg (ed.), pp. 151–170. Munich: edition text+kritik, 2009.
Rosenthal, Ruvik. *Rehov Ha-prachim 22*. Jerusalem, Tel Aviv: Keter Publishing House, 2003.
Yehoshua, Abraham B. *Molcho*. Tel Aviv: Hakibbutz Hameuchad, 1987; (English transl. Hillel Halkin, *Five Seasons*. New York: Doubleday, 1989).

Culture and Arts –
Reflecting a New Jewish Presence

Hanni Mittelmann
Reconceptualization of Jewish Identity as Reflected in Contemporary German-Jewish Humorist Literature

The emergence of a Jewish-German entertainment literature, which presents the topic of Jewish identity and culture in a humorous way, is a rather recent phenomenon in the contemporary German book market. We find a plethora of new collections of Jewish jokes such as *Sex am Sabbat?* ('Sex on Shabbath?') by Ilan Weiss[1] and *Jetzt mal Tacheles. Die jüdischen Lieblingswitze* ('Tacheles. Paul Spiegel's Favorite Jewish Jokes'), collected by Dina and Leonie Spiegel (the daughters of Paul Spiegel, the late president of the Central Council of Jews in Germany).[2] There are also more academic treatises on the Jewish joke, such as *No, warum nicht? Der jüdische Witz als Quelle der Lebenskunst* ('Nu, why not? The Jewish Joke as the Source of the Art of Living')[3] by Austrian psychotherapist Elisabeth Jupiter. In addition, however, there are also quite a number of semi-autobiographical books and novels, which throw a humorous light on the not-exactly-easy coexistence of Germans and Jews. Among them is Lena Gorelik's novel with the impossibly long title *Lieber Mischa... der du fast Schlomo Adolf Grinblum geheissen hättest, es tut mir leid, dass ich Dir das nicht ersparen konnte: Du bist ein Jude* ('Dear Mischa... who was almost called Schlomo Adolf Grinblum, I am sorry that I can't spare you the fact: You are a Jew').[4] Another in this vein is a book by Oliver Polak entitled *Ich darf das, Ich bin Jude* ('I Am Allowed to Do This, I am a Jew') and another book and CD by the same author called *Jud Süss Sauer, die Show* ('Jew, Sweet Sour. The Show')[5] that try to provide humorous 'instruction' to the uneasy German reader of how to deal with a Jew, if said reader should encounter one in the workplace, at a party, or at the tennis club. According to Michael Wuliger – author of an 'etiquette book' entitled *Der koschere Knigge. Trittsicher durch die deutsch-jüdischen Fettnäpfchen* ('The Kosher Knigge. Sure-footed through the German-Jewish Mess') – the statistical probability of a German meeting a Jew is 1:400, which is, after all (as he puts it) twice as likely as the odds to hit the jackpot in the lottery.[6]

---

1 Weiss (ed.), Sex am Sabbat?, 2010.
2 Spiegel / Spiegel (ed.), Jetzt mal Tacheles, 2009.
3 Jupiter, No, warum nicht?, 2010.
4 Gorelik, Lieber Mischa, 2012.
5 Polak / Haas, Ich darf das, Ich bin Jude. 2008; Polak, Jud süss Sauer, 2010.
6 Wuliger, Der koschere Knigge, 2009.

My goal here is to discuss this type of literature as a reflection of the ongoing reconceptualization of Jewish identity in contemporary Germany by the younger generation of Jews living there.

The previous generation of post-Second World War Jewish-German writers such as Henryk Broder, Rafael Seligmann, Doron Rabinovici, Lea Fleischmann, Maxim Biller, Peter Stephan Jungk, and others who burst onto the literary scene in Germany and Austria in the 1980s, were the offspring of their traumatized survivor parents. These authors described their life in the land of the murderers of their grandparents with satiric wit and biting irony. They saw themselves, as Rafael Seligmann phrased it, as the "grandchildren of Tucholsky"[7] and thus connected to the discursive tradition of sarcastic-ironic Jewish humor, which existed in Germany from the time of Heinrich Heine and Ludwig Börne, ending in 1933 with Kurt Tucholsky. This type of humor, which was revived by these writers in the 1980s, was frivolous, aggressive and controversial. It was an oppositional humor, sharp-edged with wicked darts directed against a Germany that they deemed to be unredeemable. It was a literature which expressed a deep-seated alienation and distrust of Germany, reflected in titles such as *Dies ist nicht mein Land. Eine Jüdin verlässt die Bundesrepublik* ('This Is Not My Country. A Jewess Leaves the Federal Republic of Germany'), written by Lea Fleischmann.[8]

By contrast, the books penned by the new young generation of German-Jewish writers reflect a change of mentality (*Mentalitätswechsel*) as Wuliger termed it in an article bearing the title *Aus das Trauma* ('The Trauma is Over').[9] This new generation is "no longer afraid of Germany" (*Keine Angst vor Deutschland*), the actual title of a volume by historian Michael Wolffsohn, published in 1990 that proclaims that there has been a change (*Wende*) both in German mentality and in Jewish self-perception.[10]

This second and third generation of German-Jewish writers as represented by Gorelik, Polak, Wladimir Kaminer, Vladimir Vertlib, Arye Sharuz Shalikar, Vanessa Fogel, and others is somewhat removed from the traumatic events of the past. For them the Holocaust is a fact of German history which they also know about from the stories of their grandparents. It is a part of their lives just as it is a part of the lives of their German contemporaries. This historical knowledge of the past is not, however, burdened with fear or hatred or attribution of guilt. It does not influence their self-image or their self-perception. Thanks to this new generation, Germany's Jews – thus Wuliger claims in his article *Aus das Trauma*

---

[7] Seligmann, Mit beschränkter Hoffnung, 1991, p. 127.
[8] Fleischmann, Dies ist nicht mein Land, 1980
[9] Wuliger, in: Jüdische Allgemeine Zeitung, June 23, 2011.
[10] Wolffsohn, Keine Angst vor Deutschland, 1990.

('The Trauma is Over') – have outgrown their old role as victims. This certainly accounts for their emerging humorous representation of self and their relaxed view of German-Jewish relations.

An equally important reason that might account for this type of attitude is that these young Jewish writers have a migratory background. They come from the former Soviet Union or from Israel, England, or America, and have developed a different take on identity and the relation of their own culture to their host-culture. This generation with its multiple cultural, national, and linguistic identities no longer knows the cognitive search for a unified identity which was so typical for modernity. Rather, it celebrates a postmodern pluralism and the freedom of a hybrid identity that has developed from this generation's Russian, Israeli, or American identities. The experience of liminality and cultural hybridity is part of their lives. Yet, there is no longer the melancholy of torn identities that existed among German Jews before the Second World War and among the second postwar generation whose loyalties were torn between Israel and Germany. This youngest generation confidently displays its affinities for different cultures. As children of postcolonialism and globalization, they do not deny their ethnicity as the titles of the afore-mentioned books demonstrate. They give the cultural differences that exist prominence, make them visible, but at the same time create new cultural models of a transcultural identity that both confirm and dissolve the 'uniqueness' (*Eigene*) and 'the alien' (*Fremde*).[11]

Using the title of an article by the philosopher Paul Ricoer *Von der Trauerarbeit zur Übersetzung* ('From the labor of mourning to translation') as a reference, one could say that this young generation of Jewish writers has indeed moved from the mourning in which the previous post-Holocaust generation had to engage, to the labor of transcultural "translation."[12] Thanks to their multiple cultural backgrounds, they have become mediators between the cultures and are attempting to create the equivalence of the non-identical, through the narration of their own histories. Their narrative identity is no longer characterized by the identity of the self (*ipse*), but by changeability and mobility and by exchangeability (*Bewegtheit*). The exchange of cultures, or rather the "translation" of cultures, as Paul Ricoer puts it, becomes the new goal.[13] These young writers want to create equivalences, but not identities. They create comparisons between what seemingly cannot be compared. As Ricoer frames it, their writings point to the 'undeniable phenomenon of human plurality' ("das unwiderlegbare Phänomen der menschlichen

---

[11] Krohn, Vorwort. In: Krohn (ed.), Jahrbuch für Exilforschung, 2007, p. X.
[12] Ricoer, Vielzahl der Kulturen. In: Krohn (ed.), 2007, p. 3.
[13] Ricoer, 2007, p. 4.

Pluralität") but also aim to 'mediate between the plurality of cultures and the unity of humanity.'[14]

Changed historical and social circumstances in Germany have affected a change in German mentality and the self-perception of the Jews living there. This is also due to the influence of American culture on postwar Germany. Writers like Philip Roth, Saul Bellow, and Mordechai Richler, but also the Hollywood films produced by Woody Allen which represent the American-Jewish tradition of humor, have found their way onto the German cultural scene. Moreover, and above all, from the mid-1980s, with the advent of German commercial television, Germans have been exposed to TV sitcoms like *Alf*, *The Nanny*, *Seinfeld*, and *Roseanne* right in their living rooms, presenting Germans with the American melting pot vision of society. The 'strangers are welcome' structure underlying these American-Jewish sitcoms and soap operas suggested that the 'other' does not have to be viewed as threatening.[15] Rather, the 'other' can have an enriching and humanizing influence on a staid society set in its ways, as the figures of the alien Alf and the Nanny prove. Both add a bit more color to the conventional lives of the families of which they have become part, and provide these families with new perspectives on life and living.

These humorous and positive representations of the 'alien' also influenced the young Jews who were growing up in Germany at that time, and were looking for role models with whom to identify. For the previous postwar generation of young Jews it was the Israeli Jew who had become the shining example for a desirable Jewish identity. He soon became deconstructed by writers like Rafael Seligmann and Maxim Biller. Now the American Jew and his role in American society came into view. The younger generation of German Jews became acquainted with the social constellation of integrative American identity politics, which was fundamentally open towards immigrants, and invited them to participate in the creation of a common American culture. From this attitude emerged the self-confident Jewish-American self-image, of which Jews living in Germany could only dream. The image of the American Jew transmitted by literature, sitcoms and movies produced in postwar America was described by Sander Gilman with wit and candor, as follows:

> America is fun for the Jews – they become powerful, win Nobel prizes and engage in the building of cultural institutions such as video archives of the Holocaust. They are smart Jews, but not tough Jews. They have it easy. They are superficial and not engaged in the reconstitution of a new Jewish culture, for Jewish culture in America has become mainstream.[16]

---

[14] Ricoer, 2007, p. 4.
[15] Kniesche, Projektionen von Amerika, 2008, p. 219.
[16] Gilman, America and the newest Jewish writing, 2000, p. 161.

America is seen by young Jews living in Germany as a place of tolerance and acceptance of minorities, of Jews and artists. It has become the model for this generation, which started to demand implementation of the American vision of an integrative society. The experience of America helped these young Jews who lived in Germany and Austria to acquire a new self-image and a new literary program.

What they learned from the American-Jewish experience was also that entrance into mainstream society can be won through laughter – by the employment of the famous Jewish humor which in America had become part of the American mainstream culture – just as jazz had been transformed from an African American music genre into a part of American music.[17]

Modeled after the American-Jewish example, entertaining humor seems to have become an important discursive voice of the Jewish minority group in Germany. Through laughter, one tries to establish one's self as a member of a society from which one otherwise would be excluded. Unlike the satirical and sarcastic wit employed by the previous generation, which in its essence was intolerant towards everything German, the humor engaged in by this young generation is not aggressive and alienating.[18]

The newest type of humor is much more accepting and also socially more acceptable. It is an inclusive type of humor programmed to end the isolation in which the Jewish community has lived since after the war, and encourages vying for acceptance and integration. This inclusive and conciliatory type of humor, however, has nothing to do with assimilatory self-dissolution. Unlike the prewar generation of German Jews, this young post-Holocaust generation no longer sees it necessary to pay this price for social acceptability. It wants acceptance and not "tolerance," as proclaimed by the title of a new book by Lena Gorelik, a young writer who immigrated to Germany from Russia at the age of eleven: *"Sie können aber gut Deutsch!" Warum ich nicht mehr dankbar sein will, dass ich hier leben darf, und Toleranz nicht weiterhilft* ('"You really speak an excellent German!" Why I no longer want to be grateful for being allowed to live here and why tolerance doesn't help').[19] By narrating themselves and their own culture, these young Jews living and writing in Germany attempt to achieve acknowledgement and acceptance of their own uniqueness (*Eigenes*), as well as to create a sense of similarities (*Ähnlichkeiten*).[20]

---

[17] Rabbi Moshe Waldoks, interview by Andreas Mink, in: Aufbau. Das jüdische Monatsmagazin, January 3, 2007, p. 8.
[18] Chase, Two Sons of 'Jewish Wit', 2001, p. 44.
[19] Gorelik, "Sie können aber gut Deutsch", 2012.
[20] Ricoer, 2007, p. 5.

Through humorous representations of the alien and foreign, modeled after the American-Jewish sitcoms, these writers attempt to make the unfamiliar 'other' accessible and remove the aura of a 'foreign threat.'[21] Thus, the sitcom-figure Alf became an important identificatory figure for Oliver Polak in his youth. From this 'big-nosed cousin with the body covering sidelocks' ("grossnasiger Vetter mit den Ganzkörper-Gebetslocken"),[22] Polak learned that one can stage the 'alien' – and specifically the Jewish alien, who was and is always eyed by Germans with suspicion – in an engaging way.[23] By undermining xenophobic views and dogmatic thinking with humor, the unknown and alien start to lose their threatening power and can even be experienced as endearing and amiable. The stand-up comedy of Oliver Polak which is built on this concept, always plays before sold-out audiences. This seems to prove that this approach is somewhat effective.

The new type of humorous self-representation also aims to stress the commonality of humanity and 'the similarity of the different.' This is what Wuliger, for instance, wants to impress upon the German reader with his little 'etiquette book.' In an interview about the work, he states that the German reader will discover that he himself shares with the Jew many more traits than he would suspect:

> Soccer is more interesting to him [the Jew] than the situation in Gaza; he is interested more in the performance qualities of his car than in the problem of overcoming the past (*Vergangenheitsbewältigung*); he prefers listening to ABBA rather than to Klezmer music; and rather than the Talmud, he reads *Kicker*, a football magazine.

> (Die Bundesliga interessiert ihn mehr als die Lage in Gaza, über die Fahreigenschaften seines Wagens denkt er häufiger nach als über die Vergangenheitsbewältigung. ABBA hört er lieber als Klezmermusik. Und öfters als den Talmud liest er den Kicker).

Therefore, Wuliger recommends to the German reader, should he meet a Jew: 'don't get on the Jew's nerves by telling him or her how distressed you were after a visit to the Holocaust memorial or impart to him your deep insights into the Middle East conflict' ("nerven Sie den armen Mann – oder die Frau – nicht mit der Betroffenheit beim Besuch des Holocaustmahnmals oder Ihren Ideen zum Nahostkonflikt"). Wuliger also recommends not to inquire about the details of the laws of *kashrut*, which Jews most probably do not know anyhow. After all, he writes 'no Catholic would be happy to get into a debate on the theological aspects of transubstantiation while he is drinking his beer' ("Sie würden ja auch, wenn

---

21 Ricoer, 2007, p. 5.
22 Polak / Haas, 2008, p. 53.
23 Polak / Haas, 2008, p. 53.

Sie Katholik sind, beim Bier keine Debatte über die theologischen Aspekte der Transsubstantiation führen wollen").[24]

These young writers write from a posture of self-confidence and loving acceptance of their ethnic background. They no longer know the Jewish self-hatred of previous generations which (as we know from Freud) expressed itself so often in self-criticism. The autobiographical novels by Lena Gorelik, in which she describes with loving self-irony some of the more grotesque sides of Jewish culture and traditions is one case in point; the communal structures of Jewish ethnicity, which were still the target of snide criticism by the previous generation of Jewish writers who depicted them as oppressive and repressive, are now portrayed as civilizing, protective structures. Even the Jewish mother – the *Yiddische Mame*, the object of vicious attacks by writers like Seligmann – is now seen not as the source of castration anxieties, but rather as the source of strength and an individual sense of value.[25] Assimilation is no longer a topic in this literature. Rather, these new books deconstruct the German dominant, leading culture (*Leitkultur*), whose own grotesque aspects form the backdrop for descriptions of some equally grotesque aspects of Jewish culture.

By making their own culture the object of satire, these young writers free themselves from the ethnic stereotypes imposed on them by others, but they also free themselves from the restrictions and taboos of their own culture. This type of self-representation both destabilizes and transcends anti-Semitic prejudices, but it also negates the philosemitic projections that have created the idealized folkloric images of the Jew, common in postwar German culture. The parodist subversion of such stereotypes points to the fragility of the construction of the image of the Jew, but also demands the observance of the common norms of a civil society regarding the 'other,' and thereby confirms them.

The humorous entertainment produced by these young Jewish writers is mainly conciliatory, but clearly also displays a disciplinary aspect (i.e. patterns and strategies found in academic analysis of humor) about which Henry Bergson speaks in his theory of humor.[26] The background to this humor is, just like in traditional Jewish ghetto humor, the experience of rejection and exclusion by the dominant society. Therefore, as in traditional Jewish humor, the aim is to neutralize the enemy through laughter – to bring conscious or half-conscious prejudices that are deeply rooted in the collective folklore of German society, into the open and reveal their ludicrousness and their absurdity. Thus, in his chapter 'Pointers

---

[24] Wuliger, in: Cicero Online, August 12, 2010.
[25] Wisse, The Schlemiel as Modern Hero, 1980, XI.
[26] Farb, Speaking Seriously About Humor, 1981, p. 765.

for the First Encounter with a Jew' (*Tipps für das erste Kennenlernen*), Wulinger disarms some of the more common stereotypes about Jews:

> Mr. Blumberg, who has been introduced to you at the birthday party of a colleague who has already advised you beforehand ('he is a Jew, but very nice') might possibly disappoint you. He neither wears a black hat nor sidelocks. If he has a beard than he probably sports then of the fashionable three-day-variation. He speaks perfect German without a Yiddish accent. He also does not carry an Uzi. Actually he looks totally normal. Don't show your surprise. 'You really don't look it' is not a good way to start the conversation with him. 'I always wanted to get to know a Jew' is also not the best way.
>
> (Herr Blumberg, der Ihnen bei der Geburtstagsparty eines Kollegen vorgestellt wird und vom Gastgeber vorher bereits avisiert wurde ('Er ist Jude, aber sehr nett'), wird Sie deshalb möglicherweise enttäuschen. Er trägt weder einen schwarzen Hut noch Schläfenlocken. Wenn er einen Bart hat, dann in der modischen Drei-Tage-Variante. Er spricht Hochdeutsch ohne jiddischen Akzent. Eine Uzi hat er auch nicht umgeschnallt. Eigentlich wirkt er ganz normal. Lassen Sie sich Ihre Überraschung nicht anmerken. 'Sie sehen gar nicht so aus', ist kein guter Gesprächseinstieg. 'Ich wollte immer schon mal einen Juden kennenlernen' auch nicht).[27]

The laughter elicited here is based on norms of civil thinking and behavior that exclude those who won't abide by them. It aims to create solidarity within the group that can laugh together, and excludes those who do not join in the laughter from membership in a civilized, liberal, and humanistic society.[28] The goal of this laughter is, to quote Walter Benjamin, 'the destruction of all that which threatens the humane' ("die Vernichtung dessen, was das Humane bedroht").[29]

Through this humanizing and creative type of humor these young writers open communication channels between Germans and Jews. They turn fear into laughter and thus achieve a social potency which is usually denied the Jew or attributed to him in an exaggerated way. "The phallic power of the word," as Lacan phrased it, dismantles hierarchies and takes the "mastery of discourse,"[30] – the power of definition, back from the dominant society.

This seemingly harmless Jewish entertainment literature is, after all, not as harmless as it might appear. It is entertaining, but not harmless. It displays a subversive quality which has always been part of Jewish humor. It is a literature of dialectics and destabilization and not only a feel-good-about-the-Jews-literature that absolves the Germans from their past. Its aim is not a superficial reconciliation. The past always remains present and begs to be acknowledged and dealt

---

27 Wuliger, 2009, p. 7.
28 Farb, 1981, p. 765.
29 Braese, Das teure Experiment, 1996, p. 215.
30 Chase, 2001, p. 45.

with. Therefore, a writer like Oliver Polak can propose in his book *Ich darf das. Ich bin Jude* the following tongue-in-cheek 'deal' to the German reader:

> Let us disregard this embarrassing story which is already over 60 years old. Let us make a deal for the duration of your reading this book: I will forget the thing with the Holocaust and you forgive us Michel Friedman. Fine! Then we can make a fresh start.
>
> (Ich meine: wie lange ist diese dumme Geschichte jetzt her? über 60 Jahre, oder? Treffen wir doch für die Dauer der Lektüre folgende Vereinbarung: Ich vergesse die Sache mit dem Holocaust – und Sie verzeihen uns Michel Friedman. Fein! Dann können wir ja noch mal ganz von vorne anfangen.)[31]

From their newly-established position of self-empowerment, these young Jewish writers open the dialogue with the Germans on the writers' own terms, and establish themselves as equals. They transcend the narratives and politics of the victim in the name of equality, solidarity, and universal humanity. They aim to dissolve the tension between the two groups, offering to establish new, relaxed relations between Germans and Jews.

Of course, whether this new Jewish humorist literature will achieve its goal of a more normal German-Jewish relationship is still in question. Michael Wuliger provides us with a yardstick for possible progress in German-Jewish relations:

> The German-Jewish relationship will be normal on that day when somebody meets a Jewish asshole and proclaims afterwards: 'What an asshole' and not: 'What a typical Jewish asshole'
>
> (Das deutsch-jüdische Verhältnis wird an dem Tag ein normales sein, wenn jemand einem jüdischen Arschloch begegnet und hinterher sagt: 'So ein Arschloch' und nicht: 'Ein typisch jüdisches Arschloch').[32]

Wuliger is convinced that it will still take quite a while until this is achieved. In conclusion, one can say that this new, humorous depiction of German-Jewish relations releases the Jews from their role as victims, and attempts to free Germans from fear of their own shadow. Laughter is indeed not the worst beginning with which to open a new dialogue. To quote Walter Benjamin in his essay about satirist Karl Kraus: 'There is no better way than laughter to initiate thinking. And especially the vibrations of the diaphragm [through laughter] usually offer a better chance to thinking than the stirring of the soul' ("Nur nebenbei angemerkt, dass es fürs Denken gar keinen besseren Start gibt als das Lachen. Und

---

[31] Polak / Haas, 2008, p. 11.
[32] Wuliger, 2009, p. 7.

insbesondere bietet die Erschütterung des Zwerchfells dem Gedanken gewöhnlich bessere Chancen dar als die der Seele").[33]

References

Braese, Stephan. *Das teure Experiment. Satire und NS-Faschismus*. Opladen: Westdeutscher Verlag, 1996.
Chase, Jefferson. Two Sons of 'Jewish Wit': Philip Roth and Rafael Seligmann. *Comparative Literature* 53 (2001): pp. 42–57.
Farb, Peter. Speaking Seriously About Humor. *The Massachusetts Review* 22 (1981): pp. 760–776.
Fleischmann, Lea. *Dies ist nicht mein Land. Eine Jüdin verlässt die Bundesrepublik*. Hamburg: Hoffmann & Campe, 1980.
Gilman, Sander. America and the newest Jewish writing in German. *The German Quarterly* 73 (2000): pp. 151–162.
Gorelik, Lena. *Lieber Mischa... der du fast Schlomo Adolf Grinblum geheissen hättest, es tut mir leid, dass ich Dir das nicht ersparen konnte: Du bist ein Jude*. Berlin: List, 2012.
Gorelik, Lena. *"Sie können aber gut Deutsch!" Warum ich nicht mehr dankbar sein will, dass ich hier leben darf, und Toleranz nicht weiterhilft*. Munich: Pantheon, 2012.
Jupiter, Elisabeth. *No, warum nicht? Der jüdische Witz als Quelle der Lebenskunst*. Vienna: Picus, 2010.
Kniesche, Thomas W. *Projektionen von Amerika. Die USA in der deutsch-jüdischen Literatur des 20. Jahrhunderts*. Bielefeld: Aisthesis, 2008.
Krohn, Claus Dieter. Vorwort zu den Beiträgen. In: *Übersetzung als transkultureller Prozess. Exilforschung. Ein internationales Jahrbuch* 25, Claus-Dieter Krohn (ed.), p. IX–XI. Munich: edition text + kritik, 2007.
Mink, Andreas. "Von Chelm nach Hollywood. Interview mit Rabbi Moshe Waldoks." *Aufbau. Das jüdische Monatsmagazin*, January 3, 2007, pp. 8–10.
Polak, Oliver, Jens Oliver Haas. *Ich darf das, Ich bin Jude*. Cologne: Kiepenheuer & Witsch, 2008.
Polak, Oliver. *Jud Süss Sauer, die Show*. Audio CD. SME Spassgesellschaft/Sony Music, 2010
Ricoer, Paul. Vielzahl der Kulturen. Von der Trauerarbeit zur Übersetzung. In: *Übersetzung als transkultureller Prozess. Exilforschung. Ein internationales Jahrbuch* 25, Claus-Dieter Krohn (ed.), pp. 3–6. Munich: edition text + kritik, 2007.
Seligmann, Rafael. *Mit beschränkter Hoffnung. Juden, Deutsche, Israelis*. Hamburg: Hoffmann & Campe, 1991.
Spiegel, Dina, Leonie Spiegel (ed.). *"Jetzt mal Tacheles". Die jüdischen Lieblingswitze von Paul Spiegel*. Mannheim: Artemis & Winkler, 2009.
Weiss, Ilan (ed.). *Sex am Sabbat? Moderne Jüdische Witze*. Berlin: Patchworldverlag, 2010.
Wisse, Ruth R. *The Schlemiel as Modern Hero*. Chicago: Chicago University Press, 1980.
Wolffsohn, Michael. *Keine Angst vor Deutschland*. Erlangen, Bonn, Vienna: Straube, 1990.

---

33 Walter Benjamin, als Motto zitiert nach Braese, 1996.

Wuliger, Michael. *Der koschere Knigge. Trittsicher durch die deutsch-jüdischen Fettnäpfchen*. Frankfurt a. M.: Fischer, 2009.

Wuliger, Michael. "Die meisten Juden halten Adorno für einen Rotwein." *Cicero Online*, August 12, 2010. http://www.cicero.de/die-meisten-juden-halten-adorno-für-einen-rotwein/41089 (accessed March 29, 2015).

Wuliger, Michael. "Aus das Trauma. Deutschlands Juden sind der alten Opferrolle entwachsen – dank der Zuwanderer." *Jüdische Allgemeine Zeitung*, Juni 23, 2011. http://www.juedische-allgemeine.de/article/view/id/10625 (accessed March 29, 2015).

Karsten Troyke
Hava Nagila[1]

A Personal Reflection on the Reception of Jewish Music in Germany

As far as I can assess, there was not the slightest interest in Jewish music in Germany after 1945. Firstly, no one knew what Jewish music was and secondly, there was only a very vague idea of what it meant to be a Jew. Bedevilled by the National Socialists (Nazis) and defamed in books and the media, the German public had forgotten the role traditionally played by Jews in art and culture. Poems (and songs) by Heinrich Heine*, although an integral part of German culture, were marked as "writer unknown" – for example, *Ich weiß nicht was soll es bedeuten, dass ich so traurig bin* ('The Loreley'[2]).

Compositions by Gustav Mahler*, although rooted in the German tradition of late-Romantic music, had been forgotten. German-Jewish actors, cabaret stars, and popular composers had been murdered or had fled. Although many people still remembered the songs, hardly anyone knew that Jews had written them – for example, *Ich bin von Kopf bis Fuss auf Liebe eingestellt* written by Friedrich Hollaender*, known in the English-speaking world as *Falling in Love Again*. Actually, this is not really Jewish but German culture. The pre-Nazi influence of German-Jewish artists on the art and culture scene in Germany cannot be over-estimated. The situation was similar in literature, science, philosophy, and sociology. Capitalism had raised high hopes among German Jews for chances of equality through assimilation. These hopes were destroyed by the race theories which were at the core of the German version of fascism. People who had grown up under the Nazis – or who adhered to their ideology – believed that somehow Jews were inferior human beings, or, at the very least, did not fit into German culture. This attitude was still widespread in 1945 and even the better educated people had most likely forgotten Alban Berg*, Sigmund Freud* or Rosa Luxemburg*.

But I want to talk about music. Popular music. As most people did not know what Jewish was, Jewish music did not exist for them. American hits came to Germany with the occupation powers and were popular. People liked the

---

1 *Hava Nagila* (הבה נגילה, in English *Let us rejoice*) is a Jewish traditional folk song in Hebrew. The commonly used text was probably composed by Abraham Zevi (Zvi) Idelsohn in 1918 to celebrate the British victory in Palestine during the First World War, as well as the Balfour Declaration.
2 In 1824 Heinrich Heine wrote the poem *Die Lorelei* ('The Loreley'), which was set to music in 1837 by Friedrich Silcher and is today one of the most famous Rhine songs.

English-language compositions written by Jews, but no one in Germany realised that the 'strange German' in the song *Bay mir bistu sheyn*[3] was, in fact, Yiddish. Even Zarah Leander*, the star of a number of Nazi films, sang this song in 1950, but with Swedish verses.

Holocaust survivors, who often came from Poland, loved Yiddish hits. They listened to records from Paris, London, or America. Some cantors and musical singers took up these songs and Shellac Records with ghetto songs became available. Soon, people from the DP camps[4] saw a chance to build a future for themselves in the Netherlands, France, and so forth – and even in Germany. Thus, the songs of East European Jews were brought to Germany. (In the 1920s there was a rich Yiddish migrant culture in Berlin, with theatre, recordings, and books. All this had been destroyed and forgotten by 1945.)

These were the real Jewish songs (for only in Yiddish does this word translate as 'Jewish'). Very often Yiddish, being so similar to German, was the language used for communication in the Jewish communities being rebuilt in Germany – founded largely by Polish Jews, while at the same time the language was rejected in Israel as the language that belonged to an awful past. Jossy Halland* sang *Heymish Zayn*[5] ('To Feel At Home') in the Amsterdam cabaret *Lilalo*.[6] In Paris, records were produced with Henry Gerro*, Benzion Witler*, the Malavsky family,* and others.

The first time the German public noticed that there was such a thing as Jewish music was through a recording by Harry Belafonte*. This was *Hava Nagila* which became a world-wide hit in 1955, in Germany also. Later pop singers from Israel such as Camilla Corren* sang Yiddish songs in German. In West Germany Lea-Nina Rodzynek (known as *Belina*)* sang the original Yiddish songs. She originated from Poland, had survived a concentration camp, was able to flee and then

---

3 *Bay Mir Bistu Sheyn* (Yiddish: בײַ מיר ביסטו שײן, 'For Me You're Beautiful') is a popular Yiddish song composed by Jacob Jacobs (lyricist) and Sholom Secunda (composer) for a 1932 Yiddish comedy musical, *I Would If I Could* (in Yiddish, מען קען לעבן נאָר מען לאָזט נישט, 'You could live, but they won't let you'). In 1937, Sammy Cahn heard a performance of the song, sung in Yiddish by African-American performers in New York. There have been several songs in the Soviet Union that use the tune. In Nazi Germany it was also a hit until its Jewish origins were discovered in 1938, and it was promptly banned.

4 A displaced persons camp or DP camp is a temporary facility for displaced persons forced to migrate. The term is mainly used for camps established after the Second World War in West Germany and in Austria, as well as in the United Kingdom, primarily for refugees from Eastern Europe and for former inmates of the Nazi German concentration camps.

5 *Heymish Zayn* (Yiddish, היימיש זײן) is a song with music and lyrics by Jacques Halland. It was performed by him exclusively in almost every program at his cabaret. It deals with nostalgia for a lost home, for the shtetl. It was recorded for his vinyl LP *Lilalo*, Germany, 1984.

6 *Lilalo* was a Yiddish cabaret that operated in Amsterdam (1959–1983).

hide from the Nazis. She gave concerts accompanied by a classical guitarist. She appeared existentialist, much like Juliette Greco*, and sang *Es brent*[7] by Mordechai Gebirtig* on television in Germany.

East Germany (the GDR) – founded as an anti-fascist state – had Lin Jaldati*, a singer who had survived Auschwitz, knew Yiddish and could perform Yiddish songs. She, too, sang *Es brent*. She was Dutch, had come to East Berlin from the Netherlands with her (Communist) husband and was prepared to use her abilities 'to help build a better world.' She, too, sang the old Yiddish songs of poverty and oppression; Paul Robeson*, the famous Afro-American singer from the USA, was her guest when he visited the GDR in 1960. He had the famous Yiddish partisans' song *Zog nisht keynmol az du geyst dem letstn veg*[8] ('Never say this is your final road') in his repertoire.

At this time a folk-song revival began in the USA. Pete Seeger* and his group *The Weavers* became important again; Joan Baez* made *Dona Dona*[9] world-famous; and the first Newport Folk Festivals[10] took place. Most of the protagonists were Jewish. All of the Left-wing parties and groups in the USA were led by Jewish politicians and the world was in upheaval - despite the Cold War. In the GDR, where I lived, people made private copies from records smuggled in from the West such as those sung by Theodore Bikel*, who sang Yiddish folk and theatre songs, and songs from Israel. People talked of Robert Zimmerman who had just become world-famous as Bob Dylan* – a Jewish lad from Minnesota. It somehow became a good thing to be Jewish.

Havatselet Ron*, born in Aden (Yemen), was the only Israeli singer who came to the socialist East at the beginning of the 1960s and she, too, sang *Hava nagila*, Yiddish folk-songs, and German hits. She stayed only two years. Later, her tapes were found in the radio archives marked: "Nicht senden!" ('Not for broadcasting!')

---

7 *It is Burning*, (Yiddish, עס ברענט, in reference to a shtetl. The second Yiddish verse says literally אונדזער שטעטל ברענט - our shtetl is burning), *Es brent* is a Yiddish poem-song written in 1938 by Mordechai Gebirtig. The poem was originally written about the pogrom of Przytyk, which took place on March 9, 1936. Cracow's underground Jewish resistance adopted *Es brent* as its anthem. It is frequently sung in Israel and around the world on Holocaust Remembrance Days.
8 *Zog Nisht Keynmol* (Yiddish: זאָג נישט קיינמאָל, also referred to as *Partizaner Himen*, or the *Partisan Anthem*) is the name of a Yiddish song considered one of the chief anthems of Holocaust survivors and is sung in memorial services around the world. The lyrics of the song were written in 1943 by Hirsh Glick, a young Jewish inmate of the Vilna Ghetto.
9 *Dona Dona* (Yiddish דאַנאַ דאַנאַ, also known as דאָס קעלבל *Dos Kelbl – The Calf*) is a Yiddish theater song about a calf being led to slaughter. *Dona Dona* was written for the Aaron Zeitlin stage production *Esterke* (1940–1941) with music composed by Sholem Secunda.
10 The Newport Folk Festival is an annual American folk-oriented music festival held in Newport, Rhode Island, which began in 1959 as a counterpart to the previously established Newport Jazz Festival.

The Soviet Union's support for pan-Arabism and the Ba'ath Party (as a result of Russian arms exports) had prevented diplomatic relations between the GDR and Israel. The Yiddish (not the Hebrew) songs seemed to have fallen out of history and appeared to have nothing to do with Israel. Thus, Yiddish songs, particularly the partisan songs, were sung in Left-wing circles in both East and West Germany. This continued even after 1967 (the Six Day War) when most Left-wing German intellectuals turned against Israel. Esther and Abi Ofarim* became very popular in East *and* West Germany. Apart from German songs, they performed American and Israeli folk songs and 'Songs of the World.' I think it was their charm, at least in Germany, that helped overcome traditional clichés about Jews. In 1963 a young man in West Berlin became known for singing very old Yiddish folk-songs: Peter Rohland*. He was the first non-Jewish German to delve into the subject of Yiddish songs (beside German folk songs), and he did not remain the only one. Unfortunately, he died in 1966.

There were so few Jews in the Socialist half of Germany that one cannot speak of their political influence. In the West, however, there was at least a verbal alliance with Israel and recognition of Jewish interests. Despite this, no one could really define what 'Jewish culture' was. In West Germany (FRG, or in German BRD) people started lamenting their loss of German-Jewish culture with its assimilationist tradition. At the same time, Jews in Germany were considered responsible for the politics of the Israeli government. In the East (GDR, or in German DDR) the milieu was worse: Newspapers reported *daily* about the 'aggressor Israel.' Under such circumstances, singing a Yiddish song became a political act. I remember the words of a singer in East Berlin in 1982. She said on stage that "singing Yiddish songs has absolutely nothing to do with the aggressive machinations of the State of Israel," then she sang the *Lid fun Sholem*[11] ('Song of Peace').

In Christian communities, the simpler Hebrew songs from the pioneer period were then (and still are) very popular: *Hevenu shalom aleichem* and *Shalom chaverim*. This new whiff of brotherhood was probably caused by the Second Vatican Council of the early 1960s, when the Pope spoke of the common heritage of Christians and Jews, while in the Protestant Church there was (and still is up to the present day) a special empathy for everything Jewish, or for what they con-

---

11 דאָס ליד פֿון שלום, in Yiddish 'The Song of Peace' is the original lyrics added to the song שפּיל זשע מיר אַ לידעלע (*Play a Little Song for Me*) written by the Jewish Soviet poet Yosl Kotliar (1908 in Berdichev–1962 in Vilna). It appeared in his collection of poems אויסגעלייזטע ערד (*Redeemed Land*), that was published in 1948 in Vilna. The music was composed by Henech Kon before the Second World War. During the Holocaust the song was adapted to reflect the experience of ghetto life, and then after the war was adapted again with new lyrics about liberation. Several of Kotliar's poems have been turned into songs, and made famous by many well-known Yiddish singers.

sider to be Jewish. Particularly in the GDR, the Protestant churches were open to all people who were otherwise publicly stigmatised: punks, environmentalists, anyone in opposition, and others.

In the 1980s, many young people in East and West Germany suddenly started singing Yiddish songs. In the United States, young Jews had already started to do so. This later became known as the 'Klezmer[12] revival.' In West Germany a folklore group called *Zupfgeigenhansel*[13] performed at concerts, presenting old German folksongs together with Yiddish ones. At this time German folk songs were freed from the dust of Nazi ideology. Old songs were rediscovered and the slogan became: 'Let's sing!'

Hardly anyone from the Jewish community was interested in this new folklore movement. The earlier proclaimed symbiosis of German and Jewish culture had nothing to do with this. Yiddish songs were sung by the *chazan* (cantor) and at the most during Passover at small gatherings. "The *goyim* want to replace us! They don't understand what they are talking about, let alone singing about!"

Truly, the young Germans actually knew very little about what it meant to be Jewish. Thus, many of those musicians were happy when the Klezmer revivalists came to Europe to give concerts. These Americans were usually the grandchildren of Jews who had arrived in the United States from Eastern Europe in the 1920s and 1930s. They had inherited old records from their grandparents, rearranged the songs on them and sometimes co-operated with the great Yiddish singers from the 1940s and 1950s. The Klezmer revivalists became the role models for many young German musicians then and thus the 'Klezmer boom' began around 1990.

---

12 Klezmer (Yiddish: singular קלעזמער or *klezmer*, plural קלעזמאָרים *klezmorim*), from Hebrew: כלי זמר – *klei zemer* or musical instruments) is a musical tradition of the Ashkenazi Jews of Eastern Europe. Played by professional musicians called klezmorim, the genre originally consisted largely of dance tunes and instrumental pieces for weddings and other celebrations. In the United States the genre evolved considerably, as Yiddish-speaking Jewish immigrants from Eastern Europe who arrived in America between 1880 and 1924 encountered and assimilated American jazz. It was not until the late twentieth century that the word came to identify a musical genre. Early twentieth century recordings and writings most often refer to the style as "Yiddish music," although it was also sometimes called "Freilech music" (Yiddish, פֿרײלעך literally, Happy music). The first recordings to use the musical term 'klezmer' to refer to the music were recorded in the USA in 1977 and 1979.

13 *Zupfgeigenhansel* was a German folk duo, one of the most successful groups to emerge on the German folk scene in the 1970s. It consisted of Erich Schmeckenbecher and Thomas Friz. The group started playing in folk-clubs, mainly in southern Germany, in 1974. They then started appearing on the radio. They released their first album, *Volkslieder I* in 1976, and in 1978 they received the Artists of the Year award from the German Phonoakademie. In 1979 they published an LP of Yiddish songs – *'ch hob gehert sogn*. They disbanded in 1985.

New York groups such as *The Klezmatics*[14] were very successful in Germany, and Klezmer groups sprang up in every German city. The word *Klezmer* now became synonymous with Jewish music. Once, when I announced a concert, I was told: "I hope you have a clarinet in your band, otherwise it's not really Jewish."

Giora Feidmann*, who in Germany is "the world's most famous clarinetist," was a great success. He held many workshops in which he spoke of the musical energy inherent in everyone. He even went so far as to play Richard Wagner* at Auschwitz – with typical Feidman phrases, *krekhts* and *dreydl* (i.e. sobbing sounds and musical ornamentation).

In the 1990s, thanks to the Americans' concerts and the 'Klezmer boom,' the Jewish communities too began to take note of Klezmer – but for another reason: The collapse of the Soviet Union made it possible for thousands of Russian Jews to leave the country. Many of them settled in Germany. Today, many Jewish publications are issued in two languages: Russian and German. And these former Soviet citizens, as well, often do not know what is Jewish and what is not. Yiddish songs and Klezmer music is one way for them to embrace their new Jewish identity. There are many excellent musicians among them, often with training in classical music.

Today, the word 'Klezmer' has become a world music genre, and not only in Germany. It is now mixed with rock, jazz, Balkan music, punk, and classical arrangements, and is no longer just Jewish music. And the boom has gone. The Yiddish cabaret and folk songs have returned to the small off-theatres and the Yiddish languageis understood by fewer and fewer people.

From the 1980s up until the beginning of the 2000s almost every *Kulturklub* (cultural public place), every theatre in Germany held an evening of Yiddish music or literature at least once a year. This is no longer the case. One reason is that culture has become much more commercialised (Yiddish folklore is not something with which one can earn much money); and I see another reason: In Germany – and internationally – the attitude towards Israel is changing for the worse. Many agree with the Nobel Prize laureate Günter Grass* who blames Israel for the threats coming from the Iranian regime. At an event, I saw a German

---

14 *The Klezmatics* are a Grammy Award-winning American klezmer music group based in New York City who have achieved fame singing in several languages, most notably mixing older Yiddish tunes with other types of contemporary music of differing origins. The group was formed in New York's East Village in 1986. They have appeared numerous times on television, including on the *PBS Great Performances* series, with Itzhak Perlman.
The Klezmatics appeared live in June 2003 in collaboration with the Philharmonie of Jena, Germany. They have also participated in cross-cultural collaborations, notably with the Gypsy virtuoso Ferus Mustafov, Israeli singers Chava Alberstein and Ehud Banay, American singer Arlo Guthrie, and Moroccan musicians *The Master Musicians of Jajouka*.

actress whom I once admired, reading out news reports about Israeli attacks on Gaza and the fighting on the Lebanese border, which she interlaced with biblical account of Elijah's battles. When I asked her "Why do you do *that*?"– She replied: "I wanted to show that Jews were like that even back then."

This short chronological history is, of course, by no means complete. I have tried mainly to describe trends and moods. And I, personally, find something else noteworthy: I have sung Yiddish songs around the world. These concerts were almost always organised 'by Jews for Jews.' Only in three countries I did find large non-Jewish audiences. These countries were Sweden, Poland and – Germany.

Short biographies

Joan Baez (born Joan Chandos Báez on January 9, 1941) is an American folk singer, songwriter, musician, and activist. She has displayed a lifelong commitment to political and social activism in the fields of nonviolence, civil rights, human rights, and the environment.

Harold ('Harry') Belafonte, Jr. (born March 1, 1927) is an American singer, songwriter, actor, and social activist. Belafonte was an early supporter of the civil rights movement in the 1950s, and one of Martin Luther King Jr.'s confidants.

Belina (born as **Lea-Nina Rodzynek** in 1925 in Treblinka, Poland–December 12, 2006 in Hamburg) was a Jewish folk singer. She became famous as a singer in many Paris cellar bars where she appeared under the name "the Black Angel from Montparnasse." In 1954 she was engaged at the Yiddish theater in Paris. Her first record also appeared, but with that she was only successful in Germany.

Alban Berg (February 9, 1885–December 24, 1935) was an Austrian composer. He was a member of the Second Viennese School with Arnold Schoenberg and Anton Webern, and produced compositions that combined Mahlerian Romanticism with a personal adaptation of Schoenberg's twelve-tone technique. Berg is remembered as one of the most important composers of the twentieth century, and to date is the most widely performed opera composer among the Second Viennese School.

Theodore Meir Bikel (born May 2, 1924) is an Austrian-American actor, folk singer, musician, and composer. Bikel is President of the Associated Actors and Artists of America, and was president of The Actor's Equity in the late 1970s and early 1980s.

Carmela Corren (born 1938 in Tel-Aviv) is an Israeli-born singer and actress. Discovered in 1956 during a work venture in Jerusalem by American television producer Ed Sullivan, she came to New York to appear on his show. Later on she starred in several musical films and television productions. Beginning in the 1960s, Carmela Corren became fairly well known in Germany, as well as in Switzerland and Austria.

Bob Dylan (born Robert Allen Zimmerman on May 24, 1941) is an American musician, singer-songwriter, artist, and writer. He has been an influential figure in popular music and culture for more than five decades.

Regina Eichner, known as Jossy Halland (June 9, 1914 in Lübeck–September 14, 1986 in Argelès-sur-Mer) was a singer and comedian. She worked frequently abroad, including with Mistinguette and Edith Piaf. From 1959 she worked in the Lilalo cabaret in Amsterdam, where she created a furor as a singer of Yiddish songs. In the 1960s, she and her husband Jacques Halland appeared regularly on TV performing parts from their cabaret routines.

Giora Feidman (born March 26, 1936) is an Argentine-born Israeli clarinetist who specializes in klezmer music. He comes from a Bessarabian family of klezmer musicians. His father, grandfather, and great-grandfather made music for weddings, bar mitzvahs, and holiday celebrations in the shtetls of Eastern Europe. He began playing as principle clarinetist in the Buenos Aires Teatro Colón Symphony Orchestra, and later in the Israel Philharmonic Orchestra. In the early 1970s he began his solo career. He has performed with the Berliner Symphoniker, the *Kronos Quartet*, the Polish Chamber Philarmonic, the Munich Chamber Philarmonic Orchestra, and the Munich Radio Orchestra.

Sigmund Freud (May 6, 1856–September 23, 1939) was an Austrian neurologist who became known as the founding father of psychoanalysis. Freud qualified as a doctor of medicine at the University of Vienna in 1881. Freud continued to maintain his optimistic underestimation of the growing Nazi threat. He remained determined to stay in Vienna, even following the Nazi German *Anschluss* of Austria, on March 13, 1938, and the outbursts of violent anti-Semitism that ensued. However, he left for London on May 1938.

Mordechai Gebirtig, (born Mordecai Bertig, May 4, 1877 in Kraków, Austria-Hungary–June 4, 1942, Kraków Ghetto, Nazi-occupied Poland) was an influential Yiddish poet and songwriter. He was born in Krakow and lived in its Jewish working-class quarter all his life. He was killed by a Nazi bullet in the Kraków Ghetto on the infamous "Bloody Thursday" of June 4, 1942.

Henry Gerro (August 31, 1919 in Volyn province, now Ukraine–October 17, 1980 in Buenos Aires in Argentina), was an author, songwriter, violinist, singer and actor. In 1972 Gerro was awarded the Medal of the Israeli Defense Ministry.

Günter Wilhelm Grass (October 16, 1927 – April, 13 2015) was a German novelist, poet, playwright, illustrator, graphic artist, and sculptor. The recipient of the 1999 Nobel Prize in Literature, on April 4, 2012, Grass published a poem *Was gesagt werden muss* ('What Must Be Said') expressing his concern about the hypocrisy of German military support for Israel which might use German-made submarines to launch a nuclear attack against Iran. He demanded "that the governments of both Iran and Israel allow an international authority to freely inspect their nuclear capabilities," although he blamed Israel for planning a war against Iran, without sufficient evidence. In response, Israel declared him *persona non grata*.

Juliette Gréco (born February 7, 1927), is a French actress and popular chanson singer who became active in the Résistance. She spent the post liberation years frequenting the Saint Germain cafes, immersing herself in political and philosophical Bohemian culture.

Heinrich Heine (December 13, 1797–February 17, 1856) was a German poet, journalist, essayist, and literary critic. He is best known outside Germany for his early lyric poetry, which was set to music in the form of Lieder (art songs) by composers such as Robert Schumann and Franz Schubert. Heine's later verse and prose are distinguished by their satirical wit and irony. His radical political views led to many of his works being banned by German authorities. Heine spent the last 25 years of his life as an expatriate in Paris.

Friedrich Hollaender (October 18, 1896–January 18, 1976) was a German film composer and author. He was born in London, where his father, operetta composer Victor Hollaender, worked as a musical director at the Barnum & Bailey Circus. He had a solid music and theatre family background. He had to leave Nazi Germany in 1933 because of his Jewish descent, and first moved to Paris. He emigrated to the United States the next year, where he wrote the music for over a hundred films. In 1956 he returned to Germany.

Lin Jaldati (born Rebekka Brilleslijper on December 13, 1912 in Amsterdam–August 31, 1988 in East Berlin) was a Dutch singer, actress, and dancer. In July 1944 she was arrested and interned among others in the Westerbork transit camp, then sent to Auschwitz and to Bergen-Belsen. Back in Amsterdam, she embarked on concert tours in 1946. In 1952 her family moved to the GDR.

Zarah Leander (March 15, 1907–June 23, 1981) was a Swedish actress, singer, and alleged spy. During her lifetime she was accused of being a spy both for Nazi Germany and for the Soviet Union. As a result of her controversial choice to work for the state-owned Ufa in Adolf Hitler's Germany, her films and song lyrics were viewed by some as propaganda for the Nazi cause, although she took no public political position.

Rosa Luxemburg (March 5, 1871–January 15, 1919) was a Marxist theorist, philosopher, economist, and revolutionary socialist of Polish Jewish descent who became a naturalized German citizen. Due to her pointed criticism of both the Marxist-Leninist and more moderate social democrat schools of socialism, Luxemburg became a symbol of hetherodoxy among scholars and theorists of the political Left. She was murdered in January 1919, during military supression of the Spartacist uprising.

Gustav Mahler (July 7, 1860–May 18, 1911) was a late-Romantic Austrian-Jewish composer and one of the leading conductors of his generation. He was born in the village of Kalischt, Bohemia (then part of the Austrian Empire, now Kaliště in the Czech Republic). His family later moved to nearby Iglau (now Jihlava), where Mahler grew up. As a composer, he acted as a bridge between the nineteenth century Austro-German tradition and the modernism of the early twentieth century.

The **Malavsky family** was a Jewish-American family who appeared throughout the Jewish world in concerts of cantorial and Jewish folk music. The family first performed in San Francisco in 1945, and later throughout the United States, performing cantorial music, jazz and Jewish songs both in Hebrew and in Yiddish.

Esther Ofarim (in Hebrew: אסתר עופרים, born June 13, 1941) is an Israeli singer. She was born in Safed to a Syrian Jewish family. She began performing as a child, singing Hebrew and international folk songs. In 1960 Esther landed a small role in the film *Exodus*. In 1961, she won the Song Festival in Tel Aviv. Two years later, she won second place in the 1963 Eurovision Song Contest with *T'en vas pas*, a song representing Switzerland. Together with her husband Abi they became world famous in the 1960. Esther lives in Germany, and still gives sold out concerts in Israel and Europe.

Paul Leroy Robeson (April 9, 1898–January 23, 1976) was an American singer and actor. He was active in the Civil Rights Movement. From the 1930s Robeson included Yiddish songs prominent in his concerts.

Peter Rohland (February 22, 1933 in Berlin–April 5, 1966 in Freiburg im Breisgau) was a German singer, songwriter, and folk song researcher. Influenced by a tape with Yiddish songs of Theodore Bikel, Rohland developed a Yiddish songs program – *The Rebbe*, which premiered in 1963 with a small ensemble in one gallery in Berlin. It was successful in student and academic circles, as well as among German Jewish communities. The songs on the program were recorded for the youth radio in the studio, however, no record company was willing to edit an LP. They claimed "obvious concerns about the authenticity of the songs." Rohland died of an acute cerebral hemorrhage in the University Hospital of Freiburg at the age of only 33 years.

Havatselet Ron (in Hebrew חבצלת רון, born as Havatselet Damari in Aden in 1936, passed away 2013 in Los Angeles), was a Jewish Yemenite singer who migrated to Israel when she was eight and lived in Kfar Shalem – a poor neighborhood in South East Tel Aviv. In the 1950s she produced an LP with original Yemenite songs in Hebrew, that was a complete failure in Israel. She recorded several songs in German, Yiddish, English, and Hebrew, and used to appear on East German TV 1963/64. At the end of the 1960s she returned to Israel and retired from music.

Peter ('Pete') Seeger (May 3, 1919–January 27, 2014) was an American folk singer and activist. Seeger reemerged on the public scene as a prominent singer of protest music in support of international disarmament, civil rights, the counterculture, and environmental causes.

Richard Wagner (May 22, 1813–February 13, 1883) was a German composer, theatre director, polemicist, and conductor who is primarily known for his operas (later known as "music dramas"). Unlike most opera composers, Wagner wrote both the libretto and the music for each of his stage works. Initially considered a romantic composer, Wagner revolutionised opera with his concept of the *Gesamtkunstwerk* (total work of art), through which he sought to synthesise the poetic, visual, musical and dramatic arts, with music subsidiary to drama. He announced this path in a series of essays written between 1849 and 1852. Wagner's life was characterised by political exile, turbulent love affairs, poverty, and repeated flight from his creditors. His controversial writings on music, drama, and politics have attracted extensive comment in recent decades, especially since they express harsh antisemitic sentiments. Due to his association with antisemitism as well as the Nazis' admiration of his work, performance of Wagner's music in the State of Israel, or in front of Holocaust survivors, has provoked public rejection and sour debates.

Ben-Zion Witler (1907–1961, from Belz, Galicia), was a Jewish singer, actor, coupletist, comedian, and composer. His family moved to Vienna in 1919, and from 1926, he was active in the Vienna theater scene. Starting in 1940, he toured the United States, playing at New York City and Chicago. In 1946 he toured Argentina (Buenos Aires). He performed with Argentinian-born actress Shifra Lerer, who became his wife, appearing in North and South America, Israel, and South Africa through the 1950s.

Zachary Johnston
Aliyah Le Berlin

A Documentary about the Next Chapter of Jewish Life in Berlin

Jewish roots in Berlin date back to the year 1295. Jews have had a tumultuous existence in Berlin, Germany, and Europe to say the least. In 1573 the Brandenburg Jews were expelled from Berlin "for all eternity" (although that did not last even a century). In 1933 the Nazi government took power the same year the first Jewish Museum opened in Berlin. Twelve years and a human apocalypse later, Berlin's Jews were almost all gone. Yet, the fascist attempt to exterminate the Jews of the world was a failure, although massive damage was inflicted on Europe's Jewish population. Some 5,000 Jews, however, stayed in Berlin after the war. Over the last 70 years, Jews have been returning to Europe. Berlin is seeing the highest return rates of any city worldwide. Surprisingly, many of these Jews are coming from Israel. *Aliyah Le Berlin* ('Making *Aliyah* to Berlin') is a documentary film about the next chapter of Jewish life in Berlin.

Berlin holds a special place in the history of Judaism. Berlin was home to Moses Mendelssohn, a Jewish thinker who forever changed the face of Judaism and the direction it took, entering the modern world. There is more to Berlin's Jewish history than just Moses Mendelssohn: Leo Baeck, Regina Jonas, David Friedländer, Daniel Itzig, Zacharias Frankel, and Abraham Geiger to name just a few. Rabbis and scholars that ended up in the United States, Canada, and even the UK often came from Berlin and brought with them the reform, liberal, and conservative forms of Jewish practice that Berlin's community and schools gave birth to and nurtured. Today, these streams of Judaism dominate modern Jewish life worldwide. Through the Jewish Enlightenment (*Haskalah*) Jews received broad educations equal to other citizens, assimilated into local cultures, while at the same time establishing the foundations for transformation of Hebrew into a living tongue, with the help of Hebraists such as Bernhard Bär, Wolf Heidenheim, and Solomon Frensdorff. Even if some these men did not hail from Berlin *per se*, they worked in Berlin and collaborated directly with the schools and scholars of Berlin.

Twelve years of National Socialism sought to exterminate the Jews "for all eternity," but failed. I am not a scholar of Jewish history or philosophy. I am a non-Jewish filmmaker living in Berlin. I am not writing this chapter as a thesis on the Jewish Enlightenment. This chapter is dedicated to exploring and perhaps enlightening the reader about the current status of Israelis and Jews living and working in Berlin in the early twenty-first century – the subject of my documentary film *Aliyah Le Berlin*. In it, I have sought to understand what motivates young Israelis to settle in Berlin, but that is only a small part of the story. The story lies in what these immigrants do when they are here, how their lives are enriched and challenged by being in Berlin, and what they add to the culture of the place they have chosen to call their home.

One cannot use the term '*aliyah*' out-of-context without eliciting a knee-jerk response due to its value-loaded nature of the word, which is tied to the 'ascent' of Jews to Israel. Yet, to 'make *aliyah*' is not only a ritual, but also an aspiration, a spiritual act for the Jew. We use it here with both irony and purpose. Our aim is contrarian, to challenge the traditional concept of *aliyah*, and the Israeli concept of its counterpart – *yeridah* or 'to go down' or emigrate from Israel – suggesting that perchance one does not 'descend' when they leave Israel. Perhaps, this new age of Israeli and Jewish exploration in Germany has a higher purpose that has yet to be ascertained, that down the road the concept of *aliyah* will receive a something deeper, stronger, and broader meaning for the nation of Israel and its citizens.

To the layperson's eye, the reasons for anyone – Israeli, American, British, or other – to relocate to Berlin is self-evident. It is cheap, hip, and fun. The only major downside is a long, cold winter. Who would not want that triad of living easy? Berlin has sold itself as 'poor, but sexy' thanks to the branding efforts of Berlin mayor Klaus Wowereit – the product of a well-oiled propaganda machine of the highest form. The image appeals to young hipsters that seek individuality above conformity, while staunchly allowing even the anarchist and the most contrarian mind the freedom to beat their own path in this world. Berlin has strived through initiatives, business deals, co-operations, public relation advertising, and sheer might to create a very enticing atmosphere for creative individuals, entrepreneurs, parents, lovers – from the lost souls to the people ready to conquer the world.

Let's go back a bit first. Mendelssohn's Enlightenment is a fitting place to begin. I believe there are two outcomes of Mendelssohn's Jewish Enlightenment relevant to an examination of Israelis in Berlin today. The near *en masse* assimilation of Berlin's Jewish population into Germanic culture by the late nineteenth century, and the birth of modern Zionism were the growth medium for the emergence of the modern Hebrew language. This Jewish Enlightenment (a 'Jewish reformation,' in a sense) had an astounding effect on Judaism and its inclusion into European cultures. At the same time, these forces of modernity on Jewish life brought about new-found aspirations and desires to return to the Land of Israel and began the transformation of Hebrew back into the living vernacular of the Jewish people as part of a national revival. So, yes, Berlin is hip and cheap to live in for *all* free spirits, however, it is no coincidence that Israeli Jews and European

Jews are migrating to the city in record numbers. Something transformative has happened on German soil more than once. It is happening again.

The twentieth century brought hardship and near extermination of European Jewry, blind to the unprecedented assimilation and the deep affinity and sense of kinship with German culture that exemplified German Jews. We all know the history of the National Socialist era and the atrocities it produced. The legacy of the Holocaust that Nazism wrought has led two to three generations of Israelis to possess sweeping, albeit at times understandable, apprehensions and uneasiness even in mundane contacts with Germans. Take words such as *Achtung* ('attention') over public address systems, or *raus* ('get out') employed in normal discourse today; they ring very differently in an Israeli ear than an American or Spaniard ear. Yet, now, three generations after the close of the Nazi era, the grandchildren of men and women who lived through the horrors of the Holocaust are returning to a very place where such atrocities originated and were, at times, carried out.

It is important not to forget the estimated 5,000 German Jews who remained in Berlin at the close of the war. They were a hidden minority, quietly going about life, worshipping in rundown synagogues, remaining out of the public's view, yet, maintaining the last grasp on Berlin's Jewish heritage. Yet, this small, albeit important community provided a foundation for the expanding of Jewish life in Berlin today. Without this community's efforts to maintain synagogues, traditions, and a Berlin Jewish identity, might have been lost forever.

Israelis have been coming to Berlin since the 1950s. This is not something new. The reasons for this influx have always been as varied as the people coming here. There were many waves of Israelis, decade-by-decade. What sets the most recent wave apart is more tangible than previous generations: Public action. Almost the converse of the quietude that typified the postwar German Jewish community, the new Jewish community is unabashedly on display (sometimes literally) for the world to see.

A New Zion?

Many of the Israelis who came to Berlin prior to the year 2000 seem to have assimilated into Berlin culture. They came before the Berlin Wall came down, to live in what was then 'trendy West Berlin': the swinging soho of the city in Kreuzberg and Schöneberg. There were artists, actors, and social misfits (not unlike today). Now, however, it is more common for an Israeli to find a home in trendy East Berlin – in neighborhoods such as Friedrichshain, Prenzlauer Berg, and Mitte (although there is no reason to fret: The old West Berlin is still represented by a large population of Israelis living in Kreuzberg and Charlottenburg).

Five years ago, I knew there were Israelis living in Berlin. Once and a while one could spy a poster for an event. A blue Star of David would catch your eye, attached to a window or lamppost. In 2012 the movement of people and ideas surfaced in Berlin under the impact of the social media. Israelis in Berlin became a 'Facebook sensation.' There are currently over 7,000 active members of Berlin Israelis' Facebook account. This forum allows Israelis to prepare for the move to Berlin – it even helps many make the decision. Most importantly, it provides a singular place where Israelis, and by default Jews from all over, can navigate life in the German capital in a familiar and 'safe' place (the group is private). Israeli-themed club nights became regular venues for boozing and dancing. Hummus restaurants began to pop up in boroughs such as Prenzlauer Berg, Mitte, and Kreuzberg with unabashed Israeli themes and menus. Entrepreneurial spirits began holding events and artists began to be represented at citywide art shows. Hebrew can often be heard on the streets or while waiting at an *U-Bahn-Station* ('subway station'). With this population came life, art, music, food, and a population searching for new meaning – heralding a new era.

Another facet of Berlin's Jewish life that attracts many Jewish people from Europe and Israel is the Abraham Geiger College. Israelis, Hungarian, French, German, and Polish Jews (among others) have come to enroll in its Jewish Studies programs. In Berlin, one encounters 'hipster rabbinical students' – many of whom have not felt at home in study or worship available in their home countries and have chosen Berlin to follow their spiritual path. This raises an interesting point: Many people perceive Israelis flocking to Berlin as a form of escapism, or running away from Israeli politics or society. Yet, when one looks deeper into what these Israelis are doing in Berlin, it becomes clear that they are not running away; they are running *towards* their Israeliness, Jewishness and even Hebrew.

There are initiatives such as *Hamakom* ('The Place') created by Israelis, German and Croatian Jews as a forum for Jewish thought that some have found absent from mainstream Israeli Judaism. Berlin provides an open, seemingly liberated atmosphere for Judaic exploration. For many Israelis coming to Berlin, they suddenly find spirituality coming to the fore in their lives. Many Israelis have conveyed that in Israel 'being Jewish' is often taken for granted, normative to a point of banality, and often without any Jewish spiritual dimension. When they arrive in Berlin and find themselves living in a culture where Judaism (and Hebrew) is not central to the society, the desire for spirituality is sparked and its role in their lives becomes amplified. Of course, this is not true for every Israeli living in Berlin. In fact, the opposite is true for some, and their retreat from Israel is also an abandoning of their Jewish identity; but I would argue, based on my research, that they are the minority. To find evidence of this, one does not have to look far: Initiatives like *Hamakom* host events devoted to study of Torah, Talmud and Jewish philosophy, and prayer. *Hamakom* works with rabbinical students, other initiatives, and even the World Zionist Organization to bring the beauty of Judaism to a new generation of people that seek a (re)connection with God, or wish to incorporate the traditions of Judaism as a culture in their own lives in Berlin, or simply seek an open and egalitarian space for Judaism in their daily lives. It would be false to say these people are running from Israel and Judaism.

Moreover, by organizing events that bring various ethnicities of Jews, Germans and Israelis together, a healing process has been set in motion, although this may not have been a direct objective of *Hamakom* or any initiative operating in Berlin today. Thus, one witnesses how, for the first time, Germans are being asked to talk about the guilt they carry, alongside Israelis and Jews conversing about the same issues. This is not just happening in brief 'sponsored forums' – meeting grounds where each party flies back to their respective homeland after the discussion. This is happening in a place where the homes they go back to are in Berlin. That makes a difference.

The Emergence of a 'Berliner Hebrew'

Modern Hebrew was born in Berlin, its seeds planted by the Jewish Enlightenment. Hebrew does not 'hide' in present-day Berlin. There is Hebrew on memorials, of course, but Hebrew is also being used in a new and interesting way. It is being used as a vehicle to examine the city of Berlin – its culture, politics, and very essence. A prime example of this phenomenon is *Spitz Magazine*, a well-received and well-constructed Hebrew-language publication that endows Israelis and Hebrew-speaking Russians or Germans (and others who know Hebrew) with the ability to conduct a discourse about Berlin in their own tongue. After all, a qualitative and serious discourse and the insights it can provide about Berlin life, politics, and society rest on nuances of language.

Hebrew, like all languages, is in constant flux. All language is descriptive, not prescriptive. What one sees now in Hebrew print and speech is Berliner or German words and phrases sneaking into the lexicon. One has to ask, when will 'Berliner-slang Hebrew' be official? Is it already so? When will these Berliner-slang terms make their way back to Israeli Hebrew? Or will Israeli Hebrew evolve in a way Berliner Hebrew may not? Or will the divergences be more geographical, as in American, Indian, and British English? Modern Hebrew being born, in part, in Berlin and, now returning to Berlin, is no coincidence. It makes sense that people like Tal Alon via *Spitz Magazine* finds success bringing her Hebrew language to a lost 'ancestral' home of sorts. Hebrew simply does not share the same connection to other cities outside of Israel the way it does Germany and Berlin. Julius Fürst, Bernhard Bär, Wolf Heidenheim, and Solomon Frensdorff (amongst others) birthed Hebrew into the modern world – not from Israel, but from Berlin and Germany. These scholars provided the foundational labor that would lead men like Eliezer Ben-Yehuda to turn Hebrew into the practical, utilitarian modern language it is today.

There is another language that adds to the ease of integration and interactions in Berlin: English became unofficially a 'second vernacular' in Berlin after 2006 when Germany hosted the World Cup. English became a normal part of day-to-day life in Berlin after public transportation added English to announcements and signage – amongst various other manifestations of English usage around the city. The city's image was boosted from the international exposure, and Mayor Wowereit's active and trendy campaigns. Airlines began flying more frequently between Israel and Berlin. English became the vehicle by which both Israelis and Berliners communicate with one another, although as more Israelis perfect their German, this trend will wane. This also provided a common tongue for Jews of various origins to integrate into the city. In the Jewish community Hebrew is their common tongue, while outside of that circle, English is the *lingua franca*. Most Jews and Israelis know these two languages.

Mastery of Hebrew is becoming a standard for children at home, and even in kindergarten, primary, and secondary schools. Berlin has no shortage of Jewish-themed schools for children of all ages and denominations. Children of Israeli-born parents or mixed parents often speak Hebrew with one parent at home and learn German in kindergarten or school – while some are sent to schools where English or French is the primary languages. There are a myriad of child-oriented frameworks for newborns to young adults across Berlin offering classes, playgroups, and general activities in Hebrew. It is fairly simple for a parent to find a Jewish holiday event in Hebrew somewhere in Berlin, if not half a dozen events – depending on how religiously observant one happen to be. This, again, is empowered by social media and this generation's total embrace of it. Advertising, one could say, has never been freer for the individual to use.

The Hebrew Library serves as a bastion of Hebrew culture for adults and children. Currently held in the curator's home, Michal Zamir's *Hebrew Library* is a place for Israelis (and Hebrew-speakers or learners) to find Hebrew books and expand their own collections. It also hosts events, generally in Hebrew, that brings Israeli authors, scholars, and artists to Berlin. For children, there is a monthly reading club whose content usually centers on Jewish holidays, allowing children to mingle and speak Hebrew outside their homes or educational institutions. A common thread among the Israelis behind these initiatives and collectives is that the profit motive is viewed as secondary to the opportunity to access a Hebrew-Israel and Jewish ambience.

Hummus and What Follows...

There is no denying that Berlin is a multicultural city. Berlin is a city with a mosaic quality, marked by its culinary variety – from Turkish kebab huts to Vietnamese pho houses, Russian supermarkets, and American burger joints, to bars of every genre one could dream of. All of them are teeming with artists, musicians, writers, businessmen, diplomats, tourists, and everything in between.

Israeli culture has been introduced and accepted within this Berlin mix. One does not have to look far to find hummus and pita. If you want an Israeli night, where Hebrew is the dominant language heard floating about the club as Israeli music blasts from speakers, you do not have to look far either. Most immigrants bring parts of their cultural baggage with them whatever their destination, and Israelis in Berlin are no exception; what is exceptional about Israelis and Jews in Berlin is the shared past. Seventy-five years ago, a Star of David in Berlin signified something foreign and sinister to Berliners; now it is a signpost for a great night at a club, or a film festival, or a good falafel. But the Israeli mark on the local cultural scene is not just about hummus and Stars of David. Israeli chefs are creating world-class cuisine... in Berlin. Artists are presenting Berlin through their Israeli or Jewish eyes in a way Berlin has never been perceived before. Musicians are revitalizing the old or creating things fresh and untried. Berlin provides the permissive atmosphere, but Israelis are the ones taking advantage of Berlin's openness. These new creations transcend national-ethnic origins or tradition, and promote and speak on behalf of the evolution of a society as a whole. People are asking themselves what it means to be Israeli, to be Jewish, to be a Berliner. How does one era of the past affect me more than another era of the past? The answers to those questions bubble to the surface in the way people are choosing to live their lives, create their art, and raise their children in Berlin.

Another aspect of Israeli life in Berlin is the development of a transnational identity. It has become fairly easy and affordable to keep one foot in Berlin and one foot in Israel. The idea of an expat going off to some foreign land and never being heard from again is dead in the social media age. It is easier to 'import' foods from home when you can just fly home, fill up a suitcase, and fly back to Berlin. Yet, there is more to this transnational identity on a deeper level, one that draws on a shared past that all Israelis have. Israel is a country of immigrants, where a significant portion of the population has experienced 'other lives' before they made *aliyah* to Israel. In the act of immigration newcomers shed large parts of their origin identity to become Israeli, whether these new Israelis hailed from Morocco or France or even the United States. While the same acculturation process exists in Berlin – the possibility of a transition from Israeli Jew to German is loaded. Despite patterns to the contrary, Jews in Israel harbor fears that the offspring of the people who shaped and built Israel at tremendous cost, will 'lose a generation' of Israelis to German assimilation. Is this fear valid? Not necessarily. Israelis are living in Berlin, some have embraced a Berliner lifestyle, but Hebrew, Judaism, and Israel are omnipresent in most of their lives. Coming from Israel, the memory of transition is still fresh and many maintain their Israeli identity and, in fact – perhaps ironically, find it easier to expand upon their Israeli identity in Germany than at home in Israel. In Germany, and Berlin, being Israeli or Jewish means something special to the individual. An aspect of your life is highlighted by default, and then the individual starts to look at their identity in a new light.

What the Future May Hold

The uprooting of a person from his place of birth to settle elsewhere is often seen as a negative for the nation abandoned and as a positive by the nation gaining a new citizen. The émigré is viewed at home as a loss to the workforce, while scientists and scholar are seen as a brain drain. One need look no further than the two Israeli citizens out of the three 2013 Nobel Prize laureates in chemistry – Arieh Warshel and Michael Levitt – whose breakthrough research was conducted in the United States, in order to grasp the enormity of the problem of a brain drain. Is the current trend of Israelis immigrating to Berlin a brain drain on Israeli society? It is hard to pin down, since Israelis in Berlin are not necessarily immigrants in the classic sense. I have used the term 'transnationals' for a reason: Israelis in Berlin travel home often, their families are still rooted in Israel, and therefore their identities and allegiances and even their center of gravity has not shifted. Israel, Hebrew, and Judaism occupy a large part of their lives in a host of ways. Current Jewish culture and Israeli culture in Berlin is about *integration*, not assimilation. By bringing these cultures to Berlin, it becomes impossible to leave them behind or abandon them in Israel.

A phenomenon can be remarkable, but, it can also be merely something that is observable – plain and simple. Israelis coming to Berlin is a phenomenon, and many people tend to ask whether or not it is a remarkable one. Over the last years there has been a mini-explosion of media and filmic coverage of this niche migrant group. Israelis moving to Berlin have fascinated Danish, French, British, American, Israeli, and German news outlets. Often, however, fascination borders more on perplexion and suspicion – dismay if you wish, than objective and acute reportage. It is common to see Israeli or German news teams, cameraman in tow, interviewing Israelis at public events. The Israeli news-gathers tend to want to know how one can survive in Berlin as an artist without money. The Germans want to know how the Israelis deal with the history… in the subtext, asking 'whether they are forgiven yet.' Today's Berliners would be proud to say they were 'the generation and the place where Israeli Jews forgave the Germans'… Yet, for many Israeli Jews, moving to Berlin is not about forgiveness and history. It is about a personal journey – an artistic endeavor, a spiritual awakening, bacchanalian nights, and ancestral stirrings. Having said that, nevertheless, for some there *is* a catharsis to be found in Berlin. It is easy to find Israelis in Berlin whose family was not directly affected by the Holocaust. Israelis from Moroccan or Iranian families, and members of minority groups have relationships with the Holocaust shaped by Israeli education, not by personal-familial experience. This is a distinction that is important to Israelis in Berlin. The baggage that comes along with Germany and Berlin and places like Wannsee or Ravensbrück have become a shared Jewish-ergo-Israeli heritage. Even if the Israeli or Jewish person living in Berlin has no direct connection to the Holocaust, its markers and echoes still ring true in their ears as they live in Berlin, amongst its ghosts.

Many Israelis are looking for a new definition of what it means to be 'Israeli' – a definition that does not focus on Jewish powerlessness and vulnerability, of genocide and victimhood. Nor do they seek an identity tied to media propaganda, sirens and traumatic 'breaking news' loops. They seek an Israeli identity and culture that venerates Jewish philosophers, artists, chemists, physicists, and writers (even the ones that do not fit into a specific national-oriented cone of influence). They seek to enlighten the world that there is more to Israel and being Israeli, or even being Jewish than settlements, occupations, and intifadas. There is a deep and beautiful culture behind the strife, one that is young and trying to find its footing in the world. Furthermore, it is not the desire of any Israeli in Berlin to ignore the Nazi past founded in Munich and executed in Berlin. Israeli Jews seem to be clearly saying that there is more to the intersection of Berlin, Judaism, Israel, and Germany than just the Holocaust, arms deals and politicalization. The past and present can also be something to be explored, utilized, and respected as a whole.

Making Aliyah to Berlin: The Documentary

Aliyah Le Berlin tells the story of Israeli, American, Hungarian, Croatian, German and Polish Jews who are returning to Berlin to start a new life, or continue an existing one. Often when an Israeli decides to move to Berlin, trepidation and worry runs through the family. ('How safe is it for Jews these days? How safe is it for MY daughter or son to walk the streets at night in a capital with such a terrifying history?') Of course, these individuals do not board a time machine and travel back to Berlin in 1942 (or another pogrom-filled era.) They are simply getting on a commercial airliner bound for a modern cosmopolis – a city that hosts one of the most vibrant art scenes on earth, becoming more multicultural every day, a place rife with opportunity and hope.

Aliyah Le Berlin weaves the stories of ten Jews (and three expert observers) as they navigate Berlin's scenes and adjust to a world where Hebrew and Judaism are not center stage. They deal with all aspects of Jewish history and life – from the birth of modern Hebrew to its current evolution towards a Berliner slang, encountering Holocaust memorials on a daily, sometimes on an hourly basis when on the streets, and rediscovering a Judaism that for some was long dormant in their own hearts.

Aliyah Le Berlin uses Moses Mendelssohn's personal history and Berlin as the 'cradle' of Jewish Enlightenment (the *Haskalah*) as a framing device to emphasize the current influx and 'neo-reformation' experienced by today's Jews in Berlin. Step-by-step, we see how Moses entered the city as a young, homeless hunchback and began learning, exploring, and creating. Similarly we follow Israelis as they run Hebrew libraries, a Hebrew magazine, and various Israeli missions to connect their islands of Israeliness and Hebrew with mainstream Berliner culture. From there, the film turns to focus on members of the community who have a direct connection with the Holocaust who are in Berlin today: Viewers meet Henry Wassermann – hero of Israel's wars, a retired scholar and expert of German-Israeli relations, and a Holocaust survivor who speaks of his life in Israel, his life in Berlin, and his memories of his deaf father's desperate and successful mission to save his family from the Nazis in Poland. After the harrowing portrayal of life in a city so closely connected to his family's near extermination, the film shifts focus to Mendelssohn's Jewish reformation and its impact on Judaism, then examine the 'neo-reformation' afoot within Judaism in Berlin today. German, Croatian, Hungarian, and Israeli Jews speak about how Judaism is changing for them, by being in Berlin. We explore their burgeoning world – filled with initiatives, events, and new community frameworks that are blossoming in the German capital. What emerges is a blend of transnationalism supported by a population that thrives in their cosmopolitanism, without jettisoning their particularism as Jews, as they seek a higher truth.

What we discovered is not a community on the run; but a community that is growing, taking liberties, and empowering Judaism, Hebrew, and Israeli culture. As a community, they ask questions about the past, the present and the future; as a movement of people, the past is being illuminated in ways that it has not been addressed for decades. People are again exploring the merits of groundbreaking philosophies and teachings of German-Jewish thinkers such as Mendelssohn, Baeck, Jonas, Fürst, and others. This film and the topics it addresses serve, in essence, as a 'reintroduction' for a broader audience to the ideas of these German-Jewish scholars, inviting German viewers to further investigate the shared legacy of the past they carry. Because of the hub of German-Jewish scholarship blossoming in Berlin, the way we talk about Germany, Berlin, and Jews is forever being changed. As a result, what Jews teach their children in the next generation will differ from what their parents and grandparents were taught. For the last 70 years when one spoke of Germany, Berlin, and Jews, the dominant theme was the Holocaust, and rightfully so; however, when the next generation learns about Berlin and Jews, the dominant theme may very well center on Berlin as Europe's largest and most vibrant Jewish community – a phoenix arisen. Will this invite a sequel to *Making Aliyah to Berlin*? In cinematography we say 'everyone loves a comeback story.'

Of all the capitals of Europe, of all Europe's diverse cities, none have as deep and profound a relationship with Judaism and Israel as Berlin has. Judaism and Berlin are invariably intertwined, for better or for worst. No other city in Europe, perhaps no other city in the world makes more sense for Jews to call home – to reclaim as their home. Jews have 795-year-long history with Berlin. The multitudes of Jews coming to Berlin today are not letting twelve dark years obliterate that history, or overshadow and dominate the future of what will come tomorrow "for all eternity."

Ghosts of the Past, Challenges of the Present: Germany Facing Old-New Anti-Semitism

Monika Schwarz-Friesel
Educated Anti-Semitism in the Middle of German Society

Empirical Findings

> 'From a realpolitik German perspective à la Merkel I must say that seven million dead Jews, as horrible as this might be, is soberly considered still better than seven billion dead people caused by the Jews' brutal world domination.'
>
> ("Aus Sicht eines realpolitischen Deutschlands a la Merkel muss man sagen, dass sieben Millionen tote Juden, so schlimm das auch wäre, aber nüchtern betrachtet besser wären als sieben Milliarden tote Menschen wegen der jüdischen brutalen Weltherrschaft.")[1]

The experience of the Holocaust and dealing with the lethal ideology that led to Auschwitz did not bring the strategies of verbally dehumanizing and demonizing the Jews to an end. Such strategies prevail and are frequently used in modern discourse even by highly educated people from mainstream society. More, anti-Semitism is on the rise, both in Germany and in Europe. In the twenty-first century, the official ban on anti-Semitic utterances has lost its influence: The articulation of traditional anti-Semitic stereotypes by projecting them on Israel has increased significantly. At the same time, there is a noticeable rejection of the results from research on anti-Semitism in mainstream society. One of the dominant strategies of dealing with actual anti-Semitism in German public discourse is to deny the very existence of it. This article shows that the age-old basic Jew hatred is alive in the middle of German society and that is by no means a sole phenomenon among Right- or Left-wing extremists. Based on extensive empirical data, it is explained how anti-Semitism under the guise of criticism of Israel is articulated also in the public space: Bashing Israel by evoking traditional judeophobic stereotypes is by now the most common strategy of contemporary anti-Semitism. In spite of the knowledge about the Holocaust, as well as to what consequences rhetoric of hate and hostility might have, Jews are frequently attacked verbally in contemporary discourse. Anti-Judaism proves to be to be both a persistent and a central way of thinking and feeling in the Western tradition – neither unshaken nor destroyed by the experience of Auschwitz.

---

[1] IBB_21.2.2013; e-mail from a social scientist with a PhD; member of the political party DIE LINKE, sent to the Israeli embassy in Berlin, February 2013.

Conceptual and Verbal Anti-Semitism: Theoretical and Methodological Considerations

There is a long and cherished illusion in modern German society that anti-Semitism after 1945 is either a past historical phenomenon or is nurtured in its contemporary form only by Right-wing extremists at the edges of society. Yet, recent empirical findings of extensive corpus studies show that anti-Semitism exists at the center of German society as well.[2]

Hostility towards Jews in modern society, known as anti-Semitism, has many manifestations: For hundreds of years, this hostility has lead to physical violence against Jews and Jewish institutions and to social discrimination of Jews.[3] It has been articulated through manifold utterances that stigmatize and abuse Jews.[4] Through the vehicle of language, anti-Semitic stereotypes have been kept alive for hundreds of years. By repetitive use of certain linguistic patterns, prejudice against Jews is preserved along the ages and transported to modern discourse, often without reflecting the consequences. Hence, anti-Semitism can be seen as a cultural code engraved in collective memory.[5]

In postwar German society, following the collapse of the Nazi regime, the issue of Jew-hatred was stigmatized and treated as a taboo in public discourse, however, the official ban and social taboo against anti-Semitism are beginning to loose their grip. A significant increase in verbal anti-Semitism can be noticed on the internet, especially on common home- and webpages etc. that are frequently used in everyday life.[6] Facilitated by the nature of electronic communication, traditional stereotypes and the old blood libels and conspiracy theories about Jews are now widely spread on the Internet.

> 'Why are Jews always so very mean?' ("Wieso sind Juden immer so böse?")[7]

This question presupposing and stating the collective malevolence of Jews as a fact was not articulated by some neo-Nazi or extremist on the internet but posted

---

[2] Schwarz-Friesel / Reinharz, Die Sprache der Judenfeindschaft, 2012; Bundesministerium des Innern (ed.), Antisemitismus in Deutschland, 2011.
[3] Low, Jews in the Eyes of the Germans, 1979; Poliakov, The History of Antisemitism, 1985; Laqueur, The Changing Face of Antisemitism, 2006.
[4] Bering, Der Name als Stigma, 1991; Reisigl / Wodak, Discourse and Discrimination, 2001; Hortzitz, Die Sprache der Judenfeindschaft, 2005.
[5] Volkov, Antisemitism as a Cultural Code, 1978.
[6] Schwarz-Friesel, "Juden sind zum Töten da," 2013.
[7] www.gutefrage.net, asked by 'MissSchool', January 1, 2011.

in a forum ('Good Question') used by high school students searching for background knowledge. It could be seen and commented on for almost two years in spite of the rebuking and critical comments by some of the users. In mainstream press, letters to the editor that contain judeophobic argumentation have tripled in the last ten years.[8]

There is an increased acceptance of anti-Semitic beliefs in the appearance of anti-Israelism in public discourse at every level of society, including the universities, the elite and mass media. Accordingly, recent polls show persistently that more than 40 percent of the persons asked hold the opinion that Israel is conducting a war of extermination against the Palestinians and are no better than the Nazis.[9] Caricatures and cartoons presenting Israelis as bloodthirsty murderers and evil tyrants oppressing and killing children are frequently exhibited in the public sphere (see, for instance the "wailing wall" [*Klagemauer*] in Cologne) and also published in the media (see the caricature of Israel as a monster published in *Süddeutsche Zeitung*[10]). Today, while racist anti-Semitism is still a tabooed subject and widely rejected in mainstream society, there are no restrictions whatsoever in rhetoric and hate speech when it comes to bashing Israel by means of verbal anti-Semitism.

Dealing with anti-Semitism in the twenty-first century leads to the following questions: Which traditional anti-Semitic stereotypes are still articulated in modern discourse? Have new stereotypes and argumentation patterns emerged and become a matter of habit? Have years of coping with the past, years of remembrance and education, socially tabooing and legally-banning anti-Semitic utterances from public discourse brought about any significant changes? Does the collective awareness regarding the dangers of discriminating rhetorics and hate speech prevent the use and articulation of such verbal means and communicative strategies in mainstream society? At least, do educated people show some responsibility in their use of language?

Our research group has been examining the verbal manifestations of contemporary anti-Semitism in Germany since 2002. We analyzed thousands of utterances in contemporary discourse on both Jews/Judaism and on Israel. The data was described within the interdisciplinary framework of cognitive science and combined with the results of the historical research on Jew-hatred.

---

8 Schwarz-Friesel / Friesel / Reinharz (eds.), Aktueller Antisemitismus in Deutschland, 2010; Schwarz-Friesel, *Explizite und implizite Formen*, 2013.
9 See ADL – Anti-Defamation League (ed.), Attitudes Toward Jews in Seven European Countries, 2009; European Union Agency for Fundamental Rights (ed.), Antisemitism, 2009.
10 Süddeutsche Zeitung, July 2, 2013, p. 15.

The underlying assumption is that language plays a crucial role in activating and re-activating judeophobic resentment and that verbal utterances give significant insight into their underlying mental stereotypes. Thus, to identify the semantics of anti-Semitic utterances is to understand the mental attitude towards Jews. Verbal structures do not only construct negative conceptualizations of Jews but they also reproduce them continually and hence validate the existence of mental anti-Semitism in the cultural and communicative memory of society. According to our definition, anti-Semitism is a hostile conceptualization of Jews based on mental stereotypes. Many of those stereotypes have a long tradition and they are passed from generation to generation by the repetitive use of verbally expressed clichés. Historical research has shown that hostility towards Jews never has been restricted to the lower classes; rather, it has always been articulated also by people with a high educational level.[11] Focusing on the nineteenth century, it shows that hostility against Jews was articulated by philosophers like Hegel, writers like Fontane, artists like Wagner, historians and professors like Treitschke, politicians and preachers like Stoecker.[12] Thus, anti-Semitism never has been, only or mainly, a phenomenon at the edges of society. In fact, history reveals that anti-Jewish thought can be found at the very foundation of Western worldviews.[13]

Fundamentally, conceptual anti-Semitism is to be understood as a negative attitude towards Jews and Judaism that is deeply influenced by representations of collective memory and has a strong emotional component. It functions as a belief system that strongly determines the world view of anti-Semites. The basis of this mental model is a distorted picture of Jews as 'the evil others' that has nothing to do with facts or experience. An utterance like an e-mail sent to the Central Council of Jews in Germany in 2009, reflects this phenomenon clearly:

> 'Personally, I don't know any person from Israel or of Jewish belief, but I hate you for being so cruel to the poor Palestinians.'
> ("Ich kenne persönlich keinen einzigen Menschen aus Israel oder jüdischen Glaubens, aber ich hasse Sie, weil Sie so grausam mit den armen Palästinensern umgehen.")[14]

The concept 'Jew' is based on an abstract representation, on a conception of Jews which has nothing to do with facts. Jews are not discriminated against because

---

[11] See Katz, From Prejudice to Destruction, 1980; Almog, (ed.), Antisemitism through the Ages, 1988; Volkov, 1978.
[12] For examples of such utterances see Schwarz-Friesel / Reinharz, 2013, chapter 3.
[13] See Wistrich, Antisemitism, 1991; Wistrich, A Lethal Obsession, 2010; Schwarz-Friesel / Reinharz, 2013; Nirenberg, Anti-Judaism, 2013.
[14] ZJD_Gaza 2009_66/816_Her.

of what they did or do, but *because* they are Jews. Their mere existence is seen as a threat to mankind, a provocation to society, a challenge to cope with. Exactly this ideology led to the 'final solution' and the gas chambers of Auschwitz. Thus, anti-Semitism is a specific, a unique phenomenon which is not to be equated with other forms of prejudice or discrimination. The uniqueness of hostility to Jews does not only lay in its long history of two thousand years but also in its mental representation and its ideological basis, which are deeply engraved in the collective memory of the West. Whatever Jews did in history, they were scolded for doing it. No single group of people, except for the Jews, has ever been singled out and blamed simultaneously for mutually-exclusive developments (e.g. capitalism and communism, or assimilation and separation at the same time). The main concept at the core of the anti-Semitic belief system is the stereotype of Jews as 'strange creatures outside normal society', as 'the evil others.'

> 'You Jews are the biggest filth of mankind.'
> ("Ihr Juden seid der größte Dreck der Menschheit.")[15]
>
> 'The Jew is not a person, he is a product of decay'
> ("Der Jude ist kein Mensch, es ist eine Fäulniserscheinung.")[16]

This total negation, using the metaphor of decay, is presently projected onto Israel. Scolding Israel but meaning all Jews is for many years, the most frequent and dominant strategy of modern anti-Semites no matter whether they belong to the Right, the Left or mainstream society.

> 'Israel is the filth of the world!'
> ("Israel ist der Abschaum der Welt!")[17]

The mental images of Jews and of the Jewish state in the mind of anti-Semites reveal a strong gap between the mental constructions and reality. They do not rely on generalizations (which is the case in other forms of prejudice) but on mental constructs, on fictions not grounded in reality. Think about the stereotype of the blood libel or on the conspiracy theories such as the *Protocols of the Elders of Zion* that are inventions, mere fictions. Anti-Semitism does not focus on single aspects or characteristics of Jews, but on the existence of Jews as Jews in general. This makes anti-Semitism unique among all other kinds of hostility towards minorities. In the mental model of the anti-Semitic worldview, Jews fill the conceptual slot of 'one not

---

15 IBD (Israeli Embassy in Germany) 2008; postcard.
16 IBD_01.08.2006_Mar_001.
17 IBD_02.08.2006_001_Gar_001.

belonging to the human race' or 'one not belonging to our society.' This categorization goes hand-in-hand with the wish of erasing the Jewish existence:

> 'Hopefully, one day all Jews will have vanished from earth.'
> ("Hoffentlich werden alle Juden mal von der Welt verschwunden sein.")[18]

The negative conceptual attitude is reflected in verbal anti-Semitism. Verbal anti-Semitism comprises all utterances that explicitly or implicitly, with or without intention, invoke judeophobic stereotypes und show patterns of anti-Semitic argumentation. Verbal anti-Semitism is a form of language use that (re)produces prejudice against Jews and keeps judeophobic resentments alive. In this respect, it is a form of mental violence against Jews by using language in order to discriminate and offend them.

Which data help us best to understand verbal anti-Semitism? The traditional research on anti-Semitism frequently focuses on a few remarks of individual persons, although this does not give us a representative insight. Alternatively, there is the reliance on opinion polls, but these have methodological shortcomings: One is the influence of the political awareness: due to political correctness candid answers may be avoided (like expressing racist views) even in anonymous opinion polls. Another is *priming*, namely, to influence the answer through the formulation of the question. Last, the loss of spontaneity and naturalness, since polls are built on artificially triggered answers to a few statements (usually two to five sentences asking people to say 'yes', 'no' or 'I don't know') that are far from covering the full range of verbal anti-Semitism and the authentic production of anti-Semitic utterances.

Thus, our method is based on corpus studies, by now one of the most important empirical methods in cognitive science.

Corpus studies supply natural, authentic data in vast quantities. The material gained is to be considered representative for the discourse phenomenon at hand. Our research is based on three kinds of corpus material: about 50,000 internet texts (from internet forums, commentary sections to online versions of newspapers, chats, YouTube, social networks, focusing on mainstream internet users); about 100,000 texts from the German mass media (the mainstream press) that covered the Middle East conflict; about 14,000 letters and e-mails sent between 2002 and 2009 to the Central Council of Jews in Germany (*Zentralrat der Juden in Deutschland*) and between 2004 and 2012 to the embassy of Israel in Berlin; about 2,000 e-mails sent between 2010 and 2012 to the embassies of Israel in Vienna, Bern, The Hague, Madrid, Brussels, London, Dublin, and Stockholm.

---

18 IBD_2006_ano_026.

The advantage of having naturally produced texts is that the writers articulate themselves in their own words, that they manifest themselves on their own initiative and are by no means influenced by outer factors as in opinion polls. Thus, we have authentic verbal utterances.

As to the letters and e-mails, more than 65 percent of the writers could be identified as belonging to the middle of society; only 3 percent as belonging to the extreme Right and about 13 percent belonged to the Left. Most of the examples discussed here are taken from this corpus. They give access to the various forms and manifestations of contemporary anti-Semitism and they reveal constant, timeless patterns of Jew-hatred and their modern adaptations.

Judeophobic Stereotypes and their Verbal Manifestations in the Twenty-first Century

The Language of Extremist anti-Semites. In discourse of Right-wing extremists and neo-Nazis, Jews are explicitly being verbally attacked and devaluated as Jews. Typical of the views of the vulgar and aggressive speech acts is a racist ideology usually linked to a strong nationalism. This kind of anti-Semitism is strongly condemned by all political parties and all institutions in Germany. Still, it is worthwhile to have a look at some representative examples of utterances typical of extremists in order to show not only the difference but also the common denominator between the racist anti-Semitism and the hostility towards Jews by mainstream writers. Stereotyping and devaluating is one of the most significant characteristics:

> 'Deicides, thieves, frauds, pack of Jews: 'chosen people'!'
> ("Christusmörder, Diebe, Betrüger, Judenpack: auserwähltes Volk!")[19]
>
> 'Simply an inferior race!!!!!!'
> ("einfach eine niedere Rasse!!!!!!!!")[20]

As in the nineteenth and early twentieth century, German Jews are not accepted as German citizens embedded in everyday life but rather discriminated as strange and inferior people not belonging to the German society:

---

19 IBD_31.07.2006_Luh_001.
20 IBD_25.10.2006_ano_001.

> 'You are a guest in this country, so behave like one and stop your persistently impertinent agitation against the hosting people.'
> ("Sie sind als gast in diesem land, also benehmen sie sich auch wie ein solcher und beenden sie ihre ständig wiederkehrende impertinente hetze gegenüber dem gastgebenden volk.")[21]

Dominant among the traditional stereotypes in texts of extremists is the concept of 'the eternal Jew', which sticks to certain negative characteristics of all Jews.

> 'That's just the way Jews have been for more than 2 thousand years.'
> ("Juden sind halt so seit über 2 Tausend Jahren.")[22]

Anti-Semitism is seen as legitimate, revealing the continuity of a very old discrimination pattern of Jew-hatred. Jews are defined not only partially but totally bad by nature, that is, their bad traits are incorrigible. Because of their bad nature Jews have to be considered not as individuals but as a collective menace.

> 'YOU AREN'T HUMAN BEINGS...!'
> ("IHR SEID KEINE MENSCHEN...!")[23]

Jews are seen as an unchanging evil in the world. Additional classical stereotypes frequently articulated, are Jews as 'deicides,' 'murderers of little children,' 'blood libel users,' 'shylocks,' 'traitors,' 'liars,' 'disloyal parasites,' 'greedy profiteers,' (*geldgierige Wucherer*), 'sly conspirators' (*hinterhältige Verschwörer*), 'vengeful Holocaust exploiters' (*rachsüchtige Nutznießer/Holocaustausbeuter*). Jews are dehumanized and referred to as 'pigs, rats, microbes, plague, boils' etc. They are demonized as 'brutes' (*Unmenschen*), 'devils' (*Teufel*), 'fiends' or 'monsters' (*Unholde*).[24]

The articulation of such medieval stereotypes goes hand in hand with a specific pattern of argumentation that confirms the belief systems of anti-Semites: Jews are hated because of the way they are.[25]

> 'Why do you have to control the whole world with all might?'
> ("Warum müsst ihr mit aller Macht die ganze Welt beherrschen?")[26]

Typical of texts of extremists are threatening speech utterances and 'solutions' that resemble the 'Final Solution' plan of the Nazis):

---

21 ZJD_22.03.2007_ano_001.
22 ZJD_12.03.2007_Kli_001.
23 IBD_00.05.2010_ano_024.
24 See Befu, Demoniziging the 'Other', 1999
25 See Wistrich (1991); Bauer, Rethinking the Holocaust, 2001.
26 ZJD_28.09.2007_Sch_001.

'Perish!!!!'
("Verreckt!!!!")[27]

'Get out of Germany, get out of Gaza, get out of this world, get out of the universe!'
("Raus aus Deutschland, Raus aus Gaza, Raus aus dieser Welt, Raus aus dem Universum!")[28]

'One day you will FINALLY be exterminated... The world prays for it.'
("Eines Tages seid ihr ENDLICH ausgerottet... Die Welt betet dafuer.")[29]

'Solution plans' apply both to Jews and to the state of Israel. One of the markers of contemporary anti-Semitism is the shifting of old stereotypes to Israel, now in the role of the new collective Jew:

'The Israelis are the rats of the world and should all be poisoned with potassium cyanide because that is how you treat rats.'
("Die Israelis sind die Ratten der Welt und sollten allesamt mit Zyankali vergiftet werden, wie man das bei Ratten so macht.")[30]

'Free the Middle East from the Jewish plague!'
("Befreit den nahen Osten von der jüdischen Pest!")[31]

'I wish the Iran would throw the bomb on Israel!'
("Möge der Iran endlich die Bombe auf Israel werfen!")[32]

Accordingly, Israel and Israelis are described as 'creature of dung, creature of plague, creature of filth, plague ulcer, criminal vermin, international disease, subhuman rabble, rabble of parasites, rabble of monsters, cripple-state, subhuman state, super-rag-filth-people, cripple-people of members of the master race' (*Mistgeburt, Pestgeburt, Dreckgeburt, Pestgeschwür, Untermenschensgesindel, Parasiten-Pack, Monsterpack, Krüppel-Staat, Untermenschenstaat, Superlumpendreckvolk, Herrenmenschen-Krüppel-Volk*), etc.

Holocaust denial that has been taken so many years to be one of the main distinguishing features of right-wing anti-Semitism no longer seems to be significant: Many right-wing extremists do not deny the Holocaust but rather regret that:

"Hitler could not fulfill his task to wipe out the Jewish devil from the earth."[33]

---

27 ZJD_10.01.2009_Her_001.
28 ZJD_Gaza2009_102/816_ano_001.
29 ZJD_Gaza 2009_401/816_Jar_001.
30 IBD_11.04.2007_Dro_001.
31 IBD_12.07.2006_ano_003.
32 IBD_03.01.2012_Hil_003.
33 Postcard to the IBB, January 2013.

Remarkably, the texts of Left-wing extremists resemble those of Right-wing extremists in all aspects discussed. The only difference found is that writers from the Left deny being anti-Semitic or racist but transfer their hostility exclusively to Israel and Zionism. Thus, they do not use the word *Jew* in their hate speech but refer to "the Zionists" or the "Zionist oppressors."

The extremist kind of verbal anti-Semitism shows four main characteristics.

First, the semantics of exclusion. Jews are singled out as people different from the group the writer belongs to:

> 'Can't Jews finally leave us Germans alone?'
> ("Können Juden Deutsche nicht endlich in Ruhe lassen?")[34]

Second, fixation by stereotypes. Herewith, all Jews are defined and described by specific characteristics.

> 'For the last two thousand years, you have been robbing land and killing people!'
> ("Seit zwei Tausend Jahren betreiben Sie Landraub und Mord!")[35]

Third, devaluation. Hence, Jews are evaluated negatively as inferior to the group of the writer:

> 'You are the most inferior thing God ever did to mankind.'
> ("Ihr seid doch das Unterste was Gott der Menschheit antun konnte.")[36]

Fourth, Jew-hatred is fiercely expressed as anti-Israelism. ('cripple-state,' 'horror-state,' 'most evil state in the world').

Summing up, Right- and Left-wing extremists tend to manifest their anti-Semitic belief systems as hatred toward Zionism and the State of Israel. This new face of anti-Semitism, however, relies on old stereotypes. The source of the hostility has not changed: At its core, anti-Semitism is still grounded on the mental figure of the 'eternal Jew' as the incarnation of cosmic evil.

However, an important question is whether there are indeed crucial differences between the fierce and radical anti-Semitism of extremists and the new forms of anti-Zionism and anti-Israelism commonly found in mainstream society.

---

[34] ZJD_29.07.2006_Bur_001.
[35] IBD_11.09.2007_Mar_001.
[36] IBD_22.07.2006_ano_007.

Educated Anti-Semitism: Stereotyping Coupled with Strategies of Denial and Legitimization

Many of the people writing to the Central Council of Jews in Germany and the Israeli embassy belong to the middle of the German society. They are economically well-off, (often highly) educated, politically belonging to one of the mainstream parties. Hence, they are teachers, lawyers, priests, managers, physicians, bankers, students, editors, politicians, journalists and many academics from the university sector, with doctorates or professorships.

They do not articulate themselves through open hate speech or vulgar death threats. Their e-mails and letters very often are long and elaborated with a certain kind of seemingly sophisticated argumentation. Most frequently, educated writers claim to write moved by moral integrity and uprightness. Their speech acts are purporting to be 'advice,' 'care,' 'written out of concern and anxiety,' or on behalf of ethical reasons:

> 'Please do not take my letter as an attack, but as an amicable piece of advice.'
> ("Betrachten Sie mein Schreiben bitte nicht als Angriff, sondern vielmehr als freundschaftlichen Rat.")[37]

Hence, they fiercely deny being prejudiced by nature and strongly negate any kind of racist or anti-Semitic attitude ("I am not an anti-Semite!" is one of the most frequent statements articulated in the corpus). They claim to write only due to the best of motives, out of worry or uneasiness, and call themselves 'humanists' (*Humanisten*).

Crucial in the argumentation of educated writers is always the strategy of legitimization: to justify their verbal anti-Semitism, they give themselves the image of being responsible, prejudice-free citizens (often explicitly referring to their high level of education as an expertise to criticize both the Central Council and the State of Israel). Another frequent strategy of legitimization is the reference to information from the mass media or from prominent figures in public life (preferably Jewish intellectuals who strongly criticize Israel[38]):

> 'Every day I have to read and hear about your disgusting, brutal and murderous actions in Israel.'
> ("Jeden Tag muss ich lesen und hören, was Sie an widerwärtigen, brutalen und mördrischen Taten in israel anrichten.")[39]

---

[37] ZJD_07.08.2006_Hön_001.
[38] On the issue of Jewish intellectuals active in anti-Israel campaigns, see Friesel, On the Complexities of Modern Jewish Identity, 2011.
[39] IBD_19.03.2009_See_001.

> '[Günther] Grass is right!'
> ("Grass hat Recht!")⁴⁰

However, a close and critical look at their texts reveals an attitude towards Jews that in content is not very different than the fierce hostility of the extremists. The correspondents from the mainstream society evoke the same old stereotypes in their texts but they either do it in a less vulgar way or they do it implicitly, using indirect speech that convey the anti-Semitic content through implicatures:

> 'Is it possible that the excessive violence in Israel, including the murder of innocent children, corresponds to the long tradition of your people?'
> ("Entspricht womöglich die exzessive Gewalt in Israel, die auch den Mord an Kindern einschließt, der langen Traditionslinie Ihres Volkes?")⁴¹
>
> 'Do you have human feelings at all?'
> ("Habt ihr überhaupt menschliche Gefühle?")⁴²

Those speech acts often come as (rhetorical) questions and their semantics include allusions to traditional judeophobic stereotypes, formerly attributed to Jews (such as the incorrigibility of Jewish behavior, the tradition of being child murderers or the lack of human feelings).

Often, there is no differentiation made between the German Jews and the Israeli Jews. Accordingly, a frequent stereotype of educated writers is that Jews are disloyal citizens who do not really belong to Germany. It connects to the nineteenth century notions of the Jews as "non-Germans". Now the concept is related to German Jews as Israelis. Often, no differentiation is drawn between Jews and Israelis, they are mentally equated, the lexemes *Jew* and *Israeli* used as synonyms:

> 'You are the last of all people who have a right to give us advice! Attacks by Right-wing extremists in Germany are regrettable, but your country is the last of all countries which has the right to denounce other countries. For your country, that is ISRAEL, permanently commits state terrorism and doesn't even know what human rights mean [...]'⁴³
> ("Betreff: Sie sind die absolut Letzten die ein Recht haben uns Ratschläge zu geben! So bedauerlich rechtsradikale Übergriffe in Deutschland auch sein mögen, Ihr Land ist das absolut Letzte das ein Recht hat andere Länder anzuprangern, weil Ihr Land, sprich ISRAEL permanent regelrecht Staatsterrorismus betreibt und sowas wie Menschenrechte nicht mal kennt [...]")

---

40 IBD_17.01.2012_Mar_001.
41 ZJD_06.09.2002_Sch_001.
42 ZJD_Gaza 2009_34/816_Zon_001.
43 ZJD_25.10.2006_Sch_001.

Common stereotyping rests on the concept of Jews as arrogant and disloyal (to the country in which they live). See the following writing to the Central Council of the Jews in Germany:

> 'I am a social scientist and your comments increasingly cause negative emotions about your association. Keep in mind the consequences your know-it-all explanations will have in the long term!'
> ("Bei mir als Sozialwissenschaftler lösen Ihre Kommentare immer mehr negative Gefühle über Ihren Verein aus. Bedenken Sie, welche Folgen Ihre besserwisserischen Ausführungen auf Dauer erzeugen!")[44]

Typical, too, is to blame the Jews for the existence of anti-Semitism:

> 'The Central Council of Jews should stop interfering because this kind of behavior creates anti-Semitism.'
> ("Der Zentralrat der Juden sollte zukünftig diese Einmischungen unterlassen, da er dadurch Antisemitismus erzeugt.")[45]

Another allegation is that hatred against Jews is justified, and that Jews are collectively responsible for actions of the State of Israel:

> 'And I get annoyed at myself for having always believed that the Jewish people were persecuted wrongfully.'
> ("Und ich ärgere mich, daß ich mein lebenlang glaubte, daß das jüdische Volk zu unrecht verfolgt wurde.")[46]

> 'In the past I did not understand what caused anti-Semitism. But your teaching examples concerning murderers and war criminals do explain this insanity.'
> ("Ich verstand früher nicht wie es zum Antisemitismus kam, aber Eure Lehrbeispiele in Sachen Mörder und Kriegsverbrecher lassen diesen Wahnsinn ein Gesicht geben.")[47]

The equation of Zionism with Nazism commonly occurs. The texts of educated writers contain many Nazi comparisons devaluating Israel, too such as *SS-Israel* and 'Your Nazi methods' (*Ihre Nazi-Methoden*). In addition, Jewish and Israeli citizens are painted with cliché-loaded brushes and negative stereotypes are expressed which rest on anti-Semitic attitudes of a time which was assumed to have been overcome. The following example is from a journalist and Left-wing politician from Munich:

---

44 ZJD_16.04.2007_Sch_004.
45 ZJD_07.05.2007_Zie_001.
46 ZJD_01.08.2006_Sch_003.
47 ZJD_01.08.2006_Sch_003.

'You learned well from Hitler and his Nazi regime.'
("Sie haben gut von Hitler und seinem NS-Regime gelernt.")[48]

Analogies such as the following are often communicated: 'The Israeli military uses methods of the SS'; 'Gaza reminds me of Auschwitz.' Drastic vocabulary like 'villain state' (*Verbrecherstaat*), 'murderous regime' (*Mörderregime*), 'orgies of violence' (*Gewaltorgien*) is used. Many writers use hyperbolic terms such as 'the most barbaric, brutal and despicable deeds,' 'worst war criminals' (*schlimmste Kriegsverbrecher*), 'the most evil wrongs' (übelste Schandtaten). Frequently, Israel is depicted as 'the most eminent threat to world peace.' This de-realized way of looking at Israel is a mere continuation of the old stereotyping Jews as cosmic evil.

Medieval motifs show up when Israelis are described and demonized as 'brutes' (*Unmenschen*), 'devils' (*Teufel*), and 'fiends' or 'monsters' (*Unholde*). Quite frequently, Jews are described as Holocaust profiteers:

'The common abuse of the Holocaust for present purposes has a counterproductive effect on a normal coexistence of Jews and Gentiles.'
("Der häufige Missbrauch des Holocausts für gegenwärtige Zwecke ist kontraproduktiv für ein normales Zusammenleben zwischen Juden und Nichtjuden.")[49]

This stereotype is often articulated in combination with the rebuke Jews would suppress any kind of free speech in Germany when it comes to Israel. Many argue that the new concept of anti-Semitism defines legitimate criticism of Israel too narrowly, and that the Jews exploit anti-Semitism in order to silence a critical debate.

'Who among us dares 'to think aloud' and to voice his personal opinion?'
("Wer wagt den bei uns,laut zu denken' und seine persönliche Meinung zu sagen?")[50]

At the same time, the cliché that the press is absolutely controlled by Jews brought up in the nineteenth century by Marr and Treitschke, is very often articulated. Obviously, the writers do not notice that these two statements stand in contrast to each other. As our analysis shows, irrational contradictions are a central part of anti-Semitic argumentation along the ages.

The following e-mail sent by a law professor to the Central Council of Jews in Germany is typical of the argumentation of many educated writers (holding Jews

---

48 ZJD_09.03.2008_Stra_001.
49 ZJD_11.03.2008_Zen_001.
50 IBB_ 10.04.2012_Per_001.

collectively responsible for actions of the State of Israel, demonizing and de-evaluating Israel and evoking traditional anti-Judaic stereotypes):

> 'Due to the fact that you have demonstrated your solidarity with Israel for the last few days without any criticism, you cannot expect anybody anymore to distinguish between the Central Council [of Jews] and Israel. ... all your crimes...The reason for this must be the Zionist idea to be the chosen people.'
> ("Da Sie sich dieser Tage ohne jede Kritik auf die Seite Israels stellen, ist nun wenigstens die Forderung aus der Welt, man müsse zwischen dem Zentralrat und Israel differenzieren. ...alle Ihre Verbechen... Hintergrund ist wohl die zionistische Idee, ein auserwähltes Volk zu sein.")[51]

Educated writers from the middle of society rely on the semantics of exclusion, fixation and devaluation just as extremists do. Further, the concept of the eternal Jew is evoked in many letters by alluding to the stereotype. Here is one from an academic with a Ph.D. in history:

> 'The world is fed up with the State of Israel's professional breeding of terrorists. [...] Why have the Jews been persecuted for centuries! This is a question you have to ask yourself. [...] Do not call me an anti-Semite because it would not be true.'
> ("Die Welt hat langsam genug von der vom Staat Israel professionell betriebenen Terroristenzucht. [...] Warum werden die Juden seit Jahrhunderten immer wieder verfolgt! Das müssen sie sich schon selber fragen. [...] Nennt mich nicht einen Antisemiten, denn das trifft nicht zu.")[52]

Using the strategy of contrast, humanistic values are evoked, while the Jews are disqualified of their lack of it:

> "We Germans, we have learned from the past! We cling to humanistic values now and refuse any kind of racism. The Jews, however, obviously did not learn from the Holocaust. They are the most disgusting racists now and behave like Nazis."[53]

> 'I can only hope for the Jews to come to their senses again as fast as possible and to start thinking and acting like human beings!'
> ("Ich kann nur hoffen, das die Juden sich so schnell wie möglich besinnen und das Humanität in ihren Gedanken und Handeln wieder einzieht!")[54]

---

51 ZJD_27.07.2006_Rau_001.
52 IBD_04.07.2006_Str_001.
53 IBD_27.03.2011_Has_001.
54 ZJD_Gaza 2009_214/816_Sch_001.

In connection with this strategy, a very dominant form of anti-Semitism among educated people involves missionary activity directed at Jews. Accordingly, many writers are prone to patronizing moral advice:

> "A friendly advice: We cling to moral values of the Western world, Christian values of love, respect, kindness. If you adept to our values, you would gradually stop being hated."[55]

> "Circumcision... Get rid of this atavistic behavior. Reach the 21.century and drop this barbarian ritual of molesting little children. Then you will be accepted in our Western civilization."[56]

Denying Jews the right to self-determination (e.g. by claiming that the existence of a Jewish state of Israel is a racist crime and circumcision is a barbaric uncivilized act to be prohibited), is a modern repetition and adaptation of the old urge in Western thought to erase genuine Jewishness.

There is a strong emotional dimension in educated anti-Semitism, reflected in utterances with intensive affective vocabulary: the writers 'feel so much empathy with the victims of the brutal Israeli violence,' they are 'utterly shocked and disgusted,' 'without words,' 'speechless due to disgust, repulsion and anger,' 'deeply moved,' 'shocked, concerned,' 'deeply felt empathy and sorrow for the suffering of the poor, mistreated Palestinians,' they express 'pity, sickening, nauseating, compassion, sincere concern,' 'burden on their conscience,' as 'humanists they sincerely suffer, are depressed, they simply felt the strong urge to write about this,' etc.

At the same time, they are 'not concerned with the contemporary anti-Semitism of only a few right-wing extremists', they are 'fed up being constantly reminded of the Holocaust' and they call 'for an end of the excessive and unnecessary culture of remembrance in Germany.' The 'deeply moved' writers almost never express feelings of empathy when they write about the victims of the Holocaust or Israelis as targets of terror attacks.

> "Enough! There must be a stop to this excessive Holocaust remembrance!"[57]

This total lack of empathy is reflected also widely on the internet, especially in commentary sections of online press. In 2011, three little Israeli children were brutally murdered in their sleep in a settlement. A comment as the following was articulated not randomly, then:

---

55 IBD_24.07.2012_Kar_001.
56 IBD_03.11.2012_Bir_001.
57 E-mail to the IBB, January 2013.

'Who sows violence reaps violence. This should be known to the Jews who are well versed in the Bible.'
("Wer Gewalt sät, erntet Gewalt. Das müßte den bibelfesten Juden doch wohl bekannt sein.")[58]

Anti-Semitic texts of mainstream educated writers are not as vulgarly formulated as extremists' writings. They avoid death threats, but instead propose indirect genocidal solutions in the name of "humanity" as in the following e-mail of a professor from humanities:

> "The state of Israel is an anomaly. It has to be dissolved in a peaceful way. Please do accept this for the sake of us all!"[59]

In the end, the "solution for the Jewish problem," no matter whether expressed as vulgar death threat, moral advice or the call for dissolving the Jewish state Israel, always means one thing: the extinction of Jewish existence.

Surprisingly, the old and by now well-known anti-Semitic stereotypes are recycled in a pattern of repetitiveness and obsession by educated writers, as well. Their knowledge of the Holocaust and of the dangers of prejudicial world views does not prevent them from articulating verbal anti-Semitism. The awareness of the Holocaust, however, drives modern educated anti-Semites to use communicative strategies of denial and legitimization in order to keep up the image of noble, upright citizens.

Of course, there is a difference between the radical and vulgar hate speech of extremist and educated people from the middle of society, but this difference lies only in the form not in the content. The semantics of anti-Jewish devaluation is the same. The common conceptual ground to be found between the Jew-hatred of extremists and the anti-Semitism (albeit denied by its communicators) of the educated Bourgeois from the middle of society is that Jews are perceived as 'the other' connected to a deep emotional mistrust and feeling of aversion.

The educated type of anti-Semitism still rests on old judeophobic concepts, but is contextually shaped by actual events (e.g., the Middle East conflict, the debate on circumcision, the coping with the German past). Those events are nothing but a trigger for the old European fantasies on Jews. Unchanged by time or experience, education and knowledge, is the semantics of devaluation and discrimination that is deeply rooted in the ideology of 'the Jew,' engraved in Western thought and emotion and preserved in collective memory. There are continuities

---

58 12.03.2011_17:23_Raimon.
59 ZJD_21.07.2009_Has_001.

on the level of the stereotypization of Jews and of Israelis as collective Jews at all political and ideological levels of society.

Reactions to Anti-Semitism on the Internet and in Public Discourse: Denying and Marginalizing the Obvious

However, there is a strong tendency to deny the very existence of contemporary hostility against Jews in the German society. The concept of anti-Semitism in public opinion still rests on the historical phenomenon of racism. Thus, 'true anti-Semitism' is seen and recognized only at the outer edges of society. It is widely ignored or vehemently marginalized that today's judeophobia has developed into new manifestations.

In Germany, this became quite evident in a public debate in April 2012, on a poem of the German Nobel laureate Günter Grass in which he attacked and bashed Israel (and not the Iran) for being a 'threat to world peace' because of its nuclear program. Although the poem borrowed judeophobic clichés and projected them on Israel, many people commenting on it were not able or willing to recognize anything anti-Semitic in the text. Since the text focused on the nuclear power of Israel and the word *Jew* did not occur once, many defended it as 'simply critical,' 'giving just facts,' or a 'manifestation of free speech.' The text showed main characteristics of modern verbal anti-Semitism in the disguise of critique of Israel. Claiming to just criticize Israeli politics, but using at the same time judeophobic stereotypes and argumentation patterns, is by now one of the most prominent and most common manifestations of contemporary Jew-hatred. The debate flamed up anew in January 2013, when Jakob Augstein, a Leftish journalist and columnist for Spiegel Online, appeared on the Wiesenthal list for "2012 Top Ten Anti-Semitic/Anti-Israel Slurs" ranking him ninth for his public attacks on the State of Israel. Instantly, many in German mainstream media rushed to defend Augstein without even having read his columns.

However, the texts of Augstein, that frequently employ a rhetoric found in the writings of classical anti-Semites, do not simply fall under the category of critical journalism, since they implicitly invoke stereotypes of classical Jew-hatred. Although Augstein admitted never having been to Israel, he frequently condemns and demonizes the country. Having no personal experience whatsoever in the conflict, he nevertheless feels competent enough to vehemently bash Israel. He stated, for instance, that orthodox Jews follow 'the law of revenge' (thus repeating a very old anti-Jewish stereotype) and implied that some ominous Jewish force determines political decisions through 'lobby groups' (hence, leaning on conspiracy theories). Further, he communicated conceptualizations and images associated with classic anti-Semitism to characterize Israel and Israelis. He called Gaza a 'camp' and abused Israel of 'breeding terrorists.' This kind of language use in the middle of society, articulated in mainstream press can trigger and re-enforce prejudice and evoke sentiments against Jews even if those processes are not intended. Since language in mass media has a mental power of its own and is capable to subconsciously influence the collective mind to a large degree, it is not a matter of the intention that lies behind a text but above all the text and its content itself, its cognitive implicatures and associations that make it verbal anti-Semitism or not.

There is a sharp distinction to be made between honest and legitimate political criticism based on knowledge of facts, without using stereotypes and verbal anti-Semitism under the guise of critique of Israel that uses argumentation patterns typical of classical anti-Semitic discourse and that applies generalizations that are hostile to Jews, and evoke old judeophobic sentiments. Nevertheless, public opinion tends to ignore or marginalize this dimension of persuasive rhetoric.

It is instructive to observe the reactions of people in Germany, as expressed on the internet both to public debates on anti-Semitism and to reports from current research on anti-Semitism.

In January 2012, an expert's report of the German parliament (*Bundestagsbericht der Expertenkommission*)[60] was published stating that approximately 20 percent of all Germans are explicitly or implicitly prejudicial against Jews. In summer 2012, the political TV series Fact reported on every day's anti-Semitism in Germany presenting empirical facts on the topic.

It turns out that we find the same strategies of denial and downplay in public discourse and on the internet that we noticed in our e-mail corpus. One typical reaction is denial:

> 'What a load of garbage! I have never heard anything against Jews in my life. Hatred towards foreigners and Germans is certainly more common. The persecution of the Jews is history, enough with invoking evil spirits... Reality is definitely different.'
> ("So ein Schwachsinn! Hab in meinem ganzen Leben noch nichts gegen Juden gehört. Ausländerhass oder Deutschhass ist wohl eher verbreitet. Die Judenverfolgung ist Geschichte, es reicht böse Geister zu beschwören... Die Realität sieht definitiv anders aus.")[61]

---

60 Bundesministerium des Innern (ed.), 2011.
61 www.focus.de, Peter, January 23, 2012.

Another reaction is relativization and trivialization:

> 'Again, they pull some experts out of the hat and make very unspecific accusations against the German population.'
> ("Da werden wieder irgendwelche Experten aus der Schublade gezogen und sehr allgemein gehaltene Vorwuerfe gegen die deutsche Bevoelkerung erhoben.")[62]

Some writers reframe the issue and communicate de-realizing re-interpretations:

> 'Whoever is brave enough to tell the truth about Israel just isn't a friend of Jews anymore.'
> ("Wer es wagt die Wahrheit über Israel zu sagen ist eben kein Judenfreund mehr.")[63]

> 'Every criticism of Israel is very easily being put on one level with anti-Semitism.'
> ("Jede Kritik an Israel wird doch sehr schnell mit Antisemitismus gleichgesetzt.")[64]

Many express aversion and weariness:

> 'I know many people who do not want to talk about the spectrum Judaism anymore.'
> ("Ich kenne viele Menschen die sich über das Spektrum Judentum nicht mehr unterhalten wollen.")[65]

In many comments that deny the very existence of contemporary anti-Semitism, anti-Semitic stereotypes simultaneously are confirmed and validated:

> 'Examine 'The Israel Lobby', you should never underestimate [...] the power of the Jews'
> ("Untersuche die 'Israel-Lobby', die Macht der Juden [...] soll man nicht unterschätzen")[66]

> 'If, as mentioned in the article, the Jews are persecuted already for more than 2000 years, the question should be put if they have not contributed something to the aversion against them.'
> ("Wenn, wie im Beitrag erwähnt, die Juden schon über 2000 Jahre verfolgt werden, muss man sich schon mal die Frage stellen, ob die nicht auch was zu der Abneigung gegen sie beigetragen haben.")[67]

A recent strategy to downplay contemporary anti-Semitism is to make fun of it. Accompanying the debate on Augstein, in the media one can see or hear commentators who tell the audience that anti-Semitism in Germany is harmless and

---

62 www.focus.de, Kritiker, January 23, 2012.
63 www.focus.de, Surfer2007, Januar 23, 2012.
64 www.focus.de, emeinung, January 23, 2012.
65 www.focus.de, Ursachenforschung, January 23, 2012.
66 www.youtube.com, liebling85, October, 2012.
67 www.mdr.de, Kommentar von hillus zur Sendung Fakt, September 18, 2012.

is not to be considered a real problem for society. Some comments even handled the whole phenomenon as a joke:

> "This can only be regarded as a joke."[68]
>
> "I want to get on that list, too!"[69]

Summary

Stereotypes and feelings of hatred against Jews still exist and are verbalized, this in spite of all the efforts to eliminate anti-Semitism and to erase the distorted and false picture of Jews and Judaism in years after the end of the Second World War. Worse, stereotypes already used in the Middle Ages to abuse Jews are to be found also in modern discourse not merely articulated by right-wing extremists but communicated at all levels of society. Verbal constructs of classical Judeophobia prove to be enduring and persistent. In contemporary discourse, one finds many words and phrases in speech act hostile to Jews that were elaborated centuries ago and passed from generation to generation.

Our corpus study shows that regarding to verbal anti-Semitism no real change has occurred regarding the semantics of exclusion, fixation and devaluation. Jews are still conceptualized by anti-Semites as 'the others,' as 'the most vile and mean creatures on earth,' and are perceived as a threat to mankind. A modern version of this conceptualization concerns the state of Israel, the most vital symbol of present-day Jewish existence and survival: the negative picture of the eternal Jew is being projected on the Jewish state. Much of what purports to be criticism of Israel in fact turns out to be the old anti-Jewish sentiments. Claiming to just criticize Israeli politics, but using at the same time judeophobic stereotypes, is by now one of the most common manifestations of contemporary Jew-hatred. In spite of the knowledge as to what consequences a rhetoric of hate and hostility may cause, it happens that Jews (and in reference shifting speech acts, Israelis) are verbally discriminated and devaluated in contemporary discourse. Verbal abuse and discrimination of Jews does not only show up within texts of extremists, but also in the middle of society. One may find verbal anti-Semitism articulated by people with high education, too. The difference between radical extremists and educated anti-Semites lies in the style, the less radical language use, but the semantics of

---

68 Tina Mendelssohn commenting the listing of Augstein by the Wiesenthal Center, KulturZeit, 2013.
69 Harald Martenstein, in: Tageszeitung, January 2013.

devaluation is the same. Anti-Semitic texts of mainstream educated writers are not as vulgarly formulated as extremists' writings. Due to political correctness and the bashing of openly articulated anti-Semitism in Western societies, implicit forms of it are preferred in public discourse. Thus, the word 'Jew' often may not even occur in verbal utterances conveying content hostile toward Jews. Anti-Semites from mainstream society prefer to use indirect speech (rhetorical questions, allusions of specific kinds and reference shifting) to express their hostility towards Jews and/or Israel. They avoid death threats, but instead propose indirect genocidal solutions in the name of "humanity." This implicit verbal anti-Semitism, however, evokes the same traditional stereotypes as in the texts from extremists. Hence, those indirect forms are as dangerous as direct, manifest forms of Jew-hatred to the collective mind of a society. Even more so, since many people are not able or willing to recognize the more subtle forms as verbal anti-Semitism, their manipulative and persuasive power might be even greater.

In the twenty-first century, anti-Judaism with both its classical patterns of conceptual stereotyping hostility and its modern adaptations, is alive and influential in the midst of the German society. Our empirical findings clearly show, that in spite of the collective awareness of the catastrophe in the Holocaust, the lethal semantics of anti-Semitism is still found in modern discourse and it is spread in the public and on the internet without meeting any vehement opposition. At the same time, today's anti-Semitism manifested as anti-Israelism is vehemently denied or marginalized.

References

ADL –Anti-Defamation League (ed.). *Attitudes Toward Jews in Seven European Countries*. New York: ADL, 2009. http://www.adl.org/Public%20ADL%20Anti-Semitism%20 Presentation%20February%202009%20_3_.pdf (accessed March 31, 2015).

Almog, Shmuel (ed.). *Antisemitism through the Ages*. Oxford: Pergamon Press, 1988.

Bauer, Yehuda. *Rethinking the Holocaust*. New Haven: Yale University Press, 2001.

Befu, Harumi. Demonizing the "Other". In *Demonizing the Other. Antisemitism, Racism and Xenophobia*, Robert P. Wistrich (ed.), pp.17–30. Amsterdam: Harwood, 1999.

Bering, Dietz. *Der Name als Stigma. Antisemitismus im deutschen Alltag 1812–1933*. Stuttgart: Bering, 1991 [1987].

Bundesministerium des Innern (ed.). *Antisemitismus in Deutschland. Erscheinungsformen, Bedingungen, Präventionsansätze. Bericht des unabhängigen Expertenkreises Antisemitismus*. Rostock: Publikationsversand der Bundesregierung, 2011.

FRA – European Union Agency for Fundamental Rights (ed.). *Anti-Semitism. Summary Overview of the Situation in the European Union 2001–2008*. Vienna: FRA, 2009. http://fra.europa.eu/fraWebsite/attachments/Antisemitism_Update_2009.pdf (accessed March 30, 2015).

Friesel, Evyatar. On the Complexities of Modern Jewish Identity: Contemporary Jews against Israel, *Israel Affairs* 17 (2011): pp. 504–519.
Hortzitz, Nicoline. *Die Sprache der Judenfeindschaft in der frühen Neuzeit (1450–1700). Untersuchungen zu Wortschatz, Text und Argumentation.* Heidelberg: Winter, 2005.
Katz, Jacob. *From Prejudice to Destruction. Anti-Semitism 1700–1933.* Cambridge/MA: Harvard University Press, 1980.
Laqueur, Walter. *The Changing Face of Antisemitism: From Ancient Times to the Present Day.* Oxford: Oxford University Press, 2006.
Low, Alfred. *Jews in the Eyes of the Germans. From the Enlightenment to Imperial Germany.* Philadelphia: Institute for the Study of Human Issues, 1979.
Nirenberg, David. *Anti-Judaism: The Western Tradition.* New York: W. W. Norton, 2013.
Poliakov, Léon. *The History of Antisemitism.* London: Elek Books, 1985.
Reisigl, Martin, RuthWodak. *Discourse and Discrimination. Rhetoric of Racism and Antisemitism.* London: Routledge, 2001.
Schwarz-Friesel, Monika, Evyatar Friesel, and Jehuda Reinharz (eds.). *Aktueller Antisemitismus in Deutschland. Ein Phänomen der Mitte.* Berlin, New York: De Gryter, 2010.
Schwarz-Friesel, Monika. „Juden sind zum Töten da" (studivz.net, 2008). Hass via Internet – Zugänglichkeit und Verbreitung von Antisemitismen im World Wide Web. In *Sprache und Kommunikation im technischen Zeitalter. Wieviel Technik (v)erträgt unsere Gesellschaft?*, Konstanze Marx, Monika Schwarz-Friesel (eds.), pp. 213–236. Berlin, New York: De Gryter, 2013.
Schwarz-Friesel, Monika. Explizite und implizite Formen des Verbal-Antisemitismus in aktuellen Texten der regionalen und überregionalen Presse (2002–2010) und ihr Einfluss auf den alltäglichen Sprachgebrauch. In *Judenfeindschaft und Antisemitismus in der deutschen Presse über fünf Jahrhunderte. Erscheinungsformen, Rezeption, Debatte und Gegenwehr*, Michael Nagel, Moshe Zimmermann (eds.), pp. 993–1008. Bremen: edition lumière, 2013.
Schwarz-Friesel, Monika, Jehuda Reinharz. *Die Sprache der Judenfeindschaft im 21. Jahrhundert.* Berlin, New York: De Gryter, 2013.
Volkov, Shulamit. Antisemitism as a Cultural Code. Reflections on the History and Historiography of Antisemitism in Imperial Germany. *Leo Baeck Institute Yearbook* 23 (1978): pp. 25–46. http://leobaeck.oxfordjournals.org/content/23/1/25.full.pdf+html (accessed March 30, 2015).
Wistrich, Robert. *Antisemitism. The Longest Hatred.* New York: Pantheon Books, 1991.
Wistrich, Robert. *A Lethal Obsession: Antisemitism from Antiquity to the Global Jihad.* New York: Random House, 2010.

Günther Jikeli
Anti-Semitism within the Extreme Right and Islamists' Circles

Anti-Semitism has long been a part of the extreme Right and Islamist movements. However, while anti-Semitism is still virulent within both movements in Germany, today, anti-Semitism often takes indirect forms. In the case of the extreme Right, it is frequently embedded in revisionist positions on the Second World War. Islamists in Germany, on the other hand, voice anti-Semitic positions with references to Israel, anti-Jewish excerpts from Islamic scripture, and hostile attitudes towards Western societies in the context of an alleged "war against Islam." Explicit anti-Semitic hate messages are often transmitted in music and the social media.

Cooperation between the two movements is marginal. However, as some examples show, similarities in anti-Semitic views can be found. Furthermore, Jewish communities face terrorist threats from radicals of the extreme Right and Islamists. The extreme Right and Islamists are not isolated from mainstream society; similar attitudes are widespread, and exist beyond the membership of organizations associated with extreme Right and Political Islam.

It comes to no surprise that anti-Semitism is deeply rooted both in the extreme Right and among Islamists. Both ideological movements have a long tradition of anti-Semitism, and it has been argued that anti-Semitism is an intrinsic part of the extreme Right and Islamism.[1]

Any examination comparing of anti-Semitism among the extreme Right and Islamists in Germany raise a number of questions. How is anti-Semitism manifested today among each, and what are the similarities and differences between them? How much influence do such groups have on mainstream society? The extreme Right and radical Islamists, by definition, operate on the fringes of society, however, the relationship between the margins and the mainstream is complicated. Although flagrant anti-Semitism is most notable on the extreme Right and among radical Islamists, anti-Semitic sentiment is manifested in all segments of society.

---

[1] For anti-Semitism in Islamism see: Tibi, Islamism and Islam, 2012; Tibi, From Sayyid Qutb to Hamasm, 2010; Mallmann / Cüppers, Nazi Palestine, 2010; Wistrich, A Lethal Obsession, 2010; Kiefer, Antisemitismus in den islamischen Gesellschaften, 2002; Müller, Auf den Spuren von Nasser. In: Benz / Wetzel (eds.), Antisemitismus und radikaler Islamismus, 2007. For antisemitism in the extreme Right see: Rensmann, Against 'Globalism'. In: Rensmann / Schops (eds.), Politics and Resentment, 2011; Pfahl-Traughber, Antisemitismus im Rechtsextremismus. In: Pfahl-Traughber / Fünfsinn (eds.), Extremismus und Terrorismus, 2011b.

Attitudes considered far Rightist are widespread in mainstream society. A survey published in 2012 found that 9 percent of the population in Germany adhere to a "closed extreme Right world view." Many more agree with some extreme Right positions or worldviews or decline to reject them. In Germany, 32.8 percent agree with the statement "Reparations from Germany often do not benefit the victims, but rather a Holocaust-Industry by clever lawyers." Only 42.4 percent completely reject that "actually, the Germans are superior to other nations by nature"; 17.8 percent agree. Only 55.6 percent of the general population rejects the statement "Jews always provoke conflicts with their ideas"; 19.5 percent agree.[2] The responses indicate that the boundaries between the mainstream and the extreme Right are not as clear-cut as one might think or wish.

Similarly, some Islamist views are widespread among Muslims. According to a 2006 survey, 36 percent of Muslims in Germany believe that there is a "natural conflict between being a devout Muslim and living in a modern society."[3] A survey among young Muslims in Germany found that about 15 percent of seven-hundred and seventeen Muslims sampled between the ages of fourteen and thirty-two can be described as "very religious and strongly rejecting the West, leaning towards acceptance of violence."[4] Furthermore, 9.4 percent of Muslims support introduction of corporal punishment in German as in Islamic religious law (*Shari'a*). Interestingly, many Muslims in Germany are party to authoritarian attitudes often attributed to the extreme Right: For example, 65.5 percent in 2005 agreed that "the state should control newspapers and television in order to guarantee morality and order." About 6 percent justify violence and terrorism in the name of Islam.[5]

Although some extremist views are shared by larger populations, such views are not accepted in public discourse. It is largely left to extremist groups to voice flagrant anti-Semitism publicly. The extreme Right is responsible for most anti-Semitic crimes; between 90–95 percent of all anti-Semitic crimes reported and about 80 percent of the violent anti-Semitic incidents that take place in Germany are attributed to the extreme Right. Nevertheless, violent Islamists also pose a direct threat to Jews and non-violent Islamist groups voice anti-Semitic views that are used to justify attacks against Jews.

---

2 Author's translation. The statements in German read "Reparationsforderungen an Deutschland nützen oft gar nicht mehr den Opfern, sondern einer Holocaust-Industrie von findigen Anwälten;" "Eigentlich sind die Deutschen anderen Völkern von Natur aus überlegen;" and "Juden sorgen mit ihren Ideen immer für Unfrieden." See: Decker / Kiess / Brähler, Die Mitte Im Umbruch, 2012, p. 29–30, 78.
3 Pew Global Attitudes Project, The Great Divide, 2006.
4 Frindte / Boehnke / Kreikenbom / Wagner, Lebenswelten junger Muslime, 2012, p. 290.
5 Brettfeld / Wetzels, Muslime in Deutschland, 2007, p. 141, 190, 177.

The Extreme Right in Germany

Keeping the shortcomings of the term "extreme Right" in mind,[6] I use this term to describe a group of individuals and organizations that harbor persistent anti-Semitic, racist, xenophobic, authoritarian, and social-Darwinist beliefs, and attitudes of inequality. An extreme Rightist world view includes that a person's "value" is determined by race and nation. Authoritarian views about the state and a "natural" social order of society and the world in general are also part and parcel of extreme Rightist world views. The organized extreme Right in Germany is opposed to democracy and poses a physical threat to those who in their eyes are not considered German – that is, foreigners or people of foreign origin and Jews. Political adversaries are also threatened. In 2012, the authorities registered 396 xenophobic violent crimes, 169 acts of violence against members of the Left and 36 anti-Semitic violent crimes by members of the extreme Right. The number of politically-motivated crimes that did not entail violence against individuals is much higher: 1,286 anti-Semitic crimes by the extreme Right, such as damage to property and hate speech were registered in 2012.

More than 22,000 individuals are affiliated with organizations of the extreme Right, almost half are considered violent.[7] While the organized and active extreme Right is relatively small, they operate in a social environment where extreme Right attitudes are no exception. Nine percent of the population in Germany – that is, an estimated seven million Germans – adhere to a "closed world view of the extreme Right." One could label them 'latent members of the extreme Right' although they do not act upon their views. It is worth noting that at present, the percentage of persons with such attitudes varies between former East and West Germany; it is higher in the east (15.8 percent) than in the west of the country (7.3 percent). Contrary to common belief, this is a rather recent phenomenon, reflecting opposite trends in west and east: While the percentage has dropped slightly in the west over the past decade, it has been on the increase in the eastern parts of the country.[8]

The German authorities closely monitor the extreme Right. Over 200 organizations and about 22,000 individuals are classified as "extreme Right" by authorities. They include 6,000 party members of the Right-wing National Democratic Party of Germany or NPD (*Nationaldemokratische Partei Deutschlands*); 1,000 party members of the *Bürgerbewegung pro NRW*; 6,000 neo-Nazis, and 7,500 indi-

---

[6] Neugebauer, Extremismus – Rechtsextremismus – Linksextremismus. In: Schubarth / Stöss (eds.), Rechtsextremismus in der Bundesrepublik Deutschland, 2001.
[7] Bundesministerium des Inneren, Verfassungsschutzbericht 2012, 2013.
[8] Decker / Kiess / Brähler, 2012.

viduals who are involved in local and sub-cultural activities of the extreme Right, notably in the music scene. In recent years, *Autonome Nationalisten* ('autonomous nationalists') have formed independent neo-Nazi groups who have developed innovative forms of activism, often copying from autonomous groups of the extreme Left.[9]

Some organizations encourage violence by openly arousing hatred, and even using violence themselves, while others (such as the NPD) try to avoid illegal activities and statements that could incite. A few (three since 2000) have formed armed terrorist groups. Between 2000 and 2006 three members of the National Socialist Underground or NSU (*Nationalsozialistischer Untergrund*) were responsible for the murder in Germany of nine people of immigrant origin and one police officer. The group has also been accused of two bomb attacks and fourteen bank robberies, and of developing and selling an anti-Semitic Monopoly-style board game called "Pogromoly" that features death camps and gas chambers. The failure of German authorities to dismantle this terrorist organization has been widely criticized and a parliamentary investigation committee was established.[10] The NSU did not focus on terrorism against Jews, but a NSU member named Böhnhardt was convicted in 1997 and sentenced to more than two years in prison for an anti-Semitic act (hanging a mannequin with a Star of David painted on it from an overpass). Another terrorist group was the *Schutzgruppe* ('Protection Group') of the *Kameradschaft Süd* ('Comradeship South') in Munich. Both names refer to organizations of the National Socialist movement. In 2003, the *Schutzgruppe* planned a major bomb attack at the cornerstone laying ceremony of the Jewish cultural center in Munich. The third extreme Right terrorist group since 2000 was the *Freikorps Havelland* ('Free Corps Havelland'); Free Corps were paramilitary right wing organizations of ex-soldiers in the Weimar Republic – a group of eleven youth who were responsible for serious arson attacks in Brandenburg targeting snack bars run by people of migrant background.

Yet, the majority of the extreme Right activities are rallies, publications, and nurturing of a neo-Nazi musical subculture, although some entities do participate in democratic elections. Besides their propaganda value, political rallies form a core element in the extreme Right's operations, serving as a form of power projection, both internally and externally. In 2012, there were 95 neo-Nazi rallies and 167 in 2011. The rallies focused on charges of "state repression," targeting those perceived as political enemies, spreading anti-Islamic content and address-

---

[9] Bundesministerium des Inneren, 2013, pp. 54–56; Bundesministerium des Inneren, Verfassungsschutzbericht 2011, 2012.
[10] The results and recommendations were published 22 August 2013. See http://www.bundestag.de/bundestag/ausschuesse17/ua/2untersuchungsausschuss/ (accessed April 4, 2015).

ing social issues. An abiding theme has branding bombardment of German cities during the Second World War by the Allies as crimes against humanity perpetrated against innocent Germans. (In other years, "solidarity with Palestine" has also been a prominent issue, in part to paint Jews as victimizers.) Annual marches in recent years in Dresden and Magdeburg to commemorate carpet bombing of these cities serve as an important mobilization ploy for neo-Nazis. The demonstrations have attracted up to a thousand participants every year. In January 2013, however, there was a successful counter-demonstration of about 12,000 people in Magdeburg and the neo-Nazis were forced to relocate their march in the suburbs instead of the center of Magdeburg. The annual march in Dresden also faces large and successful counter-demonstrations, at least since 2010. Another major annual event in recent years is "National Anti-War Day" in Dortmund held in early September, organized by neo-Nazis as part of revisionist propaganda that denies German responsibility for the outbreak of the Second World War in regard to the German invasion of Poland on 1 September 1939 (a demonstration that has also sparked a 'challenge' from civil society).

The main publications of the extreme Right in Germany include the monthly NPD journal *Deutsche Stimme* ('German Voice'), the *National-Zeitung* ('National Paper'), and a number of major Right-wing websites. The largest online portal of the extreme Right *Altermedia.de* was forced to close down in September 2012 and now only operates via Twitter. Parallel to these, thousands of other neo-Nazi and extreme-Right websites are active, particularly regional news portals such as *MUPINFO* in Mecklenburg-Vorpommern and websites run by local independent neo-Nazi groups who use the social media and video clips to disseminate neo-Nazi content.

Hate propaganda includes hate-infused lullabies for children as young as three. Music for older schoolchildren contains blatantly hate-filled messages; incitement to kill Jews is widespread.[11] According to the accounts of some experts working in schools, about a third of young people in Germany have listened to such music at least once.[12] In their efforts to disseminate hate music as a core element in extreme Rightist propaganda, activists even go so far as to distribute CDs outside schools. In music, the messages of the extreme Right are voiced more openly and aggressively than in other media.[13]

A number of extreme Right parties have had some success in local and regional elections. Currently – following the amalgamation of the NPD and the

---

11 Bundesministerium des Innern, Antisemitismus in Deutschland, 2011a.
12 Rafael, Interview with Hans Joachim Stockschläger, June 10, 2009.
13 Berliner Senatsverwaltung für Inneres und Sport and Abteilung Verfassungsschutz, Rechtsextremistische Musik, 2012.

German People's Union (*Deutsche Volksunion* or DVU) – the NPD constitutes the dominant party of the extreme Right in Germany. They hold approximately 300 seats in municipal councils across Germany (in all of the German Länder except Hamburg) and, in 2013, won 13 seats in regional parliaments in Saxony and Mecklenburg-Vorpommern.

What are the main themes 'marketed' by such groups? What role does anti-Semitism play? Anti-Semitism is only one of a number of themes promoted by the extreme Right and its anti-Semitic messages are muted to avoid legal action. In fact, the main issues of the extreme Right have shifted over the years. While it was primarily about asylum seekers in the 1990s, the extreme Right has always responded to burning political issues on the current agenda. Thus, in their propaganda, extreme Right organizations have come to focus on five main topics which they address and interlace with their own brand of xenophobia, racism, and anti-Semitism:

- revisionist issues, most prominently German victimhood during the Second World War
- migration, Islam, asylum seekers, multiculturalism
- repression by authorities (police persecution and the justice system)
- the alleged 'Jewish lobby' in the United States and Germany, and anti-Zionism
- poverty, social welfare policy, and related social issues

Anti-Semitism manifests itself in a number of forms. The most prominent is revisionist positions that diminish the Holocaust and German responsibility for the mass killings of Jews. Tropes that are often described as "secondary anti-Semitism" and Holocaust inversion (contextual reversals of victim and victimizer) are popular in the extreme Right (probably, in part, because such statements are generally not persecuted and can be paraded as 'legitimate' criticism). Nevertheless, often the line to Holocaust denial (a crime in Germany) is crossed.[14] Conspiracy theories of a 'Jewish lobby' in Germany and in the United States (political anti-Semitism) are often voiced in the context of the global crisis. Among some, anti-Zionism and "solidarity with the Palestinians" tends to boil-up parallel to periodic flare-ups in the Israeli-Palestinian conflict. While some factions regard

---

14 Member of Parliament in Mecklenburg-Vorpommern Udo Pastörs (NPD) was convicted for defamation of victims of National Socialism and survivors in 2012 and 2013. He also used the Nazi-term *Judenrepublik* ('Jew Republic') to describe Germany in the context of the current global financial crisis. Extracts of his talk are documented at http://daserste.ndr.de/panorama/aktuell/pastoersnpdhetzrede102.html (accessed April 1, 2015).

this conflict as marginal,[15] for others anti-Zionism is an important component in their anti-imperialist and anti-American worldview.[16] Racist anti-Semitism, however, is less common today, even among neo-Nazis, and religious anti-Semitism is marginal.[17]

Campaigns against Muslims or against the alleged "Islamization of Germany" – for example, the NPD campaign in 2010 – do not necessarily lead to negative views of Muslim countries, let alone positive views about Israel. Udo Voigt, the NPD leader until 2011, explained: "The enmity against Islam in domestic politics does not exclude the appreciation of the Islamic world externally as the last bastion against the capitalization and Americanization of the world."[18]

The extreme Right generally avoids blunt anti-Semitic statements in public and employs insinuations and innuendos which in the subtext are easily understood for their anti-Semitic intentions. Code words such as "Wall Street," "the lobby," "US-East Coast," "high finance," or "forces in the back" are understood as synonyms for "the Jews."[19]

In recent official statements (that is, on the NPD website and in newspapers) the word 'Aryan' can hardly be found and anti-Semitism is coded, although easily detectable. Henrik Ostendorf, the former executive of the NPD journal *Deutsche Stimme*, provides an example of how messages are transmitted: Discussing the strategy of the extreme Right, between "change through participation" and attacks "against the system" (that is open opposition to democracy in Germany), Ostendorf said that the "national camp" should "be creative and even has to work with the devil if necessary, as long as he is not from Jerusalem."[20] The NPD clearly

---

[15] The president of the *Junge Nationaldemokraten* (the NPD youth organization), Michael Schäfer, stands for such a position that he elaborated in their main publication *Aktivist* (2/2012). A marginal group of "National Socialists for Israel" was founded in 2008 but it has not been active since. In their pamphlet Reinhard Heydrich was quoted "As a National Socialist I am a Zionist." See: Beck, in: Zukunft, July 25, 2008. The marginal group of pro-Israeli Neonazi puts itself in the tradition of Nazis who supported Zionism to get rid of the Jews before they turned to the extermination of Jews.
[16] The Neonazi network "Freies Netz Hessen" campaigns against Israel with the slogan "Israel kills… and the world looks on," using music, websites, social media, stickers, tags, and publicly displayed banners.
[17] Pfahl-Traughber, 2011b.
[18] Author's translation, Voigt, Kommentar. Kriegsjahr, January 2010; quoted in: Pfeiffer, Islamfeindschaft als Kampagnenthema, 2012, p. 230.
[19] For a detailed report on symbols and signs used by the extreme Right and banned organizations see Bundesamt für Verfasssungsschutz, Symbole und Zeichen der Rechtsextremisten, 2013.
[20] Author's translation, Deutsche Stimme, Januar 2011, p. 3; quoted in Bundesministerium des Inneren, Verfassungsschutzbericht 2010, 2011b, p. 81.

works to overthrow democracy in Germany, while clarifying in the subtext that Jews and Israel are viewed as *the* enemies *par excellence*, worse than the devil.

Interestingly, the NPD has an official position on anti-Semitism. On its website we can read

> Is the NPD an Anti-Semitic Party?
>
> How is anti-Semitism defined? Criticism against Jewish pressure groups? We certainly have the right to criticize the loudmouth and the never-ending financial claims of the Central Council of Jews in Germany. Jews are not object to [sic. don't enjoy] a ban on criticism. We refuse to be blackmailed 60 years after the end of the war by the Holocaust-Industry, a term coined by the Jew Norman Finkelstein, to be politically patronized, and to be financially squeezed.
>
> Anti-Semitism thus means criticism of Jews? Of course, one can also criticize Jews. The cult of guilt, which has been pursued by the Jewish side for 60 years and the eternal Jewish self-stylization as victims, does not have to be tolerated by any German. There must be an end to the psychological warfare by Jewish power groups against our people. In the end, it is clear that the Holocaust-Industry just wants to squeeze the Germans financially with moral pretenses again and again.[21]

The NPD does not openly endorse anti-Semitism in a way anti-Semites did prior and during the Second World War, but the party questions the definition of anti-Semitism by using anti-Semitic tropes. A number of keywords and insinuations about Jews, power, and money are employed as well as linguistic references to the Nazis, such as the Jewish 'loudmouth' (*Jüdische Großmäuligkeit*) – a term that often appears in Nazi propaganda. Using 'the Jew Norman Finkelstein' and his biased thesis of the 'Holocaust Industry' the accusation of anti-Semitism is presented as a form of 'blackmailing.' Particularly the second paragraph refers to popular anti-Semitic tropes and the demand for an end to the debate about German guilt (*Schlussstrich*). Thus, anti-Semitism is reproduced, albeit in thinly-veiled forms, in official positions of the NPD.[22]

More direct forms of anti-Semitism can be found on websites and publications by *Kameradschaften* and *Autonome Nationalisten* and on the German section of the international *National Journal* which states: "Almost all wars, particularly the two world wars, were initiated by the Hebrew power centers. We owe the exploitation of humanity and our impoverishment to the financial crisis-fraud to the same

---

21 Author's translation, http://www.npd.de/html/1939/artikel/detail/2098/.
22 The same text was published in a NPD guidebook for NPD candidates and leaders. See: NPD Parteivorstand / Amt für Öffentlichkeitsarbeit (eds.), Argumente für Kandidaten, 2006.

people." The *National Journal* advertises the anti-Semitic book *Judenfibel* in the same issue:

> The "Judenfibel" shall contribute to recognizing the 'program against humanity,' so that the modern kings, today's elite, will not dare to let themselves be sucked in for money and other benefits by the modern Esthers and Mordechais. If we resisted those people's temptations and dropped out of such activities nobody would need to be afraid of the Jews and the world would become a happier place.[23]

The bluntest verbal forms of anti-Semitism, however, are to be found in music.[24] Band names such as *Aktion Reinhard* ('Action Reinhard'), *Endlöser* ('Endsolutioner'), *Terrorkorps* ('Terror Corps'), and albums with titles such as *SA voran* ('SA Go Ahead') and *Juden sind hier unerwünscht* ('Jews are not welcome here') speak for themselves. They view the Holocaust in a positive light. The lyrics of one song by vocalist called Teja in his (banned) album *Rachezeit* ('Time for Revenge') are as follows:

> You won't be bothered by doubts any more.
> You will be part of the insurgence.
> We will shatter the Jew tyranny

and in another song:

> Are Judas' arts just mockery?
> Don't give mercy.
> If you cannot raise the sword,
> so choke them without fear."[25]

Others, such as the band *Zug um Zug* ('Train by Train' or 'Step by Step') refer to Israel in their explicit wish for the murder of Jews, using traditional anti-Semitic stereotypes.[26]

---

23 Author's translation, National Journal, January 1, 2013.
24 For more examples of antisemitism and incitement to kill Jews in extreme Right music see: Pfahl-Traughber, 2011b, p. 141, 144.
25 Author's translation, the lyrics in German read: "Keine Zweifel werden dich noch stören. Bei dem Aufstand bist du dabei. Wir zerschlagen die Judentyrannei." and: "Sind Judas Künste nur Spott? Sind Judas Künste nur Spott? Gebt kein Pardon. Könnt ihr das Schwert nicht heben, so würgt sie ohne Scheu." Liedermacher *Teja*, CD „Rachezeit", quoted in: Bundesministerium des Inneren, 2012, p. 112.
26 "Look at the crooked noses with greedy hands down there in the far country. They instigate wars and destroy the world, it's all about money this pack. 2000 years ago we knew, the gallows is the just reward. And today it does not look different, I'll say it clear, Judea out. Train by train

Islamists in Germany

Islamists, by definition, strive for a society governed according to Islamic law.[27] In their view, laws should not be made by elected leaders, rather *Shari'a* law should rule.[28] Islamists therefore reject democracy although some Islamist organizations use democracy and elections in order to gain political power. Islamists, like the extreme Right, aim for a fundamental change in the political system. Yet, most Islamist organizations in Germany operate within a legal framework and reject the use of violence.

Anti-Semitism and a fundamental opposition to the Western world[29] is part and parcel of Islamist movements both historically and today, and in different parts of the world.[30] Islamist organizations in Germany are no exception.[31] We

---

into the camp, train by train, total deportation. Train by train to hell. Train by train for a pure nation." Author's translation. The original text reads: "Seht ihr da unten im fernen Land, die krummen Nasen mit gieriger Hand. Sie zetteln Kriege an und zerstören die Welt, es geht diesem Pack nur ums Geld. Vor 2000 Jahren wusste man schon, der Galgen ist der gerechte Lohn. Und heute sieht es nicht anders aus, ich sage es deutlich, Judäa raus. Zug um Zug ab ins Lager, Zug um Zug totale Deportation. Zug um Zug ab in die Hölle. Zug um Zug für eine reine Nation." Quoted in: Bundesministerium des Innern, 2013, p. 126.

27 Islamists do not acknowledge that interpretations of Islamic scripture are unavoidable if they are read and used today. Tarek Fatah argues that political Islam and building a society on Shari'a law is delusional and goes against Islamic teachings. See: Fatah, Chasing a Mirage, 2008.

28 Armim Pfahl-Traughber distinguishes Islamism from Political Islam. The term "Political Islam" also includes political movements that seek guidance in Islam but fully accept democracy. See: Pfahl-Traughber, Akteure des Islamismus. In: Biskamp / Hößl (eds.), Islam und Islamismus, 2013, p. 67.

29 A recurrent theme in Islamist writings and teachings is that the West *first and foremost* concerns itself with fighting Islam and destroying the Muslim identity. See: Shavit, Islamism and the West, 2013. This is often framed in religious terms, that is as a war between Christianity (and Judaism) and Islam. See: Jikeli, Antisemitismus und Diskriminierungswahrnehmungen, 2012a.

30 See: Tibi, 2012; Pfahl-Traughber, Antisemitismus im Islamismus. In: Pfahl-Traughber / Fünfsinn (eds.), Extremismus und Terrorismus, 2011a; Wistrich, 2010; Mallmann / Cüppers, 2010; Küntzel, Jihad and Jew-Hatred, 2007; Kepel / Milelli / Ghazaleh, Al Qaeda in Its Own Words, 2008; Farschid, Antisemitismus im Islamismus. In: Pfahl-Traughber (ed.), Jahrbuch für Extremismus- und Terrorismusforschung 2009/2010, 2010; Rensmann / Schoeps (eds.), Feindbild Judentum, 2008.2011 While anti-Semitism is voiced most openly by Islamists, anti-Semitism is endemic in almost all Muslim-majority countries. Surveys show that negative views of Jews are shared by well over 70 percent of the population in countries with Muslim majorities and by more than 90 percent in Muslim-Arab countries. Pew Global Attitudes Project, Muslim-Western Tensions Persist, 2011. These anti-Jewish attitudes are often embedded in negative views of the Western world in general, see: Friedman, in: The New York Times, November 28, 2009. Characteristics of contemporary antisemitism in Arab and Muslim-majority countries have been described as chimeric lies about Jews, such as making "the Jews" responsible for the attacks of September 11, 2001, the

find ample evidence of anti-Semitism in the history of Islamist organizations from their beginnings in the early twentieth century, in its ideology and in the writings of ideological leaders such as *Sayyid Qutb*, *Hassan al-Banna* ('Muslim Brotherhood'), *Sayyid Abul Ala Maududi* (*Jamaat-I Islami*, the 'Islamic Assembly' or 'Party'), and *Ruhollah Khomeini* (Iran). Anti-Semitism is also present in current publications and other activities. Islamist organizations are often internationally connected and Islamists in Germany are strongly influenced by foreign organizations. There are, however, also some specific developments particular to Germany and some dynamics that are singularly German.

Islamist movements, mostly by the Muslim Brotherhood, which is not considered radical, influence the majority of Islamic organizations in Europe.[32] Prominent leaders of the Muslim Brotherhood such as former Egyptian president Mohammed Morsi or Egyptian Islamic theologian Yusuf al-Qaradawi, who is also head of the European Council for Fatwa and Research, have made blatantly anti-Semitic statements in public.[33] What is the influence of such voices in Germany?

German authorities have numerated 42,550 persons in 2012 affiliated with Islamist organizations. The largest Islamist and second-largest Muslim organization in Germany[34] is the Islamic Community *Milli Görüş* or IGMG (*Islamische Gemeinschaft Milli Görüş*) with over 300 mosques and local associations and 31,000 registered members in Germany, almost exclusively individuals of Turkish origin. An alleged representative body on a national level called the *Islamrat* is almost identical to

---

phenomenon of Holocaust denial, and a revival of the "Protocols of the Elders of Zion," including the blood libel. See: Foxman, Muslimischer Antisemitismus. In: Rensmann / Schoeps (eds.), Feindbild Judentum, 2008; Wistrich, Muslim Anti-Semitism, 2002.
31 See: Bundesministerium des Inneren, 2011a; Tibi, 2012; Jikeli, European Muslim Antisemitism, 2015.
32 Rubin, The Muslim Brotherhood, 2010; Johnson, A Mosque in Munich, 2010; Maréchal, The Muslim Brothers in Europe, 2008; Jikeli, Antisemitism Among European Muslims. In: Rosenfeld (ed.), Resurgend Antisemitism, 2013; Jikeli, 2012a.
33 Mohammed Morsi described Jews as descendants of apes and pigs in 2010 and Yusuf al-Qaradawi said on Al-Jazeera in 2009: "Throughout history, Allah has imposed upon the [Jews] people who would punish them for their corruption. The last punishment was carried out by Hitler. By means of all the things he did to them – even though they exaggerated this issue – he managed to put them in their place. This was divine punishment for them. Allah willing, the next time will be at the hand of the believers." Both is documented by the Middle East Media Research Institute. See: ww.memri.org.
34 The largest Islamic organization in Germany, DITIB (*Diyanet İşleri Türk İslam Birliği*), is closely related to the Turkish government and traditionally secular. However, since Turkey is run by an Islamist government (and an antisemitic Prime Minister) since 2003, there have been some Islamist tendencies also within DITIB.

the IGMG. The organization is part of the international organization *Milli Görüş* (literally, "a national view") founded by Necmettin Erbakan in Turkey in the 1960s, once the political mentor of Turkey's Prime Minister Recep Tayyip Erdoğan. *Milli Görüş* ideology is rooted in a nationalistic form of Islamism that aspires to create a "Greater Turkey" under Islamic rule, loosely based on the borders of the former Ottoman Empire. The organization was and still is strongly influenced by Erbakan, despite his death in 2011. IGMG celebrated an "Erbakan Week" in February 2012 and IGMG leaders frequently cite and emulate Erbakan's life and teachings.[35] Erbakan repeatedly and publicly voiced anti-Semitic views. He shared his views with German readers in an interview with the German daily *Die Welt* in 2010 – including charges that the world is run by "Zionist Imperialists" claiming "for five-thousand seven-hundred years Jews have ruled the world." In the interview, he further expanded this canard with a number of additional Jewish conspiracy theories.[36]

IGMG publishes two magazines for a Turkish-German audience (in Turkish). A (brief) review of recent issues of the periodical supports the prognosis that the IGMG currently avoids blatant anti-Semitic statements. While Holocaust denial and anti-Semitic conspiracy theories are common in the Turkish-Dutch Milli Görüş publication *Doğuş*,[37] the IGMG in Germany seems to be more cautious in this respect. On the other hand, the Turkish Milli Görüş newspaper *Milli Gazete*, which publishes European editions printed in Germany, has repeatedly published crude anti-Semitic conspiracy theories.[38] The IGMG in Germany has strong links to radical groups such as the pro-Hamas organization IHH. Links have not been cut even after the latter was outlawed in Germany.[39] Signs of anti-Semitic ideology can also be found at book fairs in mosques associated with the IGMG where viciously anti-Semitic literature has been displayed.[40]

The second-largest Islamist organization in Germany is the Muslim Brotherhood (MB) which numbers 1,300 members all told, in different organizations. One of the main MB organizations is the Islamic Community in Germany (*Islamische Gemeinschaft in Deutschland* or IGD), founded in 1958 during a campaign to build

---

[35] There is no evidence for Werner Schiffauer's thesis that the IGMG is now "post-Islamist" and that the younger generation dissociates itself from Erbakan's ideology, see: Schiffauer, Nach dem Islamismus, 2010. Although Islamist statements were made more frequently and more openly before the mid-1990s Erbakan's positions have not been questioned and the IGMG in Germany is still closely associated with the Turkish Milli Görüş movement, see: Pfahl-Traughber, 2013.

[36] In this Interview, Erbakan also criticized Erdoğan and accused him for being "a cashier of Zionism." Kálnoky, in: Welt Online, August 11, 2010.

[37] Stremmelaar, Dutch and Turkish Memories of Genocide, 2013.

[38] Pfahl-Traughber, 2011b, p. 124–125.

[39] Am Orde / Beucker / Schmidt / Wiese, in: Tageszeitung, July 18, 2010.

[40] Demirel, in: DAVID, June 2006.

the Freimann Mosque in Munich.[41] The different MB networks form an important part of the Muslim umbrella organization, the Central Council of Muslims in Germany (*Zentralrat der Muslime in Deutschland* or ZMD). The ZMD also includes the Turkish-Islamic Union for Religious Affairs (*Union der Türkisch-Islamischen Kulturvereine in Europa* or ATIP), a religious spin off of the extreme Right nationalist Turkish group Grey Wolves, with approximately 8,000 members and Iran-oriented Shiites of various origins.[42]

While these organizations and federations wield influence in many mosques, Islamist internet portals are able to reach out to Muslims at home. *Muslim-Markt* is one of the main Islamic portals in German, founded and operated by German Shiites of Turkish origin. It provides religious guidance, Islamic matchmaking, links to other Islamist organizations, news (including an online Muslim-TV channel), interviews (mostly with non-Muslim authors, Islamic scholars, and clerics), and publishes special supplement issues as well under banners such as "Palestine-Special" or "[The] US Crusade against the World." Its positions are often closely-linked to those of the Iranian government.

Similar to the NPD, the *Muslim-Markt* banners a statement criticizing the definition of anti-Semitism.

> Today, those who dare criticize Israel's brutal and inhuman policies are labeled "anti-Semite[s]." The criticism is in most cases directed against the brutality of a regime of occupation and has nothing to do with racism. *Moreover, the Arabs for example are also Semites* [emphasis in the original], so Arabs can therefore hardly be antisemites. In addition, many Jewish prophets are highly respected and honored in the Holy Quran, such as Zacharias, John, David, Solomon, Moses, Aaron, and last-but-not- least Jesus and Mary who are descendents of the Jewish tribe of "Aali Imran."
>
> For the reasons mentioned we should not use the term "anti-Semitism" but *anti-Zionism* [emphasis in the original] to rightly denounce the oppression and the Zionist racial fanaticism. The man of Jewish faith Finkelstein has himself voiced criticism of Zionist financial practices and has to defend himself now against accusation of anti-Semitism [...].[43]

The statement includes the canard that Arabs cannot be anti-Semitic because they are "Semites" themselves (although there is no Semitic ethnicity, only Semitic languages such as Hebrew and Arabic). The editors use this and the fact that many Jewish prophets are also Muslim prophets (often in somewhat different ways), to imply that Muslims or Arabs cannot be anti-Semitic by nature.

---

41 Johnson, 2010.
42 Dantschke, Islam und Islamismus in Deutschland, 2006.
43 Author's translation, emphasis in original, see: http://www.muslim-markt.de/Palaestina-Spezial/diverse/verfaelschung/antisemitismus.htm (accessed April 1, 2015).

In another editorial entry *Muslim-Markt* denounces anti-Semitism as a form of racism while charging that equating anti-Zionism with anti-Semitism is "one of the worst forms of anti-Semitism."[44] The authors view accusations of anti-Semitism (misplaced and erroneous in their view) first and foremost in the context of the Israeli-Palestinian conflict. Israel, however, is put in quotation marks ('Israel') suggesting there is no genuine polity of this nature and that this is an invented construct. Interestingly enough, the *Muslim-Markt*, just like the NPD, uses Finkelstein's Jewish identity and his anti-Zionist positions as an alibi to justify its own anti-Semitic positions.[45]

The number of Salafists is small but growing, according to German authorities: 4,500 in 2012, up from 3,800 in 2011. Salafists adhere to literalist, strict, and puritanical interpretations of Islam often associated with Wahabism. In its aspiration to emulate the life of the first followers of Islam (the Salaf), Salafists believe religious rulings can and should be applied to the smallest details in life.[46] Most Salafists in Germany reject violence and their political and religious activism differs from so-called Jihadist Salafists who endorse violence. Political Salafists in Germany such as Ibrahim Abou-Nagie and the Muslim convert Pierre Vogel focus on 'proselytizing Islam' (*Dawa*); as a result, Salafism has gained a relatively high profile in Germany through public sermons, free dissemination of the Qur'an, seminars, and video messages. In 2012, the Salafist organization The Real Islam gained prominence when its members distributed hundreds of thousands of copies of the Qur'an in Germany. One of its leaders, Abu-Nagie maintains resolutely that Jews and Christians are damned and co-existence with them is not an option.[47]

No matter how rigid or intolerant their message may be, one must make a clear designation between these *legal* organizations and terror organizations such as Hamas (which has about 300 members in Germany), Hezbollah (about 950 members), the Kurdish–Iraqi Ansar-al-Islam, or the Islamic Movement of Uzbekistan – all of them fiercely anti-Semitic. The latter publishes Jihadist propaganda also in German. A spin-off, the Islamic Jihad Union, also active in Germany, was

---

44 Author's translation, see: http://www.muslim-markt.de/Palaestina-Spezial/diverse/aufruf_gegen_antisemitismus.htm (accessed April 1, 2015).
45 Emmanuele Ottolenghi notes: "In a world where antisemitism is unacceptable in social and political discourse, Israeli and/or Jewish intellectuals complying with the calls of Israel's detractors and demonizers constitute an alibi for antisemitism." See: Ottolenghi, Antisemitism and the Centrality of the Jewish Alibi. In: Rosenfeld (ed.), Resurgent Antisemitism, 2013.
46 Salafism is, despite its backward ideology, attractive in the modern word, particularly because it provides simple rules and values. Bundesamt für Verfassungsschutz, Salafistische Bestrebungen in Deutschland, 2012.
47 See interview with Abu-Nagie by Holger Schmidt, broadcast on radio SWR Info, May 24, 2012.

responsible for the terror attacks against the American and Israeli embassies in Uzbekistan in 2004. These organizations use Germany as a fundraising platform and as an area of retreat. Hezbollah has participated openly in a number of rallies in Germany, mostly in the context of the Israeli-Palestinian conflict. Hamas operates indirectly in Germany – other organizations acting as proxies for Hamas to garner support for its needs and objectives. The Palestinian Return Center – an organization with close links to Hamas – organized a conference in 2011 in Wuppertal that attracted 3.000 participants. The Islamist Party of Liberation (*Hizb ut-Tahir*) which aspires to establish a global Islamic theocracy has been banned in Germany since 2003 due to its anti-Semitic propaganda, however, it still publishes material in German[48] and continues to stir-up hatred against Jews, Israel, and Americans.

The direct security threat from Islamists for Jewish institutions in Germany became evident in 2002, after German authorities foiled a terrorist attack targeting the Jewish community center in Berlin and Jewish restaurants in Düsseldorf. The attacks were planned by members of the Al-Queda affiliated terror cell 'Unity of the Faithful' (*El-Tawhid*). Since then, a number of radical Islamists have been arrested for similar plans against Jewish targets in Germany.[49] The first actual act of terrorism by radical Islamists on German soil was the killing of two American soldiers in March 2011. Others have been arrested and convicted for being member of foreign terrorist organizations; many of them are German citizens, including converts. German authorities closely monitor at least 235 radical Islamists who have received military training abroad or intend to do so. It can be assumed that this number has risen significantly with the ongoing civil war in Syria and Iraq with ISIS. Ideologically, radical Islamists see themselves at war with "Zionists" and "crusaders" – meaning Jews and the Western world.

Music is less important to Islamists in the dissemination of their ideology than to the extreme Right. A number of Islamist groups even reject listening to music for religious reasons. Nevertheless, a number of rappers, such as Deso Dogg (ex-rapper and Jihadist in Syria in 2013), Bushido, and Yasser & Ozman, both from Austria, present themselves as Muslims and disseminate Islamist and anti-Semitic messages. Yasser & Ozman released a video (in German) entitled *An alle Brüder* ('To all Brothers'), with the following lyrics:

---

[48] Hizb ut-Tahir publishes online in German at http://www.kalifat.com/ (accessed April 1, 2015).
[49] DPA – Deutsche Presse Agentur, in: Die Zeit, December 11, 2012. For an overview of terrorist incidents against Jewish Diaspora communities worldwide and Israeli citizens abroad see: Community Security Trust, Terrorist Incidents, 2011.

The world in which we live is governed by Zionists [...]
Palestine, Afghanistan and then Iraq.
That is still not enough for them.
Now they want Iran.
The Saudis are watching [...]
The traitors are allied with Allah's major enemies [...]
Therefore, finally, to all Freemasons:
I get the eye into the crosshairs and pull the trigger [...]
I will die in Jihad.

Jihadist ideology is often disseminated in Internet forums and through social media (i.e. Jihadist groups rarely use their own website), albeit less openly since 2008 due to closer surveillance by secret services. Video clips are increasingly important and are released in many languages, including German (and also produced in Germany). Regional conflicts – such as in Chechnya, Afghanistan, Iraq, and 'Palestine' – are portrayed as religious conflicts that pit Islam against Christianity and Judaism.[50] These views, however, are also shared by some 'ordinary' Muslims who are neither Jihadists nor organized in Islamist organizations.[51]

Conclusion

The two movements – extreme Right and Islamists – in Germany include a variety of organizations with different aims and *modi operandi*. They share anti-Semitic ideology to different degrees and their anti-Semitism takes various forms. Only a few organization, focus mainly on anti-Semitism in word *and* deed, some posing a direct threat to Jewish communities in Germany. Despite their relatively small numbers, the threat from the extreme Right and Islamists against Jews is serious, including terrorist attacks. Most anti-Semitic crimes, including violent attacks, are committed by the extreme Right. Islamists are usually not involved in street violence against Jews, damage to property, and desecration of Jewish cemeteries. There are attacks against Jews by some young Muslims but these Muslims are usually not members of Islamist organizations, although at times they have been influenced by Islamist ideology.[52]

---

50 Steinberg (ed.), Jihadismus und Internet, 2012.
51 Jikeli, Discrimination of European Muslims. In: Soen / Shechory / Ben-David (eds.), Minority Groups, 2012.
52 Jikeli, 2013; Arnold / Jikeli, Judenhass und Gruppendruck, 2008.

While open anti-Semitism and people who act upon extreme Rightist or radical Islamist ideology remain marginal in Germany, both ideologies find supporters in mainstream society and in mainstream Islam in Germany, respectively.

Neo-Nazi and Islamist anti-Semites rarely cooperate on an organizational level since ideological differences are far too great despite some similarities.[53] Both movements in Germany criticize the definition of anti-Semitism and some mobilize Jewish anti-Zionists to legitimize their own anti-Semitic positions.

References

Am Orde, Sabine, Pascal Beucker, Wolf Schmidt, and Daniel Wiese. "Islamismus in Deutschland: Die netten Herren von Milli Görüs." *Tageszeitung*, July 18, 2010. http://www.taz.de/!55746/ (accessed April 1, 2015).

Arnold, Sina, Günther Jikeli. Judenhass und Gruppendruck – Zwölf Gespräche mit jungen Berlinern palästinensischen und libanesischen Hintergrunds. In *Jahrbuch für Antisemitismusforschung* 17, Wolfgang Benz (ed.), pp. 17105–17130. Berlin: Metropol Verlag, 2008.

Beck, Eldad: "Falsche Freunde." *Zukunft*, July 25, 2008. http://www.zentralratdjuden.de/de/article/1836.falsche-freunde.html (accessed April 1, 2015).

Brettfeld, Katrin, Peter Wetzels. *Muslime in Deutschland – Integration, Integrationsbarrieren, Religion sowie Einstellungen zu Demokratie, Rechtsstaat und politisch-religiös motivierter Gewalt – Ergebnisse von Befragungen im Rahmen einer multizentrischen Studie in städtischen Lebensräumen*. Universität Hamburg / Bundesministerium des Inneren, 2007.

Bundesamt für Verfasssungsschutz. *Salafistische Bestrebungen in Deutschland*. Köln, 2012.

Bundesamt für Verfasssungsschutz. *Symbole und Zeichen der Rechtsextremisten*. Köln, 2013.

Bundesministerium des Inneren. *Antisemitismus in Deutschland. Erscheinungsformen, Bedingungen, Präventionsansätze. Bericht des unabhängigen Expertenkreises Antisemitismus*. Berlin, 2011a.

Bundesministerium des Inneren. *Verfassungsschutzbericht 2010*. Berlin, 2011b.

Bundesministerium des Inneren. *Verfassungsschutzbericht 2011*. Berlin, 2012.

Bundesministerium des Inneren. *Verfassungsschutzbericht 2012*. Berlin, 2013.

Community Security Trust. *Terrorist Incidents against Jewish Communities and Israeli Citizens Abroad 1968–2010*, 2011. https://cst.org.uk/data/file/2/c/Terrorist-Incidents-1968-2010.1425053936.pdf (accessed April 1, 2015).

Dantschke, Claudia. "Islam und Islamismus in Deutschland." *ZDK Gesellschaft Demokratische Kultur*, 2006. http://www.zentrum-demokratische-kultur.de/Startseite/ZDK/Islamismus/K259.htm.

---

[53] Attempts for a closer cooperation have been made. In 2002, leaders of the extreme Right, Udo Voigt and Horst Mahler, visited a Hizb ut-Tahir conference about the imminent attack on Iraq. There are also a few links on an individual level. The convert and Jihadist, Robert Baum, convicted for terrorist charges, had apparently been rejected by the army some years earlier because he had uploaded extreme Rightist propaganda on the Internet.

Decker, Oliver, Johannes Kiess, and Elmar Brähler. *Die Mitte Im Umbruch. Rechtsextreme Einstellungen in Deutschland 2012*. Bonn: Dietz, 2012.
Demirel, Aycan. "Kreuzberger Initiative Gegen Antisemitismus." *DAVID – Jüdische Kulturzeitschrift*, June 2006. http://www.david.juden.at/kulturzeitschrift/66-70/69-demirel.htm (accessed April 1, 2015).
DPA – Deutsche Presse Agentur. "Extremismus: Hintergrund: Islamistische Bedrohungen in Deutschland." *Die Zeit*, December 11, 2012. http://www.zeit.de/news/2012-12/11/extremismus-hintergrund-islamistische-bedrohungen-in-deutschland-11225016 (accessed April 1, 2015).
Farschid, Olaf. Antisemitismus im Islamismus. Ideologische Formen des Judenhasses bei islamistischen Gruppen. In *Jahrbuch für Extremismus- und Terrorismusforschung 2009/2010*, Armin Pfahl-Traughber (ed.), pp. 435–485. Brühl: Statistisches Bundesamt, 2010.
Fatah, Tarek. *Chasing a Mirage: The Tragic Illusion of an Islamic State*. Mississauga: J. Wiley & Sons, 2008.
Foxman, Abraham H. Muslimischer Antisemitismus zwischen Europa und dem Nahen Osten. In *Feindbild Judentum: Antisemitismus in Europa*, Lars Rensmann, Julius H. Schoeps (eds.), pp. 171–178. Berlin: Verlag für Berlin-Brandenburg, 2008.
Friedman, Thomas L. "America vs. The Narrative." *The New York Times*, November 28, 2009. http://www.nytimes.com/2009/11/29/opinion/29friedman.html?_r=0 (accessed April 1, 2015).
Frindte, Wolfgang, Klaus Boehnke, Henry Kreikenbom, Wolfgang Wagner. *Lebenswelten junger Muslime in Deutschland*. Berlin: Bundesministerium des Inneren, 2012.
Jikeli, Günther. *Antisemitismus und Diskriminierungswahrnehmungen junger Muslime in Europa*. Essen: Klartext, 2012a.
Jikeli, Günther. Discrimination of European Muslims: Self-Perceptions, Experiences and Discourses of Victimhood. In *Minority Groups: Coercion, Discrimination, Exclusion, Deviance and the Quest for Equality*, Dan Soen, Mally Shechory, and Sarah Ben-David (eds.), pp. 77–96. New York: Nova, 2012b.
Jikeli, Günther. Antisemitism Among European Muslims. In *Resurgent Antisemitism Global Perspectives*, Alvin H. Rosenfeld (ed.), pp. 267–307. Bloomington: Indiana University Press, 2013.
Jikeli, Günther. *European Muslim Antisemitism. Why Young Urban Males say that they don't like Yews*. Bloomington: Indiana University Press, 2015.
Johnson, Ian. *A Mosque in Munich: Nazis, the CIA, and the Rise of the Muslim Brotherhood in the West*. Boston: Mariner Books, 2010.
Kálnoky, Boris. "Erdogan ist ein Kassierer des Zionismus." *Welt Online*, August 11, 2010. http://www.welt.de/politik/ausland/article10769062/Erdogan-ist-ein-Kassierer-des-Zionismus.html (accessed April 1, 2015).
Kepel, Gilles, Jean-Pierre Milelli, and Pascale Ghazaleh. *Al Qaeda in Its Own Words*. Cambridge: Harvard University Press, 2008.
Kiefer, Michael. *Antisemitismus in den islamischen Gesellschaften: der Palästina-Konflikt und der Transfer eines Feindbildes*. Düsseldorf: Verein zur Förderung gleichberechtigte Kommunikation, 2002.
Küntzel, Matthias. *Jihad and Jew-Hatred: Islamism, Nazism and the Roots of 9/11*. New York: Telos Print, 2007.

Mallmann, Klaus-Michael, Martin Cüppers. *Nazi Palestine: The Plans for the Extermination of the Jews in Palestine* (Transl. Krista Smith). New York: Enigma Books, 2010.
Maréchal, Brigitte. *The Muslim Brothers in Europe: Roots and Discourse.* Leiden, Boston: Brill, 2008.
Müller, Jochen. Auf den Spuren von Nasser. Nationalismus und Antisemitismus im radikalen Islamismus. In *Antisemitismus und radikaler Islamismus*, Wolfgang Benz, Juliane Wetzel (eds.), pp. 85–101. Essen: Klartext 2007.
Neugebauer, Gero. Extremismus – Rechtsextremismus – Linksextremismus: Einige Anmerkungen zu Begriffen, Forschungskonzepten, Forschungsfragen und Forschungsergebnissen. In *Rechtsextremismus in der Bundesrepublik Deutschland: Eine Bilanz*, Wilfried Schubarth, Richard Stöss (eds.), pp. 13–37. Opladen: Leske & Budrich, 2001.
NPD Parteivorstand / Amt für Öffentlichkeitsarbeit (eds.). *Argumente für Kandidaten & Funktionsträger. Eine Handreichung für die öffentliche Auseinandersetzung.* Berlin 2006.
Ottolenghi, Emanuele. Antisemitism and the Centrality of the Jewish Alibi. In R*esurgent Antisemitism: Global Perspectives*, Alvin H. Rosenfeld (ed.), pp. 424–466. Bloomington: Indiana University, 2013.
Pew Global Attitudes Project. T*he Great Divide. How Westerners and Muslims View Each Other*, June 22, 2006. http://pewglobal.org/reports/pdf/253.pdf (accessed April 1, 2015).
Pew Global Attitudes Project. *Muslim-Western Tensions Persist*, July 21, 2011. http://www.ab.gov.tr/files/ardb/evt/1_avrupa_birligi/1_6_raporlar/1_3_diger/Pew-Global-Attitudes-Muslim-Western-Relations-FINAL-FOR-PRINT-July-21-2011.pdf (accessed April 1, 2015).
Pfahl-Traughber, Armin. Antisemitismus im Islamismus. Ideengeschichtliche Bedingungsfaktoren und agitatorische Erscheinungsformen. In *Extremismus und Terrorismus als Herausforderung für Gesellschaft und Justiz. Antisemitismus im Extremismus*, Armin Pfahl-Traughber, Helmut Fünfsinn (eds.), pp. 112–134. Brühl: Statistisches Bundesamt, 2011a.
Pfahl-Traughber, Armin. Antisemitismus im Rechtsextremismus. Externe und interne Funktionen, formale und ideologische Varianten. In *Extremismus und Terrorismus als Herausforderung für Gesellschaft und Justiz. Antisemitismus im Extremismus*, Armin Pfahl-Traughber, Helmut Fünfsinn (eds.), pp. 135–150. Brühl: Statistisches Bundesamt, 2011b.
Pfahl-Traughber, Armin. Akteure des Islamismus in der Bundesrepublik Deutschland. Analyse ihrer Aktivitäten im Lichte einer Gefahrenpotenzialeinschätzung. In *Islam und Islamismus: Perspektiven für die politische Bildung*, Floris Biskamp, Stefan E. Hößl (eds.), pp. 65–84. Gießen: Netzwerk für politische Bildung, 2013.
Pfeiffer, Thomas. Islamfeindschaft als Kampagnenthema im Rechtsextremismus. Erfolgspotenzial, strategische Hintergründe und Diskurstechniken am Beispiel der NPD. In *Jahrbuch für Extremismus- und Terrorismusforschung 2011/2012*, Armin Pfahl-Traughber (ed.), pp. 215–244. Brühl: Statistisches Bundesamt, 2012.
Rafael, Simone. *Jugendliche und rechtsextreme Musik: Immer neugierig, oft entsetzt und froh über Informationen.* Interview with Hans Joachim Stockschläger, June 10, 2009. http://www.netz-gegen-nazis.de/artikel/jugendliche-und-rechtsextreme-musik-3478 (accessed March, 31, 2015).
Rensmann, Lars. Against 'Globalism': Antisemitism and Counter-Cosmopolitanism in the Party Ideology of the Extreme Right in Europe. In *Politics and Resentment. Antisemitism and*

Counter-Cosmopolitanism in the European Union, Lars Rensmann, Julius H. Schoeps (eds.), pp. 117–146. Leiden, Boston: Brill, 2011.

Rensmann, Lars, Julius H. Schoeps (eds.). *Feindbild Judentum: Antisemitismus in Europa*. Berlin: Verlag für Berlin-Brandenburg, 2008.

Rubin, Barry. *The Muslim Brotherhood: The Organization and Policies of a Global Islamist Movement*. New York: Palgrave, 2010.

Schiffauer, Werner. *Nach dem Islamismus: die islamische Gemeinschaft Milli Görüs: Eine Ethnographie*. Frankfurt a. M.: Suhrkamp, 2010.

Senatsverwaltung für Inneres und Sport in Berlin, und Abteilung Verfassungsschutz. *Rechtsextremistische Musik*. Berlin, 2012.

Shavit, Uriya. *Islamism and the West: From "Cultural Attack" to "Missionary Migrant."* New York: Routledge, 2013.

Steinberg, Guido (ed.). *Jihadismus und Internet: Eine deutsche Perspektive*. Berlin: Stiftung Wissenschaft und Politik, 2012. http://www.swp-berlin.org/fileadmin/contents/products/studien/2012_S23_sbg.pdf (accessed April 1, 2015).

Stremmelaar, Annemarike. *'Dutch and Turkish Memories of Genocide: Contact or Competition?'* Expert-Meeting presented at the Changing Perceptions of the Holocaust Competing Histories and Collective Memory. Amsterdam, June 5, 2013.

Tibi, Bassam. From Sayyid Qutb to Hamas. The Middle East Conflict and the Islamization of Antisemitism. Working Paper. *The Yale Initiative for the Interdisciplinary Study of Antisemitism* 5 (2010), Charles Small (ed.). http://isgap.org/wp-content/uploads/2013/08/Tibi.pdf (accessed April 1, 2015).

Tibi, Bassam. *Islamism and Islam*. New Haven: Yale University Press, 2012.

Wistrich, Robert S. *Muslim Anti-Semitism. A Clear and Present Danger*. American Jewish Committee, 2002. http://www.ajc.org/atf/cf/%7B42D75369-D582-4380-8395-D25925B85EAF%7D/WistrichAntisemitism.pdf (accessed April 1, 2015).

Wistrich, Robert S. *A Lethal Obsession: Anti-Semitism from Antiquity to the Global Jihad*. New York: Random House, 2010.

H. Julia Eksner
Thrice Tied Tales

Germany, Israel, and German Muslim Youth

How can we understand the relationship between Germany, Israel, and German Muslim youths in the beginning of the twenty-first century? How are these three collectives – seemingly disparate in terms of their boundedness, historical relationship, and historical location – related, if at all? This article presents an excavation of how the modes of discourse about Jews, Israel, and German Muslim youth in Germany interact and impact on each other.

At the core, my discussion delineates three mutually interrelated and interdependent discourses behind the anti-Israeli positioning of (some)[1] youth from Muslim communities in Germany today. The argument made here is that German Muslim youth's positioning against Israel is by no means a 'natural' or 'cultural' given; rather, Muslim youth's responses are structured by preexisting discursive relations in Germany. It will be argued that in order to understand the anti-Israeli posture found among some German Muslim youths, one needs to understand less-obvious discursive and structural conditions that fuel and encourage such attitudes. The primary objective is thus to theorize and present the relationship of three conditions: Firstly, long-standing civilizational master narratives[2] of exclusion that have developed into a contemporary representation of Muslims as positioned in an antagonistic relationship vis-à-vis the State of Israel; secondly, a preexisting heightened and biased concern of the German media with Israel (i.e. *Israelkritik*, 'Criticism of Israel'); and thirdly, the emergence of narratives of victimization about and by disenfranchised German Muslim youths. Each will be explored in turn.

---

[1] I intentionally and repeatedly use the phrasing "(some) German Muslim youths" to indicate and reinforce that by no means all, or even the majority of German Muslim youths position themselves against the State of Israel. Rather, around 20 percent of youths who identified as Muslim were estimated to do so in surveys, see: Frindte / Boehnke / Kreikenbom / Wagner, Lebenswelten junger Muslime, 2012.

[2] Master narratives are grand narratives – real or imagined – shared by members of a given society that serve as the 'glue' of affinity behind collective identity – constructs whose authenticity and validity have been challenged by postmodern scholars.

Master Narratives of Exclusion: Europe's Others

Minorities, especially Jews, have made their home within the shifting borders of territories that have constituted Germany since the fifth century to today. Germany in the beginning of the twenty-first century is an immigration country with about 30 percent of its youth coming from immigrant communities. Most notably, today there are about four million Muslims from about 49 countries in Germany – representing approximately five percent of the population.[3] Thus, Germany's most prominent 'others' in the twentieth and the beginnings of the twenty-first century have been its substantial Jewish (prior to the Holocaust) and substantial Muslim (since the 1960s) communities. The conflicted relationship of Europe with its Jewish and Muslim minorities has been a long-standing topic of research, yet only most recently has discussion begun to mark out the ways in which antisemitic and anti-Muslim discourses in Europe are intertwined and are productive of one another.[4]

Contemporary master narratives in Germany (similar to the rest of Europe) build on and synthesize cumulative hegemonic discourses about the civilizational, cultural, religious, ethnic, and political differences between (Christian) Europe and its 'others'.[5] Traditional antisemitism, carried as part of Christian doctrines, has been central to European public discourse for centuries and new forms of antisemitism continue to claim their own place in this tradition. While anti-Muslim discourse has not been instantiated in historical tragedies such as the Holocaust, it builds on civilizational narratives, which engage related processes of 'othering.' Contemporary European master narratives engender a civilizational narrative in which the West and its history are portrayed in continuity with Christian traditions and Occidental civilization. This civilizational-cultural narrative also entails an implicit religious dimension that is based on the alleged 'Christian' roots of society. While these contours of a Christian tradition have been called a "fictitious amalgam" almost synonymous to the similarly vague notion of 'Western values,' this amalgam underlies European self-perceptions which in

---

3 Haug / Müssig / Stichs, Muslimisches Leben in Deutschland, 2009.
4 Bunzl / Senfft (eds.), Zwischen Antisemitismus und Islamophobie, 2008; Bunzl, Between Anti-Semitism and Islamophobia, 2005; Gingrich, Anthropological Analyses, 2005; Glick Schiller, Racialized Nations, 2005b; Halliday, Islamophobia reconsidered, 1999; Özyürek, The Politics of Cultural Unification, 2005; Stender / Follert / Özdogan (eds.), Konstellationen des Antisemitismus, 2010; Widmann, Der Feind kommt aus dem Morgenland. In: Benz (ed.), Jahrbuch für Antisemitismusforschung, 2008.
5 Asad, Formations of the Secular, 2003; Mignolo, The darker side, 1995/2003.

times past entailed 'otherizing' and 're-Orientalizing' Judaism, and more recently does the same to Islam.[6]

An important aspect of the German civilizational narrative is a cultural narrative: A culturalizing discourse about 'the West' identifies specific 'culture areas' (*Kulturkreise*) as stemming from nintheenth century western and central European experience which up to this day is accompanied by assertions regarding the existence of a local German guiding culture (*Leitkultur*).[7] The presence of minorities in these allegedly homogeneous German culture spaces has historically been framed as a threat, subverting and polluting the 'cultural community.' Historically, ethnic cleansing of Germany during the Holocaust is, at least in part, the product of this narrative. Similarly, contemporary German cultural-civilizational discourse positions 'German Western culture' as opposed to 'Muslim-Oriental culture'.[8] Resting on the legacy of historical conflict with Islam, Western civilization and Islamic civilization are presented as essentially rival, exclusive, and incompatible entities whose traits are conferred to their respective populations.[9] The impossibility of consensus between the value systems of the two is one of the core claims behind such representations of Islam. Anti-Muslim representations spread by global media since the 1980s promote notions of a "clash of civilizations"[10], portraying Islam as archaic,[11] and positioning it as a potential threat to Western nations, states, and societies.

They most notably include the Muslim fundamentalists' response to Salman Rushdie's novel *The Satanic Verses*; widespread demonstrations in the Arab world in 1990 in support of Saddam Hussein the angry response in 2005 sparked by the Muhammad cartoon and similar protests in 2010 sparked by the Florida Koran burning; and in 2012 the global uproar over an amateur video defiling Muhammad and Islam that *Newsweek* chose to cover under the headline "Muslim Rage."[12] The attack on the Twin Towers in New York on September 11, 2001 was a

---

[6] Salvatore, Public Religion. In: Aziz/Said/Abu-Nimer/Sharify-Funk (eds.), Contemporary Islam, 2006.
[7] Frobenius, Ursprung der afrikanischen Kulturen, 1898.
[8] Hüttermann, Moscheenkonflike, 2011.
[9] Featherstone, Occidentalism, 2009; Goody, The Theft of History, 2006; Said, Orientalism, 1979; Dumont, Are Cultures living Beings?, 1986; Grosfoguel/Mielants, The Long-Durée Entanglement, 2006.
[10] Huntington, The Clash of Civilization, 1996.
[11] Dalsheim, On Demonized Muslims and Vilified Jews, 2010.
[12] Ali, in: Newsweek, September 17, 1012; Abad-Santos, in: The Atlantic Wire, September 17, 2012. Lewis, in: Atlantic Monthly, September 1, 1990.

global turning point in the public's construction of Muslims as 'political others'.[13] Essentialized political values are transported along with these narratives: Democratic values are ascribed to those categorized as Western and (Judeo-) Christian, and fundamentalist values are ascribed to those categorized as Muslim. Along with this, the civilizational narrative has more recently quietly and seamlessly slid into a secular and democratic narrative in which the West (now including both Christianity and Judaism) is portrayed as secular and democratic, while the Muslim world is portrayed as fundamentalist, religious, and undemocratic. Competing narratives are not mutually exclusive, thus the religious dimension in the construction of the West as a Judeo-Christian civilization coexists today with a narrative of the West as secular and democratic.

Even though claims to secularist policies at the level of the European Union would imply equal opportunities and standing for all citizens and residents, independent of religious affiliation, it has been demonstrated that the Euro-Christian roots of such European secularism' often discriminate against religious minorities. On the political Right, Christianity is proclaimed to be the foundation of European culture and civilization, and Islam is presented as an antithetical other to this culture. On the political Left, Europe is characterized as secular, democratic, and a bastion of humanitarian universalistic values. Islamic religious and gender practices are criticized as antithetical to these values and repressive of the right of the individual to subscribe to secularist values. In sum, the public discussion of both the political Left and the Right is critical of the Muslim presence in Europe.[14] As such, *Muslims* may be accepted *in* Europe to varying degrees, however *Islam* is not recognized as *of* Europe (i.e., as an indigenous religion).[15] In short, public discussion of both the political Left and the Right is critical of the Muslim presence in Europe.[16]

In Germany today, the term 'Muslim' is primarily a ideologically-infused term that has come to replace the dominant term used until about 2001 to identify immigrants and minorities in Germany – 'foreigner' (*Ausländer*). The heated debate around Muslim religious and gender practices in Germany and the politicization of Islam in the context of global political developments has elevated the stigmatization of Islam and Muslim religious practices.[17] German discourses reveal concerns that Muslims are insular and not integrated and impose on them

---

[13] Abbas, After 9/11, 2004; Brown, Comparative Analysis, 2006; Ewing, Stolen Honor, 2008; Mandel, Cosmopolitan Anxieties, 2008.
[14] Öyzrürek, 2005.
[15] Asad, 2003; Özyürek, 2005, p. 511–512.
[16] Özyürek, 2005.
[17] Ewing, 2008; Eksner, Revisiting the 'Ghetto', 2013.

demands that they comply with 'German' culture and values.[18] Opinion polls reveal anti-Muslim attitudes are widespread in Germany[19], with 27 percent of the population-at-large in Germany consistently agreeing with Islamophobic positions.[20] In 2011, 52.5 percent of German respondents agreed with the statement "Islam is mostly or totally a religion of intolerance," and 17.1 percent of Germans (and 22 percent of Europeans) agreed that "Most Muslims think that Islamist terror is legitimate"[21].

Crucially, contemporary German narratives about Muslims construct a third opposition: the allegedly intrinsic opposition between Muslims and Jews. Discourses about 'Muslims and Jews' draw on complex and interwoven narratives about Europe's others[22], Israel and Palestine, and fundamentalist Islam.[23] By adopting the narrative of a conflicted relationship of Muslims with Jews (and by extension, with Israel) as deeply significant for themselves, some German Muslims link themselves to the Israeli-Palestinian conflict constellation.[24] German Muslims, especially those from Arab families, are discursively positioned as second-degree victims of a conflict that is thought to affect their close or distant families, or at least their ethno-religious networks by virtue of the larger Muslim collective. Tragic antisemitic incidents in German cities, such as those in which German Muslims adolescents physically attacked Jewish men wearing Jewish head coverings (*kipas*) in the streets, feed this discourse. Political spectacles such as Al-Quds-Day demonstrations that attract wide media coverage further showcase the public imagery of groups of angry young men from Muslim communities participating in protests against the State of Israel while shouting antisemitic and anti-Israeli slogans. Such events are portrayed by the media as a collectively-shared emotional response to the victimization of the global Muslim nation (*Umma*) by the State of Israel's actions against the population of the Palestinian

---

18 Adelson, Touching Tales, 2000; Caglar, Das Kulturkonzept, 1990; Petterson, Muslim Immigrants in Western Europe. In: Moaddel (ed.), Values and Perception, 2007; Vertovec / Rogers (eds), Muslim European Jouth, 1998; White, Turks in the New Germany, 1997;
19 Zick / Küpper / Hövermann, Die Abwertung des Anderen, 2011.
20 Leibold / Kühnel, Einigkeit in der Schuldabwehr. In: Heitmeyer (ed.), Deutsche Zustände, 2008.
21 Zick / Küpper / Hövermann, 2011.
22 Said, 1979.
23 Abbas, 2004; Ali, 2012; Amir-Moazami, Muslim Challanges, 2005; Mythen / Walklate / Khan, 'I'm a Muslim', 2009; Schiffauer, Vom Exil- zum Diaspora-Islam, 2007.
24 Amadeu Antonio Stiftung (ed.), 'Man wird wohl Israel noch kritisieren dürfen...?!', 2012; Heyder / Iser / Schmidt, Israelkritik oder Antisemitismus. In: Heitmeyer (ed.), Deutsche Zustände, 2005; Riebe, Was ist israelbezogener Antisemitismus. In: Amadeu Antonio Stiftung (ed.), 'Man wird doch wohl Israel kritisieren dürfen...?!', 2012.

Territories.[25] Thus, although these events represent the views of only a small percentage of Muslims in Berlin and in Germany as a whole[26], they have nevertheless come to be emblematic in the eyes of rank-and-file Germans of anti-Israeli sentiment subsequently ascribed in public discourse to the larger collective of Muslims in Germany.

Critics of these portrayals refer to projection of both antisemitism and anti-Israeli attitudes, assigning them to the Muslim minority group alone – a move that contextually fits well into the general societal mood that may legitimately be described as both "Islamophobic" and "anti-Muslim"[27]. It has been suggested that the focus on Muslim youth's anti-Israeli attitudes may displace[28] the concern with antisemitism in the wider population onto its Muslim minority, enabling the German public to skirt any societal discussion about similarly problematic attitudes among autochthonous Germans.

This dynamic opens up a series of wider questions about the roots of and paths taken by contemporary anti-Israeli discourse in Germany. In the course of illuminating contemporary anti-Israeli discourses in Germany, the case of German Muslim youths who have come to position themselves against the State of Israel – some of whom, curiously, do not have ties to the region themselves and do not belong to Palestinian or Lebanese immigrant communities in Germany – can only be fully understood when a prevailing milieu of Israel-Critique in mainstream German society is added to the equation – a point that requires serious examination.

Israelkritik by Germans and German Muslims

Antisemitic attitudes are a persistent problem in all strata and among all groups of German society, as well as in Europe in general.[29] In 2010, every sixth German agreed with the statement "Jews have too much influence in Germany." While responses as this reflect traditional antisemitic attitudes, the phenomenon of

---

[25] AMIRA, 'Du Opfer, Du Jude', 2008; Bundesministerium des Inneren, Antisemitismus in Deutschland, 2011; Friedrich Ebert Stiftung, 'Islamischer Antisemitismus' und 'Islamophobie', 2008.
[26] Frindte / Boehnke / Kreikenbom / Wagner, 2012.
[27] Messerschmidt, Verstrickungen. In: Fechler / Kößler / Messerschmidt (eds.), Neue Judenfeindschaft?, 2006.
[28] i.e., an unconsciously substitute a new object for something felt in its original form to be unacceptable.
[29] Zick / Küpper, Antisemitische Mentalitäten, 2011.

antisemitism in Germany is not monolithic and unchanging. The changing form and function of antisemitism in Germany today is most clearly expressed in the phenomenon of "new"[30] or "secondary" antisemitism.[31] In general terms, the term 'secondary antisemitism' describes different phenomena that result from the need to deflect guilt after the Holocaust[32] that have also been dubbed "antisemitism because of Auschwitz."[33] The main motifs include blaming the victims and claiming a shared responsibility of Jews for their persecution in the Holocaust; the attempt to reverse victim-perpetrator roles; demands to end what respondents perceive as ongoing critical and self-conscious engagement with the Holocaust in Germany; and the claim that commemorating the Holocaust serves as a means to extract financial retributions from Germany. One variation of secondary antisemitism, a central concern in the discussion at hand, is the demonization and delegitimozation of the State of Israel and its (Jewish) citizens.[34]

Israelkritik, or criticism of Israel, is an established political term in Germany and has been defined as one-sided and harsh critique of the State of Israel – both by Right- and Left-wing commentators. Contemporary critique communicated in secondary antisemitic thinking draws on, and is fueled, by anti-Jewish attitudes and myths of traditional antisemitic thought.[35] The main thrust of *Israelkritik* today is a "3-D" process that operates on three tracks: demonization, double standards, and de-legitimization. Demonization refers to the comparison of Israel to Nazi Germany and collectively blaming of all (Jewish) Israeli citizens as responsible for Israeli state actions that the accusers brand as fascist. Double standards are at work when human rights infractions are criticized if they are committed by Israeli state forces, but not if they are committed by other states. This is also reflected in the magnitude of 'outrage' directed at Israel for human rights violations, real or imagined, compared to other countries. Delegitimization questions the right of the State of Israel to exist by challenging its existence, claiming it is a leftover of colonialism, and negating the Jewish state's right to exist by branding

---

[30] The term "new antisemitism" that has been in use since the turn of the century has been rejected in the academic debate. The seemingly "new" elements – both the focus on Israel and Muslims as antisemitic agents – upon scrutinization simply represent close-up the continuation of well-known phenomena, see: Bundesministerium des Inneren, 2011.
[31] Rabinovici / Speck / Sznaider (eds.), Neuer Antisemitismus?, 2004.
[32] Leibold / Kühnel, 2009.
[33] Referring to the often-cited phrase by the Israeli psychoanalyst Zwi Rex "The Germans will never forgive us the Holocaust", cited in: Broder, Die Vordenker als Wegdenker. In: Romberg / Urban-Fahr (eds.), Juden in Deutschland nach 1945, 2000, p. 89.
[34] Porat, The International Working Definition of Antisemitism, 2011; Sharansky, 3-D-Test of Anti-Semitism, 2004.
[35] Heyder / Iser / Schmidt, 2005.

its immigration laws as non-democratic and racist, as well as charging that Israel was illegitimately founded, based on expulsion of the Palestinian-Arab population in 1948. Direct and indirect comparisons are used to liken Israel's policies and political situation to that of the South African Apartheid regime and Fascist Germany.

Such "3-D" rhetoric patterns can today be found in the German mainstream media of both the Right and Left. For example, the chief columnist of the Leftist daily *Junge Welt* ('Young World') Werner Pirker referred to Israel as an "Apartheid state" (*Apartheids-Staat*), an "artificially inseminated state" (*Staat aus der Retorte*), which is the result of an "unparalleled ethnic cleaning process" (*Ergebnis eines ethnischen Säuberungsprozesses, der seinesgleichen sucht*).[36] These positions show clear linkages to antisemitic discourses: Israel is portrayed as an artificial state without a right to exist and is built on the historical foundations of genocide and apartheid. The last in particular, invokes an indirect parallel with Germany during the Nazi era. Such statements then demonize Israel as a criminal and immoral state, while the discursive content at the same time relativizes the crimes of Nazi-Germany and reverses perpetrator-victim positions.[37] The right to 'criticize' the State of Israel is the center of the heated public debate in Germany today – a battle over where the line should be drawn differentiating legitimate criticism of the Israeli state from (secondary) antisemitic allegations. Yet, antisemitism research shows that, contrary to their claims, in practice the vast majority of those who 'critique Israel' in Germany also agree with other antisemitic statements.[38] In sum, criticism of Israel that does not carry antisemitic connotations has been shown to be "possible, but rare" in Germany.[39]

Recent empirical studies have shown that antisemitic attitudes in Germany's general population are now primarily communicated through criticism of Israel's actions in the Israeli-Palestinian conflict. A recent representative study showed that 32–68 percent of the general population in Germany reported antise-

---

36 Bundesministerium des Inneren, 2011.
37 Faber / Schoeps / Stawski (eds.), Neuer-alter Judenhass, 2006.
38 In its 2004 survey on group-focused enmity (GBM), the Bielefeld Institute for Interdisciplinary Research on Conflict and Violence found that only 10 percent of respondents who communicated a critique of Israel without antisemitic overtones did also not agree with at least one other antisemitic statement, see: Amadeu Antonio Stiftung, 2012. The majority of this minority of respondents also criticized the Palestinian attacks on Israel and were against violence as a means of conflict resolution. Their political positioning was more 'left' than 'centre', they had higher educational status than average, were less nationalist and autoritarian, and more tolerant of other groups, see: Amadeu Antonio Stiftung, 2012.
39 Amadeu Antonio Stiftung, 2012.

mitic stereotypes that are legitimized via a critique of Israeli state policies.[40] For example, more than a third of respondents "understands that people don't like Jews" in face of the "politics of the State of Israel," thereby projecting their criticism of the Israeli state onto "the Jews" in general. More than 40 percent agree that Israeli politics in regard to Palestinians can be compared to the persecution of Jews under National Socialism in Germany. Seventy percent of German respondents think that Israel presents the biggest threat to world peace today.[41] More than half support the statement that Israel is conducting a "war of annihilation" against Palestinians. What the available survey data suggests then is that secondary antisemitism that legitimizes itself through a critique of the State of Israel is widespread among the population of Germany and is an integral part of the fabric of contemporary public thought and discourse.[42]

Anti-Israeli Positioning of German Muslim Youths

I noted above the possibility that the current focus on "immigrants" (*Ausländer*), "Muslims with immigrant background" (*Muslime mit Migrationshintergrund*) and simply "the Muslims" (*die Muslime*) as the primary carriers of anti-Israeli and antisemitic attitudes[43] represents a case of discursive displacement. As case in point, although such attitudes and sentiment are omnipresent in public discussion in Germany, there are only few studies on the actual characteristics and distributions of both anti-Israeli positioning and antisemitic beliefs among Muslim youth in Germany. Two recent studies presenting survey data on this question showed that overall 25.7 percent of Muslims under the age of 25 agreed that "people of [the] Jewish belief are arrogant and greedy"[44], and that 26 percent of Muslims under the age of 25 reported antisemitic stereotypes that are legitimized via a critique of Israeli state policies.[45] Two other studies reported that Muslim youth in Germany showed higher levels of antisemitic attitudes than non-German youths, although scrutiny of the data reveals such antisemitic attitudes vary among Muslims subgroupings according to citizenship, ethnicity, and degree

---

[40] Brettfeld / Wetzels, Muslime in Deutschland, 2007; Heitmeyer (ed.), Deutsche Zustände, 2005.
[41] Riebe, 2012.
[42] Bunzl / Senfft, 2008; Bunzl, 2005; Silverstein, The Context of Antisemitism and Islamophobia, 2008; Volkov, Antisemitism as Cultural Code, 1978.
[43] Bundesministerium des Inneren, 2011.
[44] Brettfeld / Wetzels, 2007.
[45] Heitmeyer, 2005.

and type of religious orientation of the respondent.⁴⁶ Moreover, several studies indicate that there is no simple association between Muslim ethno-cultural or religious affiliation (as distinct from *fundamentalist* religious orientation of both Muslims and Christians) and the development of antisemitic attitudes. The findings of educational interventions and qualitative studies conducted primarily in Berlin with Muslim-oriented youths, i.e., youth who are religiously identified with Islam, provide further mounting evidence that expressions of Israel-directed antisemitism among Muslim-oriented youth in Germany are often closely linked to the Israeli-Palestinian conflict. The findings indicate that among many Muslim youths, anti-Israeli positioning is characterized not so much by traditional antisemitic stereotypes (that would indicate "culturally transmitted" Muslim antisemitism), rather they are founded on one-sided criticism of Israel. The actual spread and distribution of these negative Israel-directed attitudes among Muslim youths in Germany remains unclear and uninvestigated at this point in time, however.

In summary, while these studies clearly show that there are youths from Muslim communities who hold and express antisemitic beliefs, they also show that they do so to different degrees and with different ideologies of legitimization. Nevertheless, in the media and in much of current research, the phenomenon of Israel-directed positioning among Muslims in Germany is primarily explained as part and parcel of the transmission of traditional ethno-cultural values and religious beliefs in Muslim immigrant families.⁴⁷ The research literature frequently employs ethno-religious concepts (Islamic, Islamist, Islamized, Arabic, or Arabic-Islamic) to specify the phenomenon of 'antisemitism' (e.g., Islamic antisemitism, Muslim antisemitism). These terms define particular historic and cultural developments that are linked to the emergence of different variations of antisemitism in different places and among different populations.⁴⁸ The diversity of these developments is, however, erased from the dominant portrayals of monolithic groups of 'Muslims' in which antisemitism is ethno-culturally transmitted.

A second, more popular thread for explaining the anti-Israeli positioning found among some Muslims in Germany is to suggest they are the product of personal – though vicarious – experience of victimization in the Israeli-Palestinian conflict.⁴⁹ The phenomenon of anti-Israeli positioning of Muslim youth as por-

---

46 Frindte / Boehnke / Kreikenbom / Wagner, 2012; Mansel / Spaiser, Abschlussbericht, 2010.
47 Stender / Follert, 2010; Widmann, 2008.
48 Jikeli, Überlegungen zur Bewertung, 2010; Jikeli, Antisemitismus und Diskriminierungswahrnehmungen, 2012; Kiefer, Islamischer oder Islamistischer Antisemitismus. In: Benz / Wetzel (eds.), Antisemitismus und radikaler Islamismus, 2007; Wentzel, Der schwierige Umgang, 2005.
49 AMIRA, 2008; Arnold / Jikeli, Judenhasse und Gruppendruck. In: Benz (ed.), Jahrbuch für Antisemitismusforschung, 2008; Faber / Schoeps / Stawski (eds.), 2006; Messerschmidt, 2006.

trayed in contemporary public discourse in Germany suggests a curious mutant: It is thought of as both a cultural form of antisemitism passed down in families as part of a larger package of 'Muslim' cultural values and religious beliefs, and is a contemporary form of political positioning that takes recourse to (secondary) antisemitism that targets the State of Israel and its actions in the Israeli-Palestinian conflict. The related role of narratives of victimhood, which are closely intertwined with both anti-Israeli and anti-Muslim discourses in Germany today, deserve special attention.

Narratives of Victimhood

Muslim youths who grow up in Germany today are highly aware of discourses that stigmatize Muslims and live their effects in their everyday lives. Ethnicized and marginalized youth from Muslim immigrant communities experience a particular set of ideological, discursive, and structural interpellations, and in turn they arrive at specific interpretations of society's ascription of their own membership in minoritized groups, such as "foreigner," "immigrant," and "Muslim." The preceding discussion outlined the ways in which German hegemonic narratives creates a frame in which "being Muslim" becomes an identity category, with connotations particular to the German context.[50] I would argue that as a result, – for some German Muslim youths the theme of victimization has become central to a shared (counter-) identity as Muslim – both in the context of German power relations as well as in reference to the global arena.

Experiences of victimization are reflected in the everyday lives of many German Muslims. More than 30 percent of high school students who identified as Muslim reported that they experience German society as disadvantageous for Muslims (among respondents of all ages even 50 percent reported this experience).[51] Two-thirds of Muslim respondents reported incidents of victimization or discrimination within the last year. Severe victimization experiences, severe physical attacks, and damage to property were reported by 22 percent of Muslims in Germany. There is, thus, growing evidence that German Muslim youth experience exclusion, discriminization, and stigmatization. Several studies have in

---

[50] Dwyer, Contested Identities. In: Skelto / Valentine (eds.), Cool Places, 1998; Modood, 'Difference', 'Cultural Racism and Anti-Racism'. In: Werbner / Modood (eds.), Debating Cultural Hybridity, 1997.
[51] Brettfeld / Wetzels, 2007, p. 240.

turn identified victimization as a core trope in the experiences and narratives of Muslim youths.[52]

It is in this context that *local* experiences of victimization as marginalized immigrants are mapped onto *global* discourses of Muslims as 'stigmatized others.' As outlined, a culturalist discourse based in long-standing master narratives positions Muslim youths in enmity to Jews. In reference to the culturalist-civilizational discourse that saturates the German public discussion, many Muslims in Germany perceive that Germans have a negative image of Islam and that media reporting about Islam and Muslims is one-sided. Young people from Arab and Muslim immigrant communities frequently report experiencing stigmatization – being tagged as "terrorists" and "fundamentalists." Almost 85 percent of Muslim youths in this study replied that they were upset about the fact that after terrorist attacks the first suspected subjects were always Muslims – reflecting, in their eyes, a global prejudice against Muslims.[53]

Several qualitative studies and interventions conducted with Muslim youths in Germany found a conspirational perception of a "war against Muslims," often phrased in religious terms by the youth. Because of the dichotomy of perpetrator and victim underlying the idea of victimization, these ideas often include notions that "the Jews" or "the West" were the perpetrators leading a war against Muslims.[54] As evidence, 48 percent of students who identified as Muslim in a recent study stated that the "oppression of Muslims in Palestine" made them feel sad,[55] while 85 percent of respondents of all ages who identified as Muslim agreed with this statement.[56]

Educators and social workers share the youth's narrative of victimization and identify a parallel between their experiences as part of a marginalized and disenfranchised Muslim minority of Germany and the situation (i.e. victimization) of Palestinian 'Muslims' of Israel and the Palestinian territories. Thus, the situation of Palestinians in the Middle East, as well as the global stigmatization of Muslims in anti-Muslim and Islamophobic discourse is perceived as further affirmation of their own experiences of exclusion and marginalization, and allows some of these youths to position themselves as victims of the Western media. The emerging identities of some German Muslim youths are thus framed explicitly in

---

[52] Jikeli, Discrimination of European Muslims. In: Soen / Shechory / Ben-David (eds.), Minority Groups, 2011; Karlin, Righteous Victims, 2010; Mythen / Walklate / Khan, 2009.
[53] Brettfeld / Wetzels 2007, p. 240.
[54] Jikeli, 2011.
[55] A methodological caveat is that the last statement is a single item out of a scale for which neither reliability nor validity is known. The finding might hence not be valid as reported.
[56] Brettfeld / Wetzels 2007, quote p. 241.

orientation to the Israeli-Palestinian conflict constellation today. The Israeli-Palestinian conflict is presented as a placeholder conflict onto which some German Muslim youths project their experiences of marginalization and exclusion. Thus, the orientation of the youth vis-à-vis this conflict may not be motivated by politics, nor fueled by antisemitism; rather, their positions may serve as a means of identification and solidarity among marginalized and ethnicized Muslim youths in Germany.[57]

While other forms of response to marginalization do exist (such as, for example, the emergence of a social movement for de-stigmatization and the rights of minorities in Germany), the argument made here is that identification as Muslims and against Israel is structured by their positioning in pre-existing discursive relations between 'Germans and others,' and between 'Muslims and Jews.' The possibility to self-ascription as German is not really an option, in light of the country's exclusionary discourse, the lingering effects of its blood-based citizenship law (*jus sanguinis* until the year 2000), and complex naturalization requirements[58]; identification as Muslim affords youths who are ascribed as such a fitting niche. While such a niche is encouraged by surrounding mainstream discourse, at the same time it is perceived as a counter-identity to the hegemonic secular-Christian identity that dominates German society.[59] Both the potential for ethnicized 'long-distance nationalism' in regard to the Palestinian Territories of youths from Palestinian and Lebanese communities in Germany[60], as well as the presumed solidarity with the overarching global Muslim nation or *Ummah* in the background[61] that tie Muslim youths in Germany to Muslims in Israel and the Palestinian territories is affirmed and legitimized by German discourse essentializing about Muslims' relationship to Israel and Palestine. Nestled in the intersecting strands of antisemitic and anti-Muslim discourse in Germany, Muslim youths are thus afforded a position from which to construct counter-identities as Muslims in Germany and from which to position themselves as antagonists of the State of Israel.

---

[57] Müller, "Ich bin ein Taliban...", 2007; Müller, "Warum ist alles so ungerecht?" In: Amadeu Antonio Stiftung (ed.), "Die Juden sind schuld," 2009.
[58] Mandel, 2008; Mushaben, A Crisis of Culture. In: Basgöz (ed.), Turkish Workers in Europe, 1985; Sabean, Power in the Blood, 1984.
[59] Amir-Moazami, 2005.
[60] Glick Schiller, Blood and Belonging. In: McKinnon / Silverman (eds.), Complexeties, 2005a; Glick Schiller, Long Distance Nationalism. In: Riccio / Brambilla (eds.), Transnational Migration, 2010.
[61] Abbas, 2012.

Conclusions

The chapter at hand has sought to deconstruct the discursive production of the anti-Israeli positioning of some German Muslim youth. It elucidates the conditions that led to the emergence of this phenomenon: the discursive context of long-standing cultural-civilizational narratives that 'other' Muslim youth, German *Israelkritik* that make Israel bashing normative, and the emergence of narratives of victimhood about and among Muslim youths. The most important insight of this reexamination is that anti-Israeli positioning found among some Muslim youth in Germany occurs within *preexisting* paths outlined by German master narratives. The emergence of a German Muslim counter-identity was shown to have strong discursive ties to the Israeli-Palestinian conflict and to build on both secondary antisemitic and anti-Muslim discourses in Germany. Furthermore, it emerges that anti-Israeli orientations among Muslim youth draw on narratives which forge a shared experience of victimization by minoritized Muslim youths in Germany and Palestinians/Muslims in the Israeli-Palestinian conflict.

Uniquely in the German case, such youth's responses to what they perceive as moral injustice of marginalization and victimization in the context of German dominant-non-dominant relations is projected onto the State of Israel. This presents an interesting variation on the theme of 'politicized identities': While Muslim youths are marginalized as Muslims and minorities in Germany, the expression of antagonism is rarely publicly directed against the German state. The absence of a large-scale grass roots Muslim social movement to demand remediation of the situation is painfully absent in the German case. This may be, in part, because expression of antagonism towards the German state and German society by marginalized and stigmatized Muslim youths is suppressed under German discourse, law, and an executive arm that uses a heavy-hand in punishing unruly minority youths (as evidenced in by disproportionably high arrest and imprisonment rates for immigrant youth, including Muslim youths[62]). In contrast – as elaborated above – expression of resentment against the State of Israel is in line with both mainstream German secondary antisemitic attitudes and the discursive positioning of Muslim youths as 'cousins' to the Palestinian and Muslim population of Israel and the Palestinian territories.

In effect, German social and discursive context legitimizes and encourages both the critique of Israel and Muslim youths' anti-Israeli attitudes as 'normal and acceptable, 'thus channels expression of anger at their disenfranchisement from the object much closer to home (both literally and figuratively) to a 'legitimized' transnational object – the State of Israel, and, by implication, its (Jewish) citi-

---

62 Brettfeld / Wetzels, 2007; Pfeiffer / Wetzels, Junge Türken als Täter und Opfer, 2000.

zens. Muslim youth's counter-identities which are engendered by their non-dominant position within the German power matrix are incorporated and contained by German mainstream discourse by their projection onto the Israeli-Palestinian conflict, and ultimately serve to stabilize unequal power structures within Germany. These counter-identities as Muslims may then in turn be used by other forms of collective protest,[63] such as anti-Israeli political actors. The anti-Israeli positioning found among some German Muslim youth is therefore distinct from more simple explanations such as the ethno-cultural transmission of "Muslim antisemitism" in immigrant families from Muslim countries, or attributing secondary antisemitism of Muslim youths in Germany to their 'natural' positioning in the Israeli-Palestinian conflict.

In closing, I believe it would be apt to take heed of the advice of Talal, who remarked:

> [...] if we find the violent practices of others abhorrent and morally reprehensible, we would do well to remember our histories are intertwined, and that we are at least partially responsible for the unequal world in which we live, and therefore for creating the conditions in which these violences have arisen.[64]

In this sense, in order to understand and to respond effectively to anti-Israeli attitudes among Muslim youths in Germany, it is necessary to inquire into how German society is implicated in the production of marginalized identities and how, within a general anti-Israeli climate, feelings of disenfranchisement are deflected onto a hegemonically 'approved' object of resentment.

References

Abad-Santos, Alexander: "Newsweek Goes for Broke with 'Muslim Rage'." *The Atlantic Wire*, September 17, 2012. http://www.thewire.com/business/2012/09/newsweek-goes-broke-muslim-rage/56923/ (accessed April 3, 2015).
Abbas, Tahir. After 9/11: British South Asian Muslims, Islamophobia, Multiculturalism, and the State. *The American Journal of Islamic Social Sciences*, 21 (2004): pp. 26–37.
Adelson, Leslie A. Touching Tales of Turks, Germans, and Jews: Cultural Alterity, Historical Narrative, and Literary Riddles for the 1990s. *New German Critique* 80 (2002): pp. 93–124.
Ali, Ayaan Hirsi. "How I Survived it and How We can Survive it." *Newsweek*, September 17, 2012. http://www.newsweek.com/ayaan-hirsi-ali-islamists-final-stand-64811 (accessed April 3, 2015).

---

63 Schiffauer, 2004.
64 Asad, 2007.

Amadeu Antonio Stiftung (ed.). *"Man wird ja wohl Israel noch kritisieren dürfen...?!" Über legitime Kritik, israelbezogenen Antisemitismus und pädagogische Interventionen*. Berlin, 2012. https://www.amadeu-antonio-stiftung.de/w/files/pdfs/aas-israelfeindschaft.pdf (accessed April 3, 2015).

Amir-Moazami, p. Muslim Challenges to the Secular Consensus: A German Case Study. *Journal of Contemporary European Studies* 13 (2000): pp. 267–286.

AMIRA. *"Du Opfer, Du Jude". Antisemitismus und Jugendarbeit in Kreuzberg*. Dokumentation der AMIRA-Tagung am 16. September 2008 in Berlin-Kreuzberg.

Arnold, Sina, Günther Jikeli. Judenhass und Gruppendruck – Zwölf Gespräche mit jungen Berlinern palästinensischen und libanesischen Hintergrunds. In *Jahrbuch für Antisemitismusforschung 17*, Wolfgang Benz (ed.), pp. 105–130. Berlin: Metropol, 2008.

Asad, Talal. *Formations of the Secular: Christianity, Islam, Modernity*. Stanford: Standford University Press, 2003.

Asad, Talal. *On Suicide Bombing*. New York: Columbia University Press, 2007

Brettfeld, Karin, Peter Wetzels. *Muslime in Deutschland – Integration, Integrationsbarrieren, Religion sowie Einstellungen zu Demokratie, Rechtsstaat und politisch-religiös motivierter Gewalt – Ergebnisse von Befragungen im Rahmen einer multizentrischen Studie in städtischen Lebensräumen*. Universität Hamburg / Bundesministerium des Inneren, 2007.

Broder, Henryk M. Die Vordenker als Wegdenker. In *Juden in Deutschland nach 1945*, Otto R. Romberg, Susanne Urban-Fahr (eds.), pp. 86–89. Frankfurt a. M.: Edition Tribüne, 2000.

Brown, Malcolm D. Comparative Analysis of Mainstream Discourses, Media Narratives and Representations of Islam in Britain and France prior to 9/11. *Journal of Muslim Minority Affairs* 26 (2006): pp. 297–312.

Bundesministerium des Inneren. *Antisemitismus in Deutschland. Erscheinungsformen, Bedingungen, Präventionsansätze*. Bericht des unabhängigen Expertenkreises Antisemitismus. Berlin, 2001.

Bunzl, John, Alexandra Senfft (eds.). *Zwischen Antisemitismus und Islamophobie. Vorurteile und Projektionen in Europa und Nahost*. Hamburg: VSA, 2008.

Bunzl, Matti. Between Anti-Semitism and Islamophobia. Some Thoughts on the New Europe. *American Ethnologist* 32 (2005): pp. 499–508.

Caglar, Ayse p. Das Kultur-Konzept als Zwangsjacke in Studien zur Arbeitsmigration *Zeitschrift für Türkeistudien* 3 (1990): pp. 93–103.

Dalsheim, Joyce. On Demonized Muslims and Vilified Jews: Between Theory and Politics. *Comparative Studies in Society and History* 52 (2010): pp. 581–603.

Dumont, Louis. Are Cultures Living Beings? German Identity in Interaction. *Man* 21 (1968): pp. 587–604.

Dwyer, Claire. Contested Identities: Challenging Dominant Representations of Young British Muslim Women. In *Cool Places. Geographies of Youth Cultures*, Tracey Skelto, Gill Valentine (eds.), pp. 50–65. London: Routledge, 1998.

Eksner, H. Julia. Revisiting the 'Ghetto' in the New Berlin Republic. Immigrant Youths, Territorial Stigmatization, and the Devaluation of Local Educational Capital in Marginalized Zones in Berlin, 1999-2010. *Social Anthropology/Anthropologie Sociale* 21 (2013): pp. 336–335.

Ewing, Katherine P. *Stolen Honor. Stigmatizing Muslim Men in Berlin*. Stanford: Stanford University Press, 2008.

Faber, Klaus, Julius H. Schoeps, and Sacha Stawski (eds.). *Neu-alter Judenhass. Antisemitismus, arabisch-israelischer Konflikt und europäische Politik*. Berlin: Verlag Berlin-Brandenburg, 2006.

Featherstone, Mike. Occidentalism: Jack Goody and Comparative History. *Theory Culture & Society* 26 (2009): pp. 1–15.

Friedrich Ebert Stiftung, Politische Akademie (eds.). *'Islamischer Antisemitismus' und 'Islamophobie'. Zwei unterschiedliche Begriffe – ein Phänomen der Diskrimierung?* Policy No. 27. Berlin, 2008. http://library.fes.de/pdf-files/akademie/berlin/05925.pdf (accessed April 3, 2015).

Frindte, Wolfgang, Klaus Boehnke, Henry Kreikenbom, and Wolfgang Wagner. *Lebenswelten junger Muslime in Deutschland. Ein sozial- und medienwissenschaftliches System zur Analyse, Bewertung und Prävention islamistischer Radikalisierungsprozesse junger Menschen in Deutschland*. Bundesministerium des Inneren: Berlin 2012.

Frobenius, Leo. *Ursprung der afrikanischen Kulturen*. Berlin: Gebrüder Borntraeger, 1898.

Gingrich, Andre. Anthropological Analyses of Islamophobia and Anti-Semitism in Europe. Commentary. *American Ethnologist* 32 (2005): pp. 513–515.

Glick Schiller, Nina. Blood and Belonging: Long-Distance Nationalism and the World Beyond. In *Complexities: Beyond Nature and Nurture*, Susan McKinnon, Sydel Silverman (eds.), pp. 289–312. Chicago: Chicago University Press, 2005a.

Glick Schiller, Nina. Racialized Nations, Evangelizing Christianity, Police States, and Imperial Power: Missing in Action in Bunzl's New Europe. *American Ethnologist* 32 (2005b): pp. 526–532.

Glick Schiller, Nina. Long Distance Nationalism and Peripatetic Patriots. In *Transnational Migration, Cosmopolitanism and Dis-located Borders*, Bruno Riccio, Chiara Brambilla (eds.), pp. 27–52. Rimini: Guaraldi, 2010.

Goody, Jack. *The Theft of History*. Cambridge: Cambridge University Press, 2006

Grosfoguel, Ramon, Eric Mielants. The Long-Durée Entanglement Between Islamophobia and Racism in the Modern/Colonial Capitalist/Patriarchal World-System. An Introduction. *Human Architecture: Journal of the Sociology of Self-Knowledge* 1 (2006): pp. 1–12.

Halliday, Fred. Islamophobia Reconsidered. *Ethnic and Racial Studies* 22 (1999): pp. 892–902.

Haug, Sonja, Stephanie Müssig, and Anja Stichs. *Muslimisches Leben in Deutschland* (im Auftrag der Deutschen Islam-Konferenz). Bundesamt für Migration und Flüchtlinge, 2009. http://www.bmi.bund.de/cae/servlet/contentblob/566008/publicationFile/31710/vollversion_studie_muslim_leben_deutschland_.pdf (accessed April 3, 2015).

Heitmeyer, Wilhelm (ed.). *Deutsche Zustände*, Vol. 3. Frankfurt a. M.: Suhrkamp, 2005.

Heyder, Aribert, Julia Iser, and Peter Schmidt. Israelkritik oder Antisemitismus? Meinungsbildung zwischen Öffentlichkeit, Medien und Tabus. In *Deutsche Zustände*, Vol. 3, Wilhelm Heitmeyer (ed.), pp. 144–165. Frankfurt a. M.: Suhrkamp, 2005.

Huntington, Samuel P. *The Clash of Civilizations and the Remaking of World Order*. New York: Simon & Schuster, 1996.

Hüttermann, Jörg. Moscheekonflikte im Figurationsprozess der Einwanderungsgesellschaft: eine soziologische Analyse. In *Migrationsreport 2010. Fakten – Analysen – Perspektiven*. Marianne Krüger-Potratz, and Werner Schiffauer (ed.), pp. 39–82. Frankfurt a. M., New York: Campus, 2011.

Jikeli, Günther. Überlegungen zur Bewertung von Antisemitismus unter Muslimen in Deutschland. *transversal – Zeitschrift für jüdische Studien* 1 (2010): pp. 15–28.

Jikeli, Günther. Discrimination of European Muslims: Self-Perceptions, Experiences and Discourses of Victimhood. In *Minority Groups: Coercion, Discrimination, Exclusion, Deviance and the Quest for Equality*, Dan Soen, Mally Shechory, and Sarah Ben-David (eds.), pp. 77–96. New York: Nova, 2011.

Jikeli, Günther. *Antisemitismus und Diskriminierungswahrnehmungen junger Muslime in Europa*. Essen: Klartext, 2012.

Karlin, Daniela R. *Righteous Victims: The role of competing victim identities in the Israeli Palestinian conflict: A socialy psychological paradigm*. Dissertation George Washington University 2010. http://media.proquest.com/media/pq/classic/doc/2071061151/fmt/ai/rep/NPDF?_s=P6bt%2FlhslPoVsjxUi4BhwzQQnQ4%3D (accessed April 3, 2015).

Kiefer, Michael. Islamischer oder islamisierter Antisemitismus? In *Antisemitismus und radikaler Islamismus*, Wolfgang Benz, Juliane Wentzel (eds.), pp. 71–84. Essen: Klartext, 2007.

Leibold, Jürgen, Steffen Kühnel. Einigkeit in der Schuldabwehr. Die Entwicklung antisemitischer Einstellungen in Deutschland nach 1989. In *Deutsche Zustände*, Vol. 7, Wilhelm Heitmeyer (ed.), pp. 131–151. Frankfurt a. M.: Suhrkamp, 2009.

Lewis, Bernhard. "The Roots of Muslim Rage. Why so many Muslims deeply resent the West, and why their bitterniss will not easily be mollified" *The Atlantic Monthly*, September 1, 1990. http://www.theatlantic.com/magazine/archive/1990/09/the-roots-of-muslim-rage/304643/ (accessed April 3, 2015).

Mandel, Ruth. *Cosmopolitan Anxieties: Turkish Challenges to Citizenship and Belonging in Germany*. Durham, London: Duke University Press, 2008.

Mansel, Jürgen, Viktoria Spaiser. *Abschlußbericht: Soziale Beziehungen, Konfliktpotentiale und Vorurteile im Kontext von Erfahrungen verweigerter Teilhabe und Anerkennung bei Jugendlichen mit und ohne Migrationshintergrund*. University of Bielefeld 2010.

Messerschmidt, Astrid. Verstrickungen. Postkoloniale Perspektiven in der Bildungsarbeit zum Antisemitismus. In *Neue Judenfeindschaft? Perspektiven für den pädagogischen Umgang mit dem globalisierten Antisemitismus*. Bernd Fechler, Gottfried Kößler, Astrid Messerschmidt, and Barbara Schäuble (eds.), pp. 150–171. Frankfurt a. M., New York: Campus, 2006.

Mignolo, Walter D. *The darker side of the renaissance: literacy, territoriality, and colonization*. Ann Arbor: Michigan University Press, 1995/2003.

Modood, Tariq. 'Difference', 'Cultural Racism and Anti-Racism.' In *Debating Cultural Hybridity: Multi-Cultural Identities and the Politics of Anti-Racism*, Pnina Werbner, Tariq Modood (eds.), pp. 154–172. London: Palgrave, 1997.

Müller, Jochen. "Ich bin ein Taliban…". Islamismus und Jugendkultur. *Dossier: Islamismus*, Bundeszentrale für Politische Bildung (ed.), July 5, 2007. http://www.bpb.de/politik/extremismus/islamismus/36411/islamismus-und-jugendkultur?p=all (accessed April, 2015).

Müller, Jochen. "Warum ist alles so ungerecht?" Antisemitismus und Israelhass bei Jugendlichen: Die Rolle des Nahostkonflikts und Optionen der pädagogischen Intervention. In *"Die Juden sind Schuld". Antisemitismus in der Einwanderungsgesellschaft am Beispiel muslimisch sozialisierter Milieus. Beispiele, Erfahrungen und Handlungsoptionen aus der pädagogischen und kommunalen Arbeit*. Amadeu Antonio Stiftung (ed.). Berlin, 2009. https://www.amadeu-antonio-stiftung.de/w/files/pdfs/diejuden.pdf (accessed April 2, 2015).

Mushaben, Joyce Marie. A Crisis of Culture: Isolation and Integration Among Turkish Guestworkers in the German Federal Republic. In *Turkish Workers in Europe*, Ilhan Basgöz (ed.), pp. 125–150. Bloomington: Indiana University Press, 1985.

Mythen, Gabe, Sandra Walklate, and Fatima Khan. 'I'm a Muslim, but I'm not a Terrorist': Victimization, Risky Identities and the Performance of Safety. *British Journal of Criminology* 49 (2009): pp. 736–754.

Özyürek, Esra. The Politics of Cultural Unification, Secularism, and the Place of Islam in the New Europe. Commentary. *American Ethnologist* 32 (2005): pp. 509–512.

Petterson, Thomas. Muslim immigrants in Western Europe: Persisting value differences or value adaptation? In *Values and perception of the Islamic and middle eastern publics*, Mansoor Moaddel (ed.), pp. 71–102. New York: Palgrave, 2007.

Pfeiffer, Thomas, Peter Wetzels. *Junge Türken als Täter und Opfer von Gewalt*. Hannover: KFN, 2000.

Porat, Dina. The International Working Definition of Antisemitism and Its Detractors. *Israel Journal of Foreign Affairs* 5 (2011): pp. 93–101.

Rabinovici, Doron, Ulrich Speck, and Nathan Sznaider (eds.). *Neuer Antisemitismus? Eine globale Debatte*. Frankfurt a. M.: Suhrkamp, 2004.

Riebe, Jan. Was ist israelbezogener Antisemitismus? In *"Man wird ja wohl Israel noch kritisieren dürfen...?!" Über legitime Kritik, israelbezogenen Antisemitismus und pädagogische Interventionen*. Amadeu Antonio Stiftung (ed.), pp. 7–11. Berlin, 2012.

Sabean, David Warren. *Power in the Blood: Popular Culture and Village Discourse in Early Modern Germany*. Cambridge: Cambridge University Press, 1984.

Said, Edward W. *Orientalism*. London: Penguin Books, 1995 [1979].

Salvatore, Armando. Public Religion, Ethics of Participation, and Cultural Dialogue. In *Contemporary Islam. Dynamic, not Static*, Abdul Aziz, Mohammed Said, Abu-Nimer, and Meena Sharify-Funk (eds.), pp. 83–100. London, New York: Routledge, 2006.

Schiffauer, Werner. Vom Exil- zum Diaspora-Islam. Muslimische Identitäten in Europa. *Soziale Welt – Zeitschrift für sozialwissenschaftliche Forschung und Praxis* 55 (2004): pp. 347–368.

Sharansky, Nathan. 3 D Test of Anti-Semitism: Demonization, Double Standards, Delegitimization. *Jewish Political Studies Review* 16 (2004): pp. 3–4.

Silverstein, Paul A. The context of antisemitism and Islamophobia in France. *Patterns of Prejudice* 42 (2008): pp. 1–26.

Stender, Wolfgang, Guido Follert, Mihri Özdogan (eds.). *Konstellationen des Antisemitismus. Antisemitismusforschung und sozialpädagogische Praxis*. Wiesbaden: Springer VS, 2010.

Vertovec, Steven, Alisdair Rogers (eds.). *Muslim European Youth. Reproducing ethnicity, religion, culture*. Aldershot: Ashgate 1998

Volkov, Shulamit. Antisemitism as a Cultural Code. Reflections on the History and Historiography of Antisemitism in Imperial Germany. *Leo Baeck Institute Yearbook* 23 (1978): pp. 25–46.

Wetzel, Juliane. Der schwierige Umgang mit einem Phänomen – Die EU und der Antisemitismus. *Tel Aviver Jahrbuch für deutsche Geschichte* 33 (2005), pp. 90–109.

White, Jenny B. Turks in the New Germany. *American Anthropologist* 99 (1997): pp. 754–769.

Widmann, Peter. Der Feind kommt aus dem Morgenland. In *Jahrbuch für Antisemitismusforschung 17*, Wolfgang Benz (ed.), pp. 45–68. Berlin: Metropol, 2008.

Zick, Andreas, Beate Küpper. *Antisemitische Mentalitäten. Bericht über Ergebnisse des Forschungsprojekts Gruppenbezogene Menschenfeindlichkeit in Deutschland und Europa.* Universität Bielefeld 2011. http://www.bagkr.de/wp-content/uploads/kuepper_zick_antisemitismus_2011.pdf (accessed April 3, 2015).

Zick, Andreas, Beate Küpper, and Andreas Hövermann. *Die Abwertung der Anderen. Eine europäische Zustandsbeschreibung zu Intoleranz, Vorurteilen und Diskriminierung.* Friedrich-Ebert-Stiftung, 2011. http://library.fes.de/pdf-files/do/07905-20110311.pdf (accessed April 3, 2015).

Towards New Shores:
Jewish Education and the Religious Revival

Olaf Glöckner
New Structures of Jewish Education in Germany

Chinuch or 'education' in the Jewish world unquestionably has its primary origins in the Jewish religion. Study of the Torah, the Talmud, and other written texts of Jewish tradition is a general prerequisite for Jewish learning in the strict sense. Today as well, receiving the essentials of a Jewish education is almost unthinkable without being familiar with the writings of the Torah, a certain knowledge of Talmud commentaries, and the discourses on Jewish Law (*halakha*). On the other hand, no one would question that Jewish education has made remarkable advances under the influences of modernity and the Enlightenment since the eighteenth century. 'Being Jewish' has become a much broader concept than just studying sacred works and observing Jewish commandments (*mitzvot*). Being Jewish has broadened to encompass a process of 'finding oneself,' developing Jewish art, discovering Jewish history and applying Jewish values and norms in a world that is mainly non-Jewish. The movement toward a modern, multifaceted Jewish world with new ideas, theories, reformist movements, and cultural innovations was probably nowhere stronger than in Germany. Germany's Jews were hungry to study their own heritage and religion, but at the same time highly motivated to study their surroundings, to engage in academic, economic, artistic, and humanitarian enterprises. Distinctly patriotic and admirers of Romantic writers such as Goethe and Rilke, composers like Beethoven and Bach and philosophers such as Kant and Hegel, they were also highly motivated to learn about German arts and philosophy. Masterminds of the Jewish Enlightenment such as Moses Mendelssohn and David Friedländer believed the Jewish search for wisdom should include the exploration of the larger world. Consequently, beginning in the late eighteenth and early nineteenth century, Germany's Jews strove to provide a well-rounded education for their children. It was no accident that figures such as Israel Jacobson founded a Religious and Industrial School for Jewish Boys in the small town of Seesen, Lower Saxony in 1801. This was the first Jewish school of any type in Germany. Shortly thereafter, in 1804, Mayer Amschel Rothschild, the founder of the Rothschild banking dynasty, opened the famous Philanthropin School in Frankfurt, an educational institution for poor Jewish children that had a student body of up to a thousand pupils, and became the greatest Jewish school in German history.

Jewish intellectual perspectives

While there was ambition to provide an all-around education for children, Jewish adults discovered their thirst for education, as well. Thus, in the early nineteenth century, it also became popular to concern oneself with Jewish history and religion from primarily an intellectual perspective. Together with some colleagues, Leopold Zunz, who is considered the true originator of Jewish Studies (*Wissenschaft des Judentums*) in Germany, succeeded in 1819 in founding the Association for Jewish Culture and Science (*Verein für Cultur und Wissenschaft der Juden*). However, the most famous German institution that promoted an unprejudiced, intellectual approach to Judaism in the early twentieth century was the *Freies Jüdisches Lehrhaus*, led by Franz Rosenzweig, and frequented by such luminaries as Martin Buber, Leo Löwenthal, Bertha Pappenheim, and Gershom Scholem.

In short, it could be said that on the eve of Germany's darkest period, Jews had developed a complete system of education, offering manifold opportunities to study and be educated in all kinds of Jewish tradition and culture, including Yiddish, Hebrew, the Torah, Talmud, Jewish mysticism (*Kabbalah*), Zionism, Jewish philosophy, the Enlightenment, and religious art. Jews who lived in metropolitan centers such as Berlin, Frankfurt, or Munich and who were interested in a comprehensive Jewish education for their children, could enjoy an almost complete chain of Jewish education: kindergartens, schools, youth centers, and adult education frameworks.

During the Nazi period, not only hundreds of thousands of German Jews were killed or expelled; at the same time the Jewish infrastructure suffered almost irreparable damage. There was no expectation that Jewish life in the country of the perpetrators of the Holocaust had a future. The refounding of small Jewish communities in some of the bombed-out and heavily destroyed German cities including Berlin, Frankfurt, Cologne, and Dresden shortly after the end of the Second World War was considered a temporary measure in order to manage inheritance and compensation issues, and as a place where Holocaust survivors, refugees, and displaced, elderly or sick Jews could turn. In such a situation, educational work had no priority, and in fact was viewed as an impossibility. Refounded Jewish communities had no schools, no kindergartens, no Sunday schools, no adult education centers – nothing. Moreover, there was a severe shortage of rabbis, cantors, teachers, educators, social workers, and other professionals. Surprisingly, Jewish community life in Germany continued in the decades following the Holocaust, albeit on a small-scale, however, Jewish organizations and institutions remained rather cautious in planning new educational institutions, in light of the low birth rate among Jewish families, the rising rate of intermarriage, and increasing trends towards secularization.

New Beginnings in West Germany

Nevertheless, a few communities in West Germany were active and motivated enough to try creating some new educational institutions – first of all, for children and teenagers. In 1966, the I. E. Lichtigfeld School in Frankfurt am Main opened its doors as the first Jewish elementary school in Germany after the Second World War. In fact, the Lichtigfeld School followed in the footsteps of the former Philanthropin School in Frankfurt. Twenty years later in 1986, the Heinz Galinski School opened its doors in West Berlin, with an initial enrollment of a mere 25 girls and boys. Meanwhile, three Jewish Adult Educational Centers (*Jüdische Volkshochschulen*) opened in the West: in West Berlin in 1962, in Munich in 1983 and in Frankfurt am Main in 1988.

At this point it should be noted that nothing comparable could occur in East Germany, the former German Democratic Republic. In contrast, in southwestern Germany in Heidelberg in 1979 even a University of Jewish Studies (*Hochschule für Jüdische Studien*) was able to be established, where young Jews and non-Jews study side-by-side and explore the Jewish religion and history, Biblical and modern Hebrew, art, philosophy, literature, and Israel, together with courses in pedagogy and community management. Aside from these general programs, the University of Jewish Studies in Heidelberg seeks to recruit and train professionals for the Jewish communities in Germany, to serve as administration workers, teachers, or social workers – even rabbis. Nonetheless, despite such ambitious projects such as the Jewish University in Heidelberg, central and vibrant places of Jewish education remained a rarity in postwar and divided Germany.

Then, almost everything began to change in the course of the 1990s. The unexpected influx of Jews from the former Soviet Union not only stabilized local Jewish communities and changed their composition. It also created the opportunity to shape a new Jewry in Germany. This was greeted by some media with euphoria, however, in short order, it became clear that not all Russian-Jewish immigrants were willing to join the local Jewish communities. Some considered themselves too atheistic to 'join the club.' Others were rejected as regular members because they were Jewish 'only' from their father's side and could not meet Orthodox standards of 'who is a Jew.'

Inside the Jewish communities, many aspects of community life now had to be negotiated and hammered out between veterans and newcomers; for example, how to organize future community life, what ritual and liturgy to prefer, how to integrate Russian art and culture, and numerous other issues. It was not rare that communities and their members had to grapple with mutual prejudices, clichés and finger-pointing, and the perspective for harmonious cooperation seemed fraught with obstacles. On the other hand, some common ground between veterans and newcomers existed from the very beginning – for example, a shared feeling of solidarity with Israel and commitment to combat anti-Semitism and racism in Germany, and openness among community members in many places to conduct a political, cultural, and religious dialogue with gentiles.

Today we know that the Russian-Jewish immigration to Germany opened the way for a transformation in the character of Jewish life in Germany, the emergence of a new form of community typified by pluralism within Jewish communities stretching from Hamburg in the North to Augsburg and Munich in the South, from Essen in the West to Dresden in the East. Jewish learning was the catalyst for development of a vital and healthy pluralism: It became evident that a large number of Russian Jews had, more or less, completely lost their connection to Jewish tradition. True, they were proud of their Jewish origin; proud of being prepared to fight anti-Semitism, proud to be part of the modern intelligentsia. Yet Jewish tradition in its original forms, Jewish spiritual life, and a deeper knowledge of Judaism had disappeared under the constant pressure of the Soviet regime in the USSR. Subsequently, a large demand for both basic and advanced courses on Jewish religion and tradition developed as the number of local Russian-speaking Jews increased.

Pluralism as a Driving Factor

At the same time, the rapid growth of the Jewish communities during the 1990s led to a very diversified and pluralistic Jewish landscape. Most of the local communities remained under the aegis of the roof organization of Germany Jewry – the Central Council of Jews in Germany, and many Jewish communities continued to maintain the model of the Unified Community (*Einheitsgemeinde*), despite wide differences in belief and practice. Others were established as independent liberal communities, mostly in West Germany; many of these ultimately joined the Union of Progressive Jews in Germany (UPJ). This was not the only new development. New, dynamic incentives for the Orthodox emerged, most under the sponsorship of the Chabad Lubavitcher movement and the Ronald Lauder Foundation. Chabad alone embarked on establishing close to a dozen branches across Germany. Last but not least, some secular initiatives as well were afoot, – for example, the Jewish Cultural Association (*Jüdischer Kulturverein*) in Berlin which appealed to its own specific audience of rather secular Jewish intellectuals.

From the start, Russian Jews have been the target of all of these new movements and networks. The initiators of these new groups understood that it was vital to erect a new infrastructure of Jewish education *as soon as possible*. As a result of the rapid growth in the demographics of Jewish communities in Germany sparked by the Russian Jewish influx, a large number of Jewish educational institutions could be built on the critical mass they provided many new frameworks initiated, supported, promoted and administered by local Jewish communities. The transformation in the Jewish landscape over the last 15 years has been astonishing. A study sponsored by the L.A. Pincus Fund Jerusalem, published in 2011, recorded nearly 20 Jewish kindergartens in the country – compared to two or three before German unification in 1990. The researchers also found nine Jewish elementary schools, more than 20 Jewish youth centers, and some very active Jewish student projects in university cities, some of which aspire in the future to evolve into something similar to Hillel Houses devoted to invigorate Jewish life on campus. As the first town in postwar Germany, Berlin finally had a large enough concentration of Jews to support opening a Jewish High School (*Jüdische Oberschule*) in 1993, which now has an enrollment of more than 400 students.[1]

Finally, with the outset of the new millennium, Germany's new Jews marked the return of several Talmudic academies (*yeshivot*), followed by the opening of two new rabbinical schools – the first in Germany since the Second World War and the Holocaust. The first rabbinical school, the Abraham Geiger Kolleg (AGK) was established at the University of Potsdam – a modern institution that trains liberal rabbis and cantors.[2] Founded in 1999, the AGK carries on the tradition of the Institute for the Scientific Study of Judaism (*Hochschule für die Wissenschaft des Judentums*) founded in Berlin in 1872 which was closed down by the Nazis in 1942. It is closely associated with the Union of Progressive Jews in Germany (UPJ) but serves the interests of any Jewish community seeking a liberal or conservative rabbi. Today, students from several continents are enrolled at the AGK, including a considerable number of women. In 2011, for the first time in postwar Germany, a female rabbi was ordained. Alina Treiger, born in 1979 in the Ukrainian town of Poltava, became a rabbi in the Jewish community of Oldenburg in northwestern Germany after joining the rabbinate. Treiger viewed her work as following in the footsteps of Regina Jonas, Germany's first female rabbi who was ordained in 1935 but perished in Auschwitz in 1944.

---

[1] www.josberlin.de (accessed September 9, 2013).
[2] Concerning the Abraham Geiger Kolleg and his profile, see the article by Walter Homolka in this volume.

The Legacy of Esriel Hildesheimer

The second rabbinical school in Germany after the Second World War took a more Orthodox approach. The Rabbinical Seminary of Berlin, founded in the early 2000s, also rests on pre-War foundations that were part of German Jewry's historical educational tradition. The newly reestablished school embraces the legacy left by Esriel Hildesheimer and his renowned Berlin Rabbinical Seminary which was founded in 1873. Rabbis from all over Europe had received their training there, but it was finally closed by the Nazis in 1938. Today, the German, Russian, American, and Israeli students enrolled in the Rabbinical Seminary begin by studying for a number of semesters at the Beis Zion Yeshiva, housed in the same building as the Lauder Yehurun Educational Center in downtown Berlin. The seminary operates in close cooperation with the Central Council of Jews in Germany and provides intensive support for small and peripheral Jewish communities, primarily by sending rabbinical students to organize services on the Sabbath and holidays. In 2009, the first rabbinical students of the Berlin Rabbinical Seminary were ordained. Usually graduates are expected to begin by working as rabbis *in Germany* no matter what their familial and geographical background. In contrast to the Abraham Geiger Kolleg, women do not study at the Rabbinical Seminary, however, not far from the Rabbinical Seminary, in the neighboring quarter in Berlin, a college (*midrasha*) has opened that offers theological studies for young Jewish women from all over Germany. The program includes basic Torah studies, Jewish law (*Halacha*) Hebrew language instruction, and principles of Jewish tradition. Visitors to Berlin can join special Sabbath learning programs coupled with staying with observant Jewish families living in Berlin.[3]

A number of other distinctly Jewish institutions of higher education complement the panorama and reflect the growth of the Jewish community in Germany, with its wide array of interests and needs: At the University of Applied Science in Erfurt, the capital of the federal state of Thuringia, a School for Jewish Social Work now trains professionals in social work and pedagogy who upon graduation are sent directly to serve local Jewish communities in need of their skills. Business students and future media professionals from Germany and abroad are invited to study at the Touro College in Berlin, where they can combine studies of media and communications, and economics, with Jewish history and Holocaust Studies and Communication

---

[3] www.lauderyeshurun.de/de/midrasha (accessed September 9, 2013).

The Fascination of Limmud

Sometimes successful educational endeavors are a top-down process initiated by renowned colleges, but others are grass-root enterprises. An impressive example of the latter is the annual *Limmud* Learning Festival in Berlin and other metropolitan areas. An extension of a Jewish initiative in the United Kingdom, the *Limmud* Learning Festival in Berlin was launched in 2006 and soon was transformed into a popular three-day-event where Jews of very different religious and political backgrounds and orientations meet to learn, discuss, and celebrate together. Each year the number of participants and workshops has grown so rapidly that it almost overwhelmed local hosting capacities (24 workshops in 2006, 105 in 2008, and 170 in 2009[4]). At the *Limmud* Learning Festivals, there are no traditional structural divisions that normally separate lecturers from students; on the contrary, people sit, discuss, and learn together, and any participant can also become a lecturer. Meanwhile, *Limmud* Festivals have become a fascinating laboratory where experts and laypeople with very different religious, philosophical, artistic, and political beliefs can exchange views but also experience a unique 'learning experience' in an atmosphere of fairness and tolerance. In consideration of the extremely heterogeneous structure of the Jewish population of Germany today, workshops at the *Limmud* conferences are offered in at least three languages: German, English, and Russian. The resonance and success of the *Limmud* Festivals is even more surprising considering the fact that almost all of organizational work is done by volunteers. This might be one of the decisive factors why organizations like the Central Council of Jews in Germany, the United Jewish Appeal, the L.A. Pincus Fund, and the American Joint Distribution Committee are eager to support such an impressive Jewish grassroots movement.

Limmud is a three-day festival – a highlight of the year, but in everyday Jewish community life in Germany educational work operates on a much more modest footing. In many communities, especially medium-size and small ones, there is a deplorable lack of financial resources and qualified personnel, making educational work anything but easy. In the meantime time is passing, and if Germany's current Jewish youth does not become motivated to maintain strong elements of Jewish identity, first and foremost by education, consolidation of organized Jewish life in Germany could turn out to be a pipe dream. Some Jewish umbrella organizations try to mitigate this serious problem of decentralized, relatively-weak communities by systematic training for local lay leaders. For example, Lauder Germany provides one-year courses via distant learning, including three-

---

4 Ben-Rafael / Glöckner / Sternberg, Juden und jüdische Bildung im heutigen Deutschland, 2010.

day seminars every month. These courses, called the Jewish Life Leaders Program, should enable committed lay leaders to lead services, manage administration, solve internal conflicts, and deal with local media – handling their community's daily affairs in the absence of any professional personnel.

Similar efforts to target interested Jewish adults and teenagers who possess little knowledge of Jewish religion, tradition or Hebrew are also undertaken by Chabad Lubavitch in Germany, which runs centers in some of the different federal states. In Berlin, Chabad successfully opened an own kindergarten (*Gan Israel*), an elementary school (*Or Avner*), and a "Torah College" for young Jewish men age 16 and above, who come from outside Berlin.[5]

Jewish Studies and Theology

Beyond the realm of Jewish communities and networks, academic research and education on Jewish matters has also witnessed an impressive increase over the last two decades. Almost a dozen new academic institutions dealing with Jewish topics have been established across Germany in recent decades, among them departments of Jewish Studies at the Universities of Düsseldorf, Oldenburg, and Halle and research institutes such as the Moses Mendelssohn Center for European Jewish Studies in Potsdam, the Simon Dubnow Institute for Jewish History and Culture in Leipzig, and the European Center for Jewish Music in Hannover. Most of these scientific institutions also attract a large number of non-Jewish students and scholars, as is the case with the University of Jewish Studies in Heidelberg.[6] Academic departments of Jewish Studies and most of the research institutes focusing on Jewish history past and present are funded by their respective federal states; the federal states view it as their public duty to impart knowledge of Jewish history, religion, culture, and philosophy – as well as knowledge about Israel, to promote Jewish-Christian relations far beyond academic circles. Graduates of Jewish Studies who do not opt for an academic career, often work as

---

[5] Young students of the Chabad's Torah College in Berlin normally use the one-year-program and study in parallel to their regular school attendance (usually high school or vocational school). Lessons in the Torah, the Talmud and Jewish law (the *Shulchan Aruch*) are offered in morning and afternoon sessions, and individual students can create their own personal study curriculum.
[6] Two factors may have caused the extraordinarily large proportion of non-Jewish students and scholars: The first, a general growing interest in Jewish history and Judaism among non-Jews after the Holocaust, not only in Germany, but also in other European countries. The second, are the still relatively small numbers of young Jewish people choosing these fields of study.

publishers, journalists, film producers, and employees at Jewish museums, or as lecturers at institutions devoted to political education.

Establishing an interdisciplinary Faculty of Jewish Theology that would mesh Jewish professional education, and the humanities and social sciences has been an unfulfilled dream in Germany since the nineteenth century. Some German universities had accepted or were interested in having small departments in Jewish Studies (*Judaistik*), that would operate under and round-out their Faculties of Protestant Theology, but independent Chairs of *Jewish* Theology called by some German Jewish rabbis and intellectuals for nearly 200 years, were ignored and unwelcomed. Apart from the general debate whether chairs of theology should be included in the framework of state-funded universities at all, or whether they should operate only as independent bodies[7], the idea of a 'Jewish faculty' received fresh impetus at the outset of the new millennium when discussion developed in Germany regarding full equality among the monotheistic religions, including in the academic sector. Beginning in 2011, institutes and/or centers for Islamic theology were opened at the Universities of Tübingen, Osnabrück, Erlangen, and Frankfurt am Main, thus it became just a matter of time until the first Institute of Jewish Theology would be founded, to represent the third monotheistic religion in contemporary Germany. While leading Jewish scholars and intellectuals in Germany have voiced their belief that a 'Faculty of Jewish Theology' is long overdue, only in late 2013 did Potsdam University open a School of Jewish Theology – the first German university where Jewish theology has been granted equal footing with Christian theological faculties.

Rather indirectly, and sometimes even far from the universities, associations of Jewish culture and history have come into being that are very committed to preserving Jewish artistic and intellectual heritage, sometimes with clear aspirations to revive them. Some of these associations' grants support the work of historians, archivists, and linguists who focus on uncovering forgotten treasures of Jewish literature, philosophy, music, and theater. Larger and older associations have also underwritten establishment of special libraries, either under their own trusteeship or in cooperation with local Jewish communities. Two successful endeavors of this kind that have sparked interest among Jews and non-Jews alike are "Gesher – Integration by Culture and Education" in Dortmund headed by former Muscovite historian Tanya Smolianitski, and the Israel Jacobson Society in Hannover led by Kay Schweigmann-Greve. Both associations operate mainly on a volunteer basis.

---

[7] Underlying such debates is the controversy whether theology itself could be considered a distinct discipline of science or not.

Aside from this, in some academic and non-academic circles in Germany, the Yiddish language has again become an important topic of interest. Some departments of Jewish Studies, as those at the Universities in Düsseldorf, Trier, and Potsdam, are teaching Yiddish, while elsewhere, studying and collecting Yiddish literature has become their primary objective. The most active project in this regard is the Salomo Birnbaum Yiddish Society which was founded in Hamburg in 1995. Its founders were concerned that Yiddish was only taught at universities and they wanted to give the language a place outside purely academic institutions. The society looks forward to introducing many more people to the vast and varied treasures of Yiddish culture. Apart from offering a public space for introducing and discussing Yiddish cultural artifacts, the Salomo Birnbaum Society also supports Yiddish language classes and runs its own Salomo Birnbaum Library.[8]

Several centers of Jewish education in Germany operate with a very strong local focus, combining lectures and presentations on Jewish history with further educational training, offering complete programs for certain professional groups (for example journalists and teachers), but also periodically engaging in intellectual debates. Special mention should be made here about the Moses Mendelssohn Academy (MMA) in Halberstadt (in the federal state of Sachsen-Anhalt), which was founded in 1995 and is based on a public trust. The MMA works in close cooperation with the Moses Mendelssohn Center in Potsdam. It offers educational programs for all age groups, imparting basic knowledge of Jewish history, culture, tradition, and religion to Jews and non-Jews, especially in former East Germany. The MMA is located in the former Orthodox Rabbinical Seminary of Halberstadt, the Klaussynagoge, and also serves as a venue for international gatherings.[9] Another flourishing institution with a similar profile is the Hatikva Educational and Meeting Centre for Jewish History and Culture in Dresden (the capital of the federal state of Saxony). Hatikva[10] seeks to reach out to a universal audience, regardless of faith or worldview. Topics range from a general introduction to Judaism to classes on holidays, and daily and life cycle rituals and customs. Furthermore, Jewish sites in Dresden such as the synagogue are visited and explained. Hatikva also offers space for public discussions, with an online magazine about Jewish life in research and education called *Medaon*.[11]

The success of independent institutions and projects like Gesher, the Israel Jacobson Society, the Salomon Birnbaum Society, the Moses Mendelssohn

---

8 www.birnbaum-gesellschaft.org (accessed September 9, 2013).
9 www.moses-mendelssohn-akademie.de (accessed September 9, 2013).
10 www.hatikva.de (accessed September 9, 2013).
11 www.medaon.de (accessed September 9, 2013).

Academy, and Hatikva is fueled by a combination of the members' idealism, local and political support, professionalism, and strong cooperation between Jewish and non-Jewish participants. Since the public exchange of opinions stimulated by these projects affects a host of different sectors of the population and causes people to reflect on relations between Jews and gentiles – past, present, and future, one might consider them typical manifestations of "Jewish space" as described by Diana Pinto[12] in post-Holocaust communities in Europe.

All in all, a framework of Jewish education has emerged in Germany that was quite unthinkable 20 years ago. Especially in metropolitan centers such as Berlin and Frankfurt, a whole chain of educational institutions has developed, serving the needs of almost all age groups and even offering a selection to choose from. At the same time, a certain imbalance between Jewish centers and Jewish peripheries is evident, requiring new solutions that can provide educational support for Jewish communities located far away from cultural and academic centers.

Primary Educational Interest: Israel, Hebrew, Jewish Arts

What educational interests are typical for the Jewish population in today's Germany, and what Jewish education programs are witnessing growing demand? The abovementioned study by Ben-Rafael, Sternberg and Glöckner *Jews and Jewish Education in Germany Today* which queried more than a thousand Jewish respondents reveals some trends.[13] The differences in interests in Jewish education between those Jews living in Germany for decades and those who immigrated from the former Soviet Union in the last 20 years are rather negligible. One of the survey's key questions was what kind of educational options do Jewish parents in Germany feel are missing for their children. Quite surprisingly, 50 percent of the respondents answered that nothing (!) was missing from their children's education right now. Among those who saw shortcomings, approximately 19 percent called for more information and lectures on Israel. Nearly 17 percent wished that their children could attend Jewish camps more often during holidays, and approximately 15 percent wished their children could receive more instruction on Judaism and Jewish tradition. Also, 15 percent of the respondents would like

---

[12] Pinto, Jewish Spaces versus Jewish Places?, In: Wallenborn (ed.), Der Ort des Judentums, 2004.
[13] Ben-Rafael / Glöckner / Sternberg, Jews and Jewish Education in Germany Today, 2011. All following numbers and statistics are drawn from this study.

to see their children learn Hebrew. As for the educational needs of Jewish adults in Germany, the same pattern emerged: Nearly 38 percent of the respondents answered that nothing (!) was missing at the moment. Among those who would like an opportunity for more Jewish educational programs, 27 percent were interested in more courses and events focusing on Israel. A slightly-higher number, 29.5 percent, displayed an interest in lectures and events focusing on Jewish arts. 20 percent would enjoy more programs dealing with Judaism in general, and 15 percent would like to learn more Hebrew, similar to the number who desired this for their children.

In the final analysis, expression of interest in various Jewish issues that respondents envisioned could or should be made available (through the auspices of Jewish community institutions, the state, or private initiatives) was expected. Yet, when it came to *practice* or availing themselves of existing opportunities – what Jewish parents are doing to provide their children with a solid Jewish education – the results were a source of consternation: Almost 63 percent of the respondents confirmed that, up to now, they had yet to provide any Jewish education to their children outside their own home. On the other hand, almost 75 percent of the parents were convinced of the importance of their children receiving a Jewish education. When 75 percent of parents consider a Jewish education necessary, but only one third of the children are, in fact, enjoying such an education, the discrepancy demands an explanation. There can be different reasons for this. First, access: It could be that there is a lack of local infrastructure and programs for Jewish education, because the respondent resides in a peripheral area with a very weak Jewish infrastructure. A second possible reason for the discrepancy could be quality: Absence of Jewish educational programs of quality, prompted parents to forego enrolling their children in existing programs. A third reason could be motivation: It may be that some mothers and fathers do not do enough to motivate their children to take advantage of certain Jewish educational offers in their vicinity. Finally, a fourth reason cannot be ignored: Apprehension. Parents may be reluctant to send their children to institutions where they become visible as *Jewish* children, and thus could easily become a target for anti-Semitism.

In summary, it can be said that the Jewish educational system in Germany has undergone impressive advances during the last 15 to 20 years. Many new Jewish kindergartens, schools, adult centers, learning festivals, and grassroots projects have arisen within the short span of two decades. Currently, there are very interesting enrichment activities – ranging from Jewish religion, tradition, and history, to the State of Israel, Jewish culture, and Hebrew mastery – being offered to different age groups. This is a positive feature of Jewish life in Germany, however, in the coming years, it will be of vital importance that the imbalance between relatively strong Jewish centers with comprehensive Jewish education, and a relatively weak Jewish educational and social presence on the Jewish periphery will gradually be corrected. As the survey verified, both veteran 'German Jews' and 'Russian Jews' are equally cognizant of the problem. This is an encouraging sign – demonstrating that the German Jewish community as a whole acknowledges the challenge.

References

Ben-Rafael, Eliezer, Olaf Glöckner, and Yitzhak Sternberg. *Juden und jüdische Bildung im heutigen Deutschland*. Eine empirische Studie im Auftrag des L.A. Pincus Fund for Jewish Education in the Diaspora Oktober 2010. www.zwst.org/cms/documents/241/de_DE/PINCUS STUDIE DEUTSCH NOV 16 2010.pdf (accessed September 9, 2013).

Ben-Rafael, Eliezer, Olaf Glöckner, and Yitzhak Sternberg. *Jews and Jewish Education in Germany Today*. Leiden, Boston: Brill, 2011.

Pinto, Diana. Jewish Spaces versus Jewish Places? On Jewish and Non-Jewish Interaction Today. In *Der Ort des Judentums in der Gegenwart (1989-2002)*, Hiltrud Wallenborn (ed.), pp. 15–28. Berlin: be.bra Verlag, 2004.

Walter Homolka
A Vision Come True

Abraham Geiger and the Training of Rabbis and Cantors for Europe

More than twenty years ago, Louis Jacobs (1920–2006) stated in a landmark article entitled *Jewish Theology Today* that, regrettably, " there is no department of Jewish theology, as there is of Christian, at any university."[1] The opening of the School of Jewish Theology at the University of Potsdam (Germany) on November 19, 2013, has rendered this statement invalid. Earlier that year, the Union of Progressive Jews in Germany and Masorti Germany (associated with the Conservative stream of Judaism) signed a contract with the University of Potsdam to establish the school as a fully-fledged department of Jewish theology. Backed by the Federal State of Brandenburg, the University of Potsdam offers undergraduate programs as well as Master-level programs in Jewish theology which can lead to ordination by the liberal Abraham Geiger College or the conservative Zacharias Frankel College. Rabbinical training at both seminaries is monitored by the General Rabbinical Conference of the Central Council of Jews in Germany (ARK) which, together with the rabbinical seminaries, sets academic standards for rabbis and cantors 'made in Germany.'

What appears to be a mere bureaucratic act is, in fact, a historic milestone in the development of European rabbinical training. Similar to the theological options open to pastors, imams, and priests, Jewish theology will finally become a regular academic subject in Germany, thus eligible to receive financial support from the state.

It Began with the Enlightenment: Abraham Geiger and Academic Rabbinical Training

The beginnings of modern education for rabbis and cantors and an academic approach to Jewish theology are closely linked to the career of Rabbi Abraham Geiger (1810–1874). To honor Geiger's illustrious career and crucial leadership qualities, Germany's first post-War rabbinical seminary now carries his name. More than a century after Geiger began his struggle to Reform Judaism, Leo Baeck

---

[1] Louis Jacobs , A Jewish Theology, 1973, p. 1.

explained his achievements: "The past was discovered and with it the essence of the present was won; a new generation that was conscious again of its Judaism was gradually created."[2]

By Geiger's time, *de jure* civil emancipation had already been granted to Jews in Central Europe. This, however, came at the cost of subordinating rabbinical legal authority to the law of the land; the process of which transformed rabbis into a kind of civil servant. This acquiescence of power may have begun as early as 1820 when Ruben Samuel Gumpertz (1769–1851), a banker and one of Berlin's community elders, made it clear to the state authorities that after relinquishing all judicial authority, the rabbi was nothing more than a "guardian of the kosher" and thus could not be compared to Christian clergy. Challenging the assessment that the rabbi was essentially a ritual practice specialist, Abraham Geiger pursued the goals he inherited from his mentor Leopold Zunz (1794–1886), the Renaissance man of Jewish studies, namely, – "to fashion out of Judaism a new and freshly animated Jewry."

In 1835, Geiger published the first volume of his periodical *Wissenschaftliche Zeitschrift für jüdische Theologie* ('Academic Journal for Jewish Theology'). In his opening essay, Geiger charged rabbis with the duty to fuse "the inherited with the demands of the present." Rabbis would have to become representatives of Jewish theology. In 1838, Geiger championed an alliance of theologians and community rabbis. He was forced to separate the two roles in light of the absence of academic rabbinical education in his time and the impossibility of imagining academic excellence being linked to practical community service – something we take for granted nowadays.

Geiger argued that establishment of a Jewish theological faculty would be the litmus test of *de facto* Jewish emancipation. Geiger developed a detailed curriculum for just such an institution in 1870 and was fortuitous to live to see its implementation in 1872 when the Academy for the Science of Judaism (*Hochschule für die Wissenschaft des Judentums*) in Berlin was founded shortly before his death in 1874. While over time rabbinical studies at the Academy laid down a substantial academic foundation for rabbis, education for Jewish cantors remained academically undeveloped for a long time. A first attempt towards incorporating cantorial studies into the academy was made by Moritz Deutsch who founded a short lived cantorial seminary adjacent to the Jewish Theological Seminary in Breslau in 1856. Although there had been some cantorial instruction at the teacher training seminary at Große Hamburger Strasse in Berlin, no educational institution had specialized in systematic training of cantors since the beginning of the nineteenth century. Despite all efforts to the contrary, a substantive debate

---

2 Leo Baeck, Judentum, in: Religion in Geschichte und Gegenwart[2] 3, Tübingen 1929, 488.

on a reform of cantorial education did not emerge. Ironically, it was not until 1936, in the shadow of National Socialism, that a cantorial school was finally founded. The Jewish Private Music School Hollaender was actually a conservatoire, and was called *Beth Chasanim* ('Cantors' House'). There, for the first time, students not only received instruction in liturgical music for the synagogue but they also studied general music theory as well as Jewish history and tradition. The institution did not last however, having arisen against the backdrop of the rise of Nazism in Germany. *Beth Chasanim* only operated until 1939. In 1942, the Nazis also closed the Berlin Academy for the Science of Judaism and most of the faculty and students perished during the Holocaust. Abraham Geiger's demand for equality for rabbinical training in Germany was reduced to a mere historical footnote.

A Vision Come True: the Abraham Geiger College

Since then, Germany has experienced a renaissance of Jewish life, epitomized by the founding of the Abraham Geiger College in 1999 - a rabbinical seminary that has taken Geiger's vision to heart. In 2013, the Zacharias Frankel College for Conservative (*Masorti*) rabbis was added to the Potsdam endeavor. These developments run parallel to some orthodox non-academic rabbinical training facilities supported by the Ronald Lauder Foundation.

Fig. 1: Former German Foreign Minister Guido Westerwelle with Rabbi Students of the AGK (right). Foto: Tobias Barniske

The first class of Abraham Geiger College began its studies in 2001, the same year Abraham Geiger College became part of the University of Potsdam. Another landmark was the College's admittance to the European Union for Progressive Judaism (EUPJ) during the EUPJ's Biennial in 2001 in Barcelona. The first rabbinical ordination conducted by the Abraham Geiger College – in fact the first ordination of rabbis in Germany after the Holocaust – took place in Dresden in 2006.

In 2007 the Abraham Geiger College opened a cantorial school to train male and female cantors for German and European Jewish communities. Following final evaluation by the Central Conference of American Rabbis (CCAR) in 2010, the Abraham Geiger College became a fully-accredited ordaining institution, making its graduates eligible for membership in the CCAR, as well as in the General Rabbinical Conference (ARK).

The Abraham Geiger College itself is a non-for-profit organization and registered charity. Headed by a president and a rector, it is supported by the Leo Baeck Foundation and is an incorporated foundation under the Civil Code, as per the Foundation Law for the Federal State of Brandenburg (*Stiftungsgesetz für das Land Brandenburg*, or *StiftGBbg*) of 20 April 2004. The Leo Baeck Foundation seeks both to expand and strengthen European Jewry and create an interfaith dialogue. These objectives are specifically pursued through procurement of funding for the Abraham Geiger College (and the Zacharias Frankel College) in Potsdam to assist it in carrying out its enlightened public-spirited missions. The foundation also grants fellowships and promotes interfaith projects and activities. The Abraham Geiger College is overseen by the Board of Trustees of the Leo Baeck Foundation.

In addition to the Leo Baeck Foundation's backing and supervisory role, the Abraham Geiger College also draws funding from private and public sources including the Federal German Government, the Standing Conference of the Ministers of Education and Cultural Affairs of the Länder in the Federal Republic of Germany, the Federal State of Brandenburg, and the Central Council of Jews in Germany. Furthermore, rabbinical and cantorial studies are indirectly funded by the State of Brandenburg: Academic work takes place at the state-accredited University of Potsdam where Professor Admiel Kosman, academic director of the Abraham Geiger College, holds a chair for Talmud Studies. As a publicly-funded national institution entrusted with training non-orthodox rabbis and cantors, the finances of the Abraham Geiger College are monitored by the government:

As of the 2013 summer semester, twenty-eight students are currently enrolled at the Abraham Geiger College: seventeen students (eleven men, six women) in the rabbinical studies program, and eleven students (six men, five women) in the cantorial studies program. The student body hails from a host of countries – including Argentina, Germany, France, FSU, Hungary, Israel, Norway, Poland,

Serbia, South Africa, and Sweden, forging truly multilingual learning community. Some students speak four and even five languages fluently.

At present, rabbinical and cantorial studies are integrated into the extensive curriculum of the Jewish theology department at the University of Potsdam and are embedded in the broader university context. Studies at the College lead to a Bachelor of Arts degree upon completion of the cantorial studies program, or a Master's in Jewish theology at the University of Potsdam. Fluent Hebrew is a prerequisite. As part of their program, rabbinical and cantorial students spend one year of their studies in Jerusalem to further improve their language skills and develop high-level abilities in textual study.

An essential pillar of rabbinical and cantorial education at the Abraham Geiger College is community work or work as part of socially responsible internships. Based on the concept of practical 'hands-on' education, the curriculum stipulates that students will be placed in the community (preferably in bigger German communities and abroad) in the first year of studies; from the second year on, rabbinical and cantorial students may, if they have the personal qualification and maturity, engage in community work independently. As a rule of thumb, students travel six to ten times per year to a weekend at their placement community. Among other roles in the community, they are entitled to lead synagogue services and/or hold religious education classes for children and adults.

Fig. 2: Ordained Rabbi students of the AGK in 2011: Yuri Kadnykow, Antje Yael Deusel und Jonas Simon (from left). Foto: Tobias Barniske

A faculty of male and female rabbis and cantors from all over Europe supports the students' development with ongoing evaluation in each of the various segments of their training. Each student is assigned a mentor. Graduates are also asked to participate in a post-ordination program, which offers graduates counselling and mentoring during their first two years after ordination.

Abraham Geiger College charges no tuition fees to its students, as university education is free in Germany. Moreover, thanks to the support of the YES Fund of the Women of Reform Judaism, the Rabbinic Training Fund of the European Union for Progressive Judaism, and the Ernst Ludwig Ehrlich Scholarship Foundation, our students are able to cover their living expenses through grants and scholarships provided by our partners.

Equality at Last: The Founding of the School of Jewish Theology

The opening of the School of Jewish Theology at the University of Potsdam in the 2013 winter semester, has brought Abraham Geiger's vision to life – students of the rabbinical and cantorial programs can now study within the Bachelor of Arts program in the new theological department. The School of Jewish Theology consists of ten chairs. The faculty members conduct research and teach all the major areas of Jewish theology: Bible, Jewish Law, Rabbinic studies, liturgy, religious education, and vocational training, Jewish philosophy, Jewish history, and Jewish music.

In May of 2013, the World Union for Progressive Judaism in Jerusalem noted the achievement of Abraham Geiger College in a resolution that applauded Germany and the State of Brandenburg for this significant step – finally granting Judaism equal status with Christianity and Islam. As Rabbi Louis Jacob observed in 1973, Jewish theology differs from other branches of Jewish learning in that its practitioners are personally committed to the truth they are seeking to explore. It is possible, for instance, to study Jewish history in a completely detached frame of mind. The historian of Jewish ideas or the Jewish people or Jewish institutions need have no wish to express Jewish values in his own life.

A distinguished Jewish leader of today, Rabbi Bradley Shavit Artson, dean of Rabbinic Studies at the American Jewish University's Ziegler School of Rabbinic Studies, welcomed the fact that Abraham Geiger College and the new *Masorti* training branch of the Zacharias Frankel College have developed a joint academic program in Potsdam: As a Masorti/Conservative Rabbinical School, the Zacharias Frankel College is dedicated to the philosophy, principles and values as inspired by Louis Jacobs, Abraham Joshua Heschel, Mordecai Kaplan, David Lieber, and other great modern visionaries. It builds on the thinking of positive historic Judaism and German founding fathers such as Leo Baeck and Zacharias Frankel.

The Zacharias Frankel College, therefore, relates the great German tradition of positive-historical Judaism to current global Jewish life. It assumes that Judaism in Europe and other parts outside of North America will continue to flourish and that rabbis are needed who will stand at its center.[3] With Abraham Geiger College, Zacharias Frankel College, and the School of Jewish Theology at the University of Potsdam, Germany now offers a unique international academic training center for rabbis and cantors, a program dedicated to strengthening the 'European voice' in world Jewry.

References

Homolka, Walter. "Through Knowledge to Faith: Germany Opens Groundbreaking School of Jewish Theology." *Jewish Voice for Germany*, July 9, 2013, p. 23.
Jacobs, Louis. *A Jewish Theology*. New York: Behrman House, 1973.
Jacobs, Louis. Jewish Theology Today. In *Problems in Contemporary Jewish Theology*, Dan Cohn-Sherbok (ed.), pp. 1–20. Lewiston: Edwin Mellen Press, 1991.

---

3 Homolka, in: Jewish Voice for Germany, July 9, 2013, p. 23.

Authors and Editors

Eliezer Ben-Rafael (Prof.) is a Professor Emeritus of Sociology, Tel-Aviv University. His areas of research are ethno-cultural cleavages in Israel, collective identities, sociology of languages, and linguistic landscape and the sociology of the kibbutz. He received the Landau Prize for his life achievements in sociology and was President of the International Association of Sociology. Ben-Rafael is also the co-founder of the international scholars network "Klal Yisrael." He recently published *Confronting Allosemitism in Europe: The Case of Belgian Jews* (2014) and *Sociologie et Sociolinguistique des Francophonies Israéliennes* (2013), co-authored with Miriam Ben-Rafael.

Julia Bernstein (PhD) is a cultural anthropologist and sociologist. She is a lecturer at the Institute for Comparative Educational Studies and Social Sciences of Cologne University. The main foci of her research are, among others, migration processes, transnationalism, transformations in ex-socialist societies, identity questions, material culture, food consumption, and ethnicity. She has recently published "Winners Once a Year? Russian-speaking Jews in Germany Make Sense of WW2 and the Holocaust as Part of their Transnational Biographies", in: Marie Louise Seeberg, Irene Levin, Claudia Lenz (eds.), *Holocaust as Active Memory: The Past in the Present* (2012).

Julia Eksner (Prof.) is a learning scientist and anthropologist. Her research investigates how urban minority youths experience, interpret, and navigate the opportunities and barriers posed to them by the environments in which they come of age. She is currently a professor of education at the Frankfurt University of Applied Sciences. Her most recent publications include "Religious 'Others' and Civic Education in Germany", in: James Banks (ed.), *Diversity and Citizenship Education*, (forthcoming).

Michael Elm (PhD) lectured from 2009–2014 cultural memory studies, film and political philosophy at the Political Science Department of Ben-Gurion University of the Negev in Beersheba. Currently he is a senior research fellow at the Minerva Institute for German History (Tel Aviv University) and at the Friedrich Meinecke Institute (Free University Berlin). His main foci of research are film-, trauma- and cultural memory studies, German and European modernity, cross-cultural educational theory and Holocaust studies. Among his most recent publications is "Screening Trauma: Reflections on Cultural Trauma and Cinematic Oeuvre", in: *The Horrors of Trauma in Cinema: Violence Void Visualization*, co-edited with Kobi Kabalek and Julia B. Köhne (2014).

Haim Fireberg (PhD) is a research associate at the Kantor Center for the Study of Contemporary European Jewry, Tel Aviv University and head of research programs at the Center. His main foci of research are urban history of the Jewish Yishuv in Palestine and during the first two decades of the State of Israel, and study of virtual Jewish communities (maintaining Jewish and Israeli life in cyberspace). Fireberg is also active in monitoring and researching contemporary anti-Semitism, concentrating on Europe. His most recent publication is: *Jewish Local Governments in Palestine and the State of Israel during Wartimes* (forthcoming).

Olaf Glöckner (PhD) is a research associate of the Moses Mendelssohn Center for European-Jewish Studies at Potsdam University. His main foci of research are: Jewish migration, community building and Jewish education in Germany, and anti-Semitism in Europe. He also works as a freelance journalist, focusing on contemporary developments in German Jewry. Among his most recent publications are *A Road to Nowhere? Jewish experiences in Unifying Europe*, co-edited with Julius Schoeps (2011) and *Juden in Sachsen*, co-edited with Gunda Ulbricht (2013).

Rabbi Walter Homolka (PhD, D.H.L.) is a professor of modern Jewish thought at the School of Jewish Theology at the University of Potsdam and Rector of the Abraham Geiger College. Rabbi Homolka is the former chief area rabbi of Lower Saxony and is director of the Ernst Ludwig Ehrlich Scholarship Foundation. His most recent published work is *Jesus Reclaimed – Jewish Perspectives on the Nazarene* (2015).

Günther Jikeli (PhD) is a research fellow at the Moses Mendelssohn Center for European-Jewish Studies at Potsdam University, and at the Groupe Sociétés, Religions, Laïcités at the Centre National de la Recherche Scientifique (GSRL/CNRS), Paris. In 2013, he was awarded the Raoul Wallenberg Prize in Human Rights and Holocaust Studies by the International Raoul Wallenberg Foundation and Tel Aviv University. His latest book is *European Muslim Antisemitism. Why Young Urban Males Say They Don't Like Jews* (2015).

Zachary Johnston is an American director of documentary films living in Berlin, Germany. He was a history student at The American University in Washington, DC and studied filmmaking in Los Angeles. In 2012 Johnston embarked on the film project "Aliyah Le Berlin." Through research and interviews, Zachary Johnston has begun putting together a documentary that explores the rebirth of Jewish life in Berlin via the influx of Israelis to the city.

Elke-Vera Kotowski (PhD) is a research associate at the Moses Mendelssohn Center for European Jewish Studies. Since 2009 she is the coordinator of the graduate program Walter Rathenau College. As a lecturer at the University of Potsdam and the Humboldt University of Berlin she provides project-oriented seminars in the field of German-Jewish history (including the development of exhibitions, publications, and conferences). Recently she published *Das Kulturerbe deutschsprachiger Juden. Eine Spurensuche in den Ursprungs-, Transit- und Emigrationsländern* (2015).

Hanni Mittelmann (Prof.) is a Professor Emerita and former chairperson of the Department for Central and Eastern European Culture and Literature at the Hebrew University of Jerusalem. She is the editor of the collected works of Austrian-Jewish writer Albert Ehrenstein and has published widely on German Jewish literature, German Zionist literature and Expressionist literature. She recently published her work *Sammy Gronemann. Ein Leben im Dienste des Zionismus* (2012).

Fania Oz-Salzberger (Prof.) is an Israeli historian and writer. She is Professor of History at the University of Haifa's Faculty of Law and the Center for German and European Studies, and Founding Director of the Posen Research Forum for Political Thought. From 2007–2012 she was Professor and Leon Liberman Chair in Modern Israel Studies at Monash University in Melbourne. Oz-Salzberger has written numerous essays on the history of ideas, the history of translation, the Hebraic origins of European political thought, and German-Israeli relations. She recently published *Jews and Words*, co-authored with Amos Oz (2012).

Julius H. Schoeps (Prof.) is a Professor Emeritus of Modern History (main focus on German-Jewish history) and director of the Moses Mendelssohn Center for European Jewish Studies at Potsdam University since 1992. His main foci of research are on modern Jewish and intellectual history, the Jewish Enlightenment, the history of Zionism, Russian Jewish migration and Nazi looted art. He recently published *Der König von Midian. Paul Friedmann und sein Traum von einem Judenstaat* (2014) and *Pioneers of Zionism: Hess, Pinsker, Rülf. Messianism, Settlement Policy, and the Israeli-Palestinian Conflict* (2013).

Monika Schwarz-Friesel (Prof.) is head of the Department of General Linguistics at the Technical University of Berlin. From 2000–2010 she held the chair in cognitive linguistics at the University of Jena. As a cognitive scientist she focuses on the interaction of language, cognition, and emotion. Her most recent research projects have dealt with verbal anti-Semitism and the metaphorical language describing Islamic terrorism in the mass media since 9/11. She is the author of several books on language and emotion, and on contemporary anti-Semitism, for example, *Die Sprache der Judenfeindschaft im 21. Jahrhundert*, with J. Reinharz (2013).

Karsten Troyke, born in East Berlin, GDR, is a singer, actor, and speaker living in Berlin. He is best known as an interpreter of Yiddish song, both at home and abroad. He has participated in radio plays, worked as a voice talent for advertising and synchronization and acted in a variety of stage plays. As an ambassador of the Yiddish song art, he has performed in a host of countries including Poland, France, Norway, Belgium, Denmark, Sweden, Croatia, Israel, the USA, and others.

Michael Wolffsohn (Prof.) is a Professor Emeritus of Modern History, University of the German Armed Forces, Munich. His main foci of research are on Israel, Israeli society, the Middle East conflict, contemporary Germany and Western Europe, international relations and historical Demoscopy. Wolffsohn has published widely, especially on German-Israeli relations and on relations between Jews and non-Jews in post-war Germany. Among his most recent published works is "'Back to the Roots': Für eine neujüdische Spiritualität," in: Erwin Möde (ed.), *Europa braucht Spiritualität* (2014).

Index

Abraham Geiger Kolleg 26, 56, 235, 236
Afghanistan 203
Akko 118
Aliyah Le Berlin 7, 152, 153, 161, 252
Amadeu Antonio Stiftung 212, 215, 220, 223, 225, 226
American Joint Distribution Committee 237
Amsterdam 125, 143, 149, 150, 186, 207
Argentina 110, 111, 149, 151
Augsburg 50, 234
Auschwitz 4, 7, 16, 23, 31, 32, 34–36, 38, 39, 40, 42, 43, 54, 57, 144, 147, 150, 165, 169, 178, 214, 235
Auschwitz-Birkenau 39
Auschwitz trial 16
Aussiedler 79, 113

Beis Zion Yeshiva 236
Ben-Gurion University 43, 251
Berlin 3, 6, 7, 14–16, 18–23, 26, 37–39, 41, 42, 44, 45, 50, 51, 53–57, 59, 98, 102, 104–109, 111, 112, 114–127, 140, 143–145, 150–162, 165, 170, 187, 202, 204–207, 213, 217, 223–226, 232–238, 241, 243, 251–253
Berlin Wall 18, 19, 21, 106, 154
Bitburg 17
Bitburg controversy 17
Bremen University 112
Buenos Aires 109, 111, 149, 151

Central Council of Jews in Germany 2, 22, 58, 105, 106, 131, 168, 170, 175, 178, 195, 234, 236, 237
Centralverein deutscher Staatsbürger jüdischen Glaubens 51
Chabad 28, 65, 113, 234, 238
Charlottenburg 14, 120, 155
Chechnya 203
circumcision 180, 181
Cologne 14, 50, 59, 80, 140, 167, 232, 251
Columbia University 30, 48, 101, 223
Commonwealth of Independent States (CIS) 97

Degussa 26, 27
Deutsche Stimme 192, 194
displaced persons 14, 15, 19, 143
Dresden 25, 30, 192, 232, 234, 240
Düsseldorf 49, 202, 205, 238, 240

East Berlin 19, 21, 23, 124, 144, 145, 150, 154, 253
Eastern Europe 1, 9, 13, 14, 19, 20, 56, 104, 112, 143, 146, 149
East Germany 13, 14, 18, 19, 21, 65, 106, 144, 233, 240
Erlangen 58, 140, 239
Ernst Ludwig Ehrlich Scholarship Foundation 252
Essen 205, 206, 225, 234
European Center for Jewish Music 238
Evreyskaya Gazeta 112, 116

Federal Republic of Germany 117, 124, 132
Frankfurt 14, 16, 24, 26, 31, 34, 43, 45, 48–50, 55, 100, 104, 106, 107, 115, 116, 123, 127, 141, 207, 223–226, 231–233, 239, 241, 251
Frankfurt am Main 26, 50, 106, 123, 233, 239
Freies Jüdisches Lehrhaus 232

Gastronomic Slavophilism 92
Gaza 136, 148, 168, 173, 176, 178, 179, 183
German Democratic Republic 13, 65, 233
German Jewish Cultural Heritage 113
German-Jewish legacy 5, 15, 47–52, 54
German-Jewish relations 58, 111, 133, 139
Gesher Theater 112
Great Patriotic War 54

Halberstadt 50, 240
Halle 238
Hamas 199, 201, 202, 207
Hamburg 45, 50, 115, 116, 140, 148, 193, 204, 223, 234, 240
Hava Nagila 7, 142, 143
Hebrew Library 157
Hezbollah 201, 202

Hillel Houses 235
Historikerstreit 17
Hochschule für die Wissenschaft des
   Judentums 55, 235
Hohenems 50
Holocaust denial 173, 193, 198, 199
Holocaust survivors 13–15, 18–20, 23, 24, 56,
   143, 144, 151, 232
Hungary 23, 105, 149

IG-Farben Trust 41
Iraq 203, 204
Islamic Movement of Uzbekistan 201
Islamist Party of Liberation (Hizb ut-Tahir)
   202
Islamrat 198
Israel 1–3, 5–9, 15, 16, 17, 19, 20, 27, 29,
   33, 48, 50, 54, 57, 59, 63, 65, 72, 73,
   75, 76, 78–81, 83–85, 89–98, 100, 101,
   104, 106, 107, 109, 113, 115, 116, 118,
   119–122, 124–127, 133, 143–145, 147,
   149, 151–153, 155–162, 165, 167–170,
   173–188, 194–196, 200–202, 208,
   212–221, 223, 226, 231, 233, 234,
   238–242, 251–253
Israeli-Palestinian conflict 193, 201, 202, 212,
   215, 217, 218, 220–222
Israel Jacobson Society 239, 240
Israelkritik 208, 212–214, 221, 224

Jerusalem 3, 5, 9, 16, 34, 48, 50, 52, 80, 86,
   117, 118, 122, 125–127, 148, 194, 235, 252
Jew-hatred 166, 167, 171, 172, 174, 181, 182,
   185, 186
Jewish Adult Educational Centers 233
Jewish Agency 15, 23
Jewish Berlin 125
Jewish educational programs 242
Jewish Enlightenment 152, 153, 156, 161, 231,
   252
Jewish Life Leaders Program 238
Jewish weekly Allgemeine 24
Jüdischer Kulturverein 234

Kabbalah 232
Kol Berlin 121

L.A. Pincus Fund Jerusalem 235
Leitkultur 137, 210
Leningrad 114
Leo Baeck Institute in New York 48, 50
Lichtigfeld School in Frankfurt am Main 233
Limmud Learning Festival 237
Los Angeles 44, 45, 51, 52, 100, 120, 151, 252
Ludwig Maximilian University 114

Mecklenburg-Vorpommern 116, 192, 193
Medaon 240
Melbourne 120, 252
Moscow 5, 17, 51, 80, 100, 104
Moses Mendelssohn Center in Potsdam 240
Munich 14, 25, 26, 30, 45, 50, 55, 59, 80, 104,
   107, 111, 114–116, 127, 140, 149, 160, 177,
   191, 198, 200, 205, 232–234, 253
Muslim Brotherhood 198, 199, 205, 207
Muslim-Markt 200, 201

Nazis 47, 49, 54, 57, 113, 142, 144, 151, 161,
   167, 171, 172, 179, 190, 192, 194, 195,
   205, 235, 236
Netherlands 143, 144
New York 5, 30, 44, 48, 50–52, 80, 100, 101,
   116, 120, 127, 143, 147, 148, 151, 186,
   187, 197, 205–207, 210, 223–226
North America 2, 56, 113
Norway 253

Odessa 54, 104, 107
Oldenburg 235, 238
Osnabrück 239

Palestine 14, 48, 52, 89, 101, 113, 120, 122,
   142, 188, 192, 200, 203, 206, 212, 219,
   220, 251
Palestinians 120, 167, 168, 180, 193, 216,
   219, 221
Palestinian Territories 212, 219, 220, 221
Poland 7, 19, 56, 105, 112, 143, 148, 149, 161,
   192, 253
Protocols of the Elders of Zion 169, 198

Rabbinical Seminary of Berlin 236
Ravensbrück 126, 160
Red Army 18, 21, 54, 111

Red Army Fraction 18
Ronald S. Lauder Foundation 26
Russian colony 107

Saarbrücken 105, 116
Salomo Birnbaum Library 240
Salomo Birnbaum Yiddish Society 240
San Francisco 52, 53, 150
Saxony 56, 193, 231, 240, 252
School of Jewish Theology 9, 239, 252
Simon Dubnow Institute 238
Six-Days War 16
South Africa 151
Soviet regime 234
Soviet Union 2, 3, 18, 20, 21, 29, 47, 51, 54, 63, 78, 79, 83–85, 89, 90, 95, 96, 101, 103, 104, 107, 108, 111, 112, 116, 117, 121, 133, 143, 145, 147, 150, 233, 241
Spitz Magazine 156, 157
Stolpersteine 50
Stuttgart 14, 105, 186
Süddeutsche Zeitung 25, 26, 30, 43, 44, 167
Sweden 7, 58, 148, 253

Tel Aviv 3, 9, 35, 112, 117, 118, 119, 122, 125, 126, 127, 150, 151, 251, 252
Tel Aviv-Yaffo 112
The Klezmatics 147
Third Reich 16, 54, 117, 122
Touro College in Berlin 236
Treblinka 57, 148
Tübingen 239

Ukraine 63, 75, 82, 84, 92, 94, 95, 98, 149
Union of Progressive Jews in Germany (UPJ) 2, 234, 235
United Jewish Appeal 237
University of Binghampton 51
University of Erlangen 58
University of Potsdam 9, 235, 252
University of Southern California 51

Vecherniy Kiev 94
Verein für Cultur und Wissenschaft der Juden 232
Victory Day 54, 111
Vienna 50, 51, 116, 140, 149, 151, 170, 186
Vilnius 107
Volgograd 104, 107

Wannsee 125, 160
Warsaw 17, 122
Warsaw Ghetto Memorial 17
Weimar Republic 55, 80, 191
West Germany 7, 13–18, 20, 32, 55, 105, 143, 145, 146, 190, 233, 234
World Jewish Congress 17, 19
World Zionist Organization 17, 156

Yeckes 48, 55, 109, 113
Yiddish culture 108, 240
Yiddish music 146, 147
Yiddish songs 7, 143–149, 151
Yom Kippur War 16

Zacharias Frankel College 26
Zupfgeigenhansel 146

Names Index

Abou-Nagie, Ibrahim 201
Adenauer, Konrad 34
Adorno, Theodor W. 35, 141
Agnon, Samuel 118, 120, 122, 126
Aleichem, Sholem 47
Allen, Woody 134, 149
Arendt, Hannah 35
Artson, Bradley Shavit 249
Asad, Talal 209, 211, 222, 223
Augstein, Jakob 182, 184, 185

Bach 2
Bach, Johann Sebastian 231
Baeck, Leo 48, 50, 55, 106, 109, 152, 162, 187, 226
Baez, Joan 144, 148
Bär, Bernhard 152, 157
Barkan, Semjon Arkadjevitsch 112, 113
Bar-On, Dan 114, 115
Be'er, Haim 125, 126
Beethoven, Ludwig van 231
Bein, Alex 52
Belafonte, Harry 143, 148
Bellow, Saul 134
Ben Amotz, Dan 123, 126
Ben-Gurion, David 17, 43, 251
Benjamin, Walter 138–140
Ben-Yehuda, Eliezer 157
Berg, Alban 126, 142, 148, 154, 155
Bergson, Henry 137
Bernstein 5, 6
Bernstein, Assaf 81, 99, 100, 116, 125, 251
Bikel, Theodore 144, 148, 151
Biller, Maxim 132, 134
Bismarck, Otto von 118
Blumenthal, Michael 114
Boehlich, Walter 52
Böhnhardt, Uwe 191
Börne, Ludwig 46, 47, 49, 132
Brandt, Willy 16, 17, 34
Broder, Henryk M. 132, 214, 223
Brodsky, Joseph 47
Bronfman, Edgar 19
Buber, Martin 47, 56, 109, 232

Bubis, Ignatz 24–26, 30
Bushido 202

Carlos 18
Corren, Camilla 143, 148

Demnig, Gunter 50
Deso Dogg 202
Deutsch, Moritz 114–116, 135, 140
Dylan, Bob 144, 149

Eichendorff, Joseph von 104
Eichmann 2
Eichmann, Adolf 16, 34
Einstein, Albert 47
Elon, Amos 46, 59, 123, 127
Erbakan, Necmettin 199
Erdogan, Recep Tayyip 205

Fassbinder, Rainer Werner 25
Feidman, Giora 147, 149
Finkelstein, Norman 195, 200, 201
Fleischmann, Lea 132, 140
Fogel, Vanessa 132
Fontane, Theodor 168
Fox, Eytan 125
Fraenkel, Ernst 27
Frankel, Zacharias 26, 152
Freier, Erich 124
Frensdorff, Solomon 152, 157
Freud, Sigmund 137, 142, 149
Friedländer, David 55, 57, 59, 152, 231
Friedman, Michel 139, 197, 205
Fürst, Julius 157, 162

Galinski, Heinz 15, 22, 23, 24, 26, 233
Gebirtig, Mordechai 144, 149
Geiger 9
Geiger, Abraham 26, 52, 56, 152, 155, 235, 236, 252
Geiger, Ludwig 26, 52, 56, 152, 155, 235, 236, 244–250, 252
Gerro, Henry 143, 149
Gilman, Sander 134, 140

Goebbels 2
Goethe, Johann Wolfgang von 2, 47, 104, 110, 231
Goldberg, Leah 122
Goldmann, Nahum 17
Gorelik, Lena 114–116, 131, 132, 135, 137, 140
Grass, Günter 147, 149, 176, 182
Greco, Juliette 144
Gumpertz, Ruben Samuel 245
Habermas, Jürgen 36, 44

Halbwachs, Maurice 36, 44, 111
Halland, Jossy 143, 149
Hegel, Georg Wilhelm Friedrich 168, 231
Heidenheim, Wolf 152, 157
Heine, Heinrich 46, 47, 49, 132, 142, 149, 150
Hermlin, Stephan 18
Heym, Stefan 18
Hildesheimer, Esriel 27, 236
Hildesheimer, Wolfgang 27, 236
Hilsenrath, Edgar 27
Hirohito 22
Hirschbiegel, Oliver 33, 34, 45
Hitler 2
Hitler, Adolf 17, 18, 33–35, 44, 45, 48, 54, 104, 150, 173, 178, 198
Hollaender, Friedrich 142, 150
Höllerer, Walter 125
Horkheimer, Max 47
Hussein, Saddam 210

Itzig, Daniel 152

Jacobs, Louis 143
Jacobson, Israel 231, 239, 240
Jacoby, Johann 46
Jaldati, Lin 144, 150
Jaspers, Karl 35
Jonas, Regina 152, 162, 235
Jungk, Peter Stephan 132
Jupiter, Elisabeth 131, 140

Kaminer, Wladimir 132
Kaniuk, Yoram 124, 127
Kant, Immanuel 20, 47, 231
Kessler, Judith 107
Khmelnicki, Bogdan 94

Khomeini, Ruhollah 198
Knobloch, Charlotte 58
Kohl, Helmut 17
Korn, Salomon 26, 106, 116
Kraus, Karl 139

Leander, Zarah 143, 150
Levitt, Michael 159
Lewandowski, Louis 56
Leyendecker, Hans 25, 26, 30
Liebermann, Max 47
Loewy, Ronny 43, 44
Löwenthal, Leo 27, 232
Löwenthal, Richard 27
Luxemburg, Rosa 142, 150

Mahler, Gustav 142, 150, 204
Marx, Karl 24, 92, 187
Mendelssohn 3, 9
Mendelssohn-Bartholdy, Felix 46, 47, 49
Mendelssohn, Moses 2, 46, 47, 49, 51, 52, 57, 109, 118, 127, 152, 153, 161, 162, 185, 231, 238, 240, 251, 252
Meyerbeer, Giacomo 46, 47
Morsi, Mohammed 198

Nachmann, Werner 24, 26
Nudelman, Rafael 54

Obama, Barack 23
Ofarim, Abi 145, 150
Ofarim, Esther 145, 150
Ostendorf, Henrik 194

Pantijelew, Gregori 113, 114
Pappenheim, Bertha 57, 109, 232
Pasternak, Boris 47
Pastörs, Udo 193
Pinto, Diana 79, 80, 241, 243
Pirker, Werner 215
Plaunt, Gunter 106
Polak, Oliver 131, 132, 136, 139, 140
Popper, Karl 18

Rabinovici 132, 214, 226
Rabinovici, Doron 226
Rathenau, Walther 51, 252

Reagan, Ronald 17, 24
Reich-Ranicki, Marcel 27
Reinhardt, Max 51
Richler, Mordechai 134
Ricoer, Paul 133–136, 140
Riesser, Gabriel 46
Rilke, Rainer Maria 231
Robeson, Paul 144, 151
Rodzynek, Lea-Nina 143, 148
Rohland, Peter 145, 151
Ron, Havatselet 44, 144, 151
Rosenthal, Ruvik 124, 127
Rosenzweig, Franz 56, 232
Roth, Philip 127, 134, 140
Rothschild, Mayer Amschel 231
Rumer-Sarajew, Michail 112, 116
Rushdie, Salman 210

Scheel, Walter 16, 17
Schiller, Friedrich 104, 110, 209, 220, 224
Schmidt, Helmut 17, 199, 201, 204, 212, 214, 224
Scholem, Gershom 56, 232
Schönberg, Arnold 51
Schopflocher, Roberto 109–111, 116
Schweigmann-Greve, Kay 239
Seeger, Pete 144, 151
Seghers, Anna 18
Seligmann, Rafael 132, 134, 137, 140
Shalikar, Arye Sharuz 132
Simon, Ernst 52, 224, 238
Smolianitski, Tanya 239
Spiegel, Paul 26, 105, 131, 140, 182

Stalin, Josef 18, 21, 108
Stöcker. Adolf 168

Tarantino, Quentin 35, 45
Thalheim 4
Thalheim, Robert 31, 32, 36, 39, 43–45
Treiger, Alina 235
Tucholsky, Kurt 132

Uchovsky, Gal 125

Vertlib, Vladimir 132
Vogel, Pierre 201
Voigt, Udo 116, 194, 204

Wagner, Richard 25, 49, 147, 151, 168, 189, 205, 208, 213, 217, 224
Warshel, Arieh 159
Weiss, Ilan 33, 131, 140
Witler, Benzion 143, 151
Wolffsohn 4
Wolffsohn, Michael 13, 17–19, 23, 26, 30, 46, 59, 132, 140, 253
Wowereit, Klaus 153, 157
Wuliger, Michael 131, 132, 136–139, 141

Yehoshua, A.B. 123, 127
Yosef, Shmuel 120, 126

Zamir, Michael 157
Zimmermann, Robert 187
Zuckerman, Louis 121
Zunz, Leopold 232

www.ingramcontent.com/pod-product-compliance
Lightning Source LLC
Chambersburg PA
CBHW050901300426
44111CB00010B/1335